A HISTORY OF TASM

This captivating work charts the history of Tasmania from the arrival of European maritime expeditions in the late eighteenth century, through to the modern day. By presenting the perspectives of both Indigenous Tasmanians and British settlers, author Henry Reynolds provides an original and engaging exploration of these fraught first encounters.

Utilising key themes to bind his narrative, Reynolds explores how geography created a unique economic and migratory history for Tasmania, quite separate to the mainland experience. He offers an astute analysis of the island's economic and demographic reality, by noting that this facilitated the survival of a rich heritage of colonial architecture unique in Australia, and allowed the resident population to foster a powerful web of kinship.

Reynolds' remarkable capacity to empathise with the characters of his chronicle makes this a powerful, engaging and moving account of Tasmania's unique position within Australian history.

Henry Reynolds is Research Professor in the Department of History and Classics at the University of Tasmania. His previous books include *An Indelible Stain?*, *Nowhere People: How International Race Thinking Shaped Australia's Identity* and *Why Weren't We Told?*

A History of Tasmania

HENRY REYNOLDS

CAMBRIDGE
UNIVERSITY PRESS

1/27/12
WW
 # 39.99

CAMBRIDGE UNIVERSITY PRESS
Cambridge, New York, Melbourne, Madrid, Cape Town,
Singapore, São Paulo, Delhi, Tokyo, Mexico City

Cambridge University Press
477 Williamstown Road, Port Melbourne, VIC 3207, Australia

Published in the United States of America by Cambridge University Press, New York

www.cambridge.org
Information on this title: www.cambridge.org/9780521548373

First published 2012

Cover design by Anne-Marie Reeves
Typeset by Aptara Corp
Printed in China by Printplus Co. Ltd

A catalogue record for this publication is available from the British Library

National Library of Australia Cataloguing in Publication data
Reynolds, Henry, 1938–
A history of Tasmania / Henry Reynolds.
9781107014589 (hbk.)
Includes bibliographical references and index.
Tasmania – History.
994.6

ISBN 978-1-107-01458-9 Hardback
ISBN 978-0-521-54837-3 Paperback

For Jarra, Jess, Matilda and Isabelle.

CONTENTS

ILLUSTRATIONS

ACKNOWLEDGEMENTS

Like any writer I am greatly appreciative of the assistance I have received in Tasmania's libraries, archives and museums, and particularly in the University of Tasmania Library, the State Library of Tasmania, the Archives Office of Tasmania, the Queen Victoria Museum and Art Gallery, and the Tasmanian Museum and Art Gallery.

I need to express my respect to some of the major historians who have preceded me and especially those 19th century forebears Melville, West, Calder, Bonwick and Fenton, as well as more recent scholars such as Robson, Plomley and Townsley. But my greatest debt is to contemporary Tasmania scholars such as Roe, Petrow, Davis, Maxwell-Stuart, Boyce, Pybus, Alexander, Chapman and the many others, too numerous to mention, who have written articles in local history journals or books on a multitude of Tasmanian topics.

I have also benefited from many conversations with friends and acquaintances who find Tasmanian history fascinating and like nothing more than to share an anecdote or compare memories about growing up on the island; these conversations were often conducted with members of the diaspora in many parts of the world.

Finally, I should acknowledge my father, the late John Reynolds, a leading member of the local history scene for 50 years. He was the first person to awaken my interest in the past and who spoke about people such as George Arthur, Martin Cash and Tom Davey as though he had met them. He also talked to everyone he met about their own knowledge of island history and stored innumerable stories away in his ever-active mind. He was, as were many people of his generation, a Tasmanian patriot.

INTRODUCTION

Introductions are normally read first, but they are usually written last, as was this one. This is necessary because it is only when the bulk of the book is written that it is possible to reflect on the experience of writing it.

A general history of a state has a number of challenges that are not necessarily obvious when the venture is first undertaken. Given the mismatch between the length of the book and the size of the undertaking, the first problem facing the historian is not so much what to include but what must be left out. Over a period of 230 years a great deal happened, even in a place as small as Tasmania, so every event included in the story has been given preference over many more that were left out. I decided quite early in the writing that this book could not possibly be a comprehensive work of reference where the reader could look up any aspect of Tasmanian history and find a neat informative summary. Where there was a choice between factual detail and thematic coherence and narrative flow, I chose the second option. As a result many themes and events are scouted and important individuals passed over.

I apologise in advance to any reader who finds that there are aspects of the past that have not received the attention they certainly deserve. Religion is one theme that escaped the notice it warrants, given the importance it played in the lives of most 19th century Tasmanians and many of their descendants in the 20th century. Education is another subject that should, ideally, have received more attention. The same is true of the high culture, with the artists,

musicians and writers who have graced the life of the island. So, with
those topics scouted, the main themes are political development,
along with economic and social change.

Even with a constricted agenda the general historian runs the risk
of trespassing into the many small territories policed by specialists
and attentive antiquarians. Tasmania has many scholars who have
studied particular periods or distinctive themes and who will find
the treatment of their field of interest superficial and inadequate.
There are also many amateur enthusiasts with a deep understanding of specific subjects. No general historian can ever match their
particular local knowledge. The problem is compounded by the
history of events within living memory that are still alive in many
minds. As part of the Tasmanian diaspora for 30 years I am sharply
aware of my lack of personal acquaintance with people and events
of the recent past. In that sense I write as both an insider and an
outsider, a situation that has advantages and disadvantages.

One major problem with any general history of Australia is the
question of when the story should begin. In the past historians
could adopt the easy assumption that history only began with the
arrival of the Europeans, which leaves out the tens of thousands
of years of Aboriginal ownership and sovereignty. We now know
from the work of archaeologists and linguists that there were a
number of migrations into Tasmania before that final flooding of
Bass Strait and that the different nations adapted to their home
territories and shaped the landscape in ways that are still apparent
today. But the Tasmanians were distinct in that they were among
the most isolated groups of human beings, who, for over 300 generations, knew nothing but the island and its peoples. This long and
ancient history has a unique appeal to many people but my interest has always been focused on the meeting between the Indigenous peoples and the invaders. It was a theme that I explored in
my book *The Other Side of the Frontier*, which was published 30
years ago. So I decided to start the story with the arrival of the
European maritime expeditions that occurred between 1772 and
1802 to try to explain what these unprecedented, unexpected events
meant for the Tasmanians. It seemed appropriate that this theme
should be near the centre of the narrative in the early chapters of the
book.

There are many developments that are common to the histories of European settler colonialism which are obviously also true of the Australian states. The separate histories overlap in many ways and this was doubly so after federation in 1901. When writing the history of one of the federated states there is always a tension between emphasising the distinctive features of the particular society in question and of looking at what it had in common with the other ones. We need to keep in mind that Australia is a federation and not a unitary state. Local state politics remained important throughout the 20th century and although the major parties were national in their reach each state had its own characteristics and distinctive electoral cycles. This was certainly true of Tasmania.

There are other inimitable features of Tasmanian history that can be detailed without distorting either the national or the local story. The inescapable fact of being a small offshore island has been a constant influence on the hard facts of economics and on people's sense of themselves as being Tasmanians first and Australians second. Islanders have usually felt no sense of identity with the vast inland plains, the red centre or the wide brown land. Nowhere else in Australia does geography conspire so closely with political sentiment: in one way or another the island has had varying forms of autonomy since 1824. The convict system was of profound importance in Tasmania, much more so than in New South Wales and Western Australia, the other colonies that received British convicts. Tasmania's economic development was also distinctive. A period of spectacular growth, stimulated by convict labour and imperial government investment, was followed by long bouts of economic depression. The island missed out on that long summer of growth from 1850 to 1890, which did so much to shape the Australian's sense of buoyant optimism.

At the centre of the island story is the tradition of out migration. For most of the time since the middle of the 19th century Tasmanians leaving the island have outnumbered incoming migrants. The tradition of often unwilling exile has deep roots. Population growth has been slow and normally below the Australian average. This has had a number of noticeable consequences. Economic stagnation has enabled the survival of a rich heritage of colonial architecture unique in Australia. It has also made it possible for the resident population to put down deep roots and to live within a complex, generations old, web of kinship undisturbed by mass migration.

One final problem facing the historian of any one of the states is to determine to whom the book should be addressed. I have not written it for fellow historians or for academics more generally but for the average educated reader. My assumption was that my task was to explain island history to outsiders as much as to Tasmanians, to other Australians and to visitors who wanted to learn something about the island and to hear what people had achieved, learn how they dealt with hardship and adversity since the European ships sailed like sinister sea birds into the ancestral lands of Tasmania's Indigenous nations.

I

First Meetings,
Extraordinary Encounters

What extraordinary encounters they were. Few human beings can have known the awe and wonder experienced by the Tasmanians living on the island's southeast coast during the last quarter of the 18th century. In common with other Tasmanians, they had lived in isolation from the rest of the world, since the time when Bass Strait flooded at least 8000 years earlier. Some memory of migration from the distant mainland may have survived as legend but for over 300 generations Tasmania was their all-embracing world, fellow islanders the only known inhabitants of the universe, their ways the time honoured pattern for the whole of humankind.

Suddenly, dramatically, it all changed. Nothing would ever be the same again. The brief visit of Tasman's two ships in 1642 had no sequel, although, between 1772 and 1802, 11 expeditions visited, explored and charted the much indented and complex coastline between Recherche Bay in the far south and the Freycinet Peninsula on the mid east coast. For European sailors Tasmania was a welcome haven, shelter from the prevailing westerly winds, with secure anchorages. It had a mild climate, broad beaches and access to timber and fresh water. Earnest navigators slipped lyrical passages about the island into otherwise prosaic log books and diaries. Even the unimaginative realised what an extraordinary impact their presence had on the coastal clans and understood how utterly exotic ordinary objects and everyday behaviour must have seemed to the Tasmanians. George Augustus Robinson was one of the few people to record the Tasmanians' stories.

Image 1.1: George Augustus Robinson.
(*Source:* Archives Office of Tasmania.)

While out in the bush his associate Kickerterpoller, or Black Tom, told him that he saw the first ship that came to Maria Island when he was a boy. His clan members were all frightened and ran away from the coast. The ship looked like a small island but they could not tell what it was. He added that his contemporaries could not 'conceive how the white men came here first'.[1] Another of Robinson's companions, Woorrady, recalled that when his Bruny Island clansmen first saw a European ship 'coming at sea' they said that it was *wrageowrapper*, the devil, and ran away in fear.[2]

Flight and hiding were common – and totally comprehensible – reactions to the arrival of Europeans. Many such occasions were reported in diaries and log books, though there must have been many more of which the white men were unaware. Wary surveillance was widely practised. Employing those two skills of life-long hunters – patient observation and silent stalking – the Tasmanians patiently watched the Europeans. Much of the time the white men were unaware that they were the object of spying operations. French scientist Labillardière reported that one of the Tasmanians had explained by unequivocal signs that he had 'come to reconnoitre us during the night',[3] while on Maria Island 10 years later Francois Peron observed: 'They redouble their vigilance against us, and they surround themselves with sentries in advanced positions who, from the tops of hills and even in very tall trees, keep watch on all that takes place in the vicinity.'[4]

For every time the Tasmanians ran from the white men there were other occasions when intense curiosity drew them towards the strangers. Woorrady explained to Robinson that when the Europeans set up camp on the shore his fellow clansmen 'went and looked at what the white people did, went and told other natives and they came and looked also'.[5] The curiosity the Europeans recorded in their books and journals was mirrored by the Tasmanians. 'We were so novel to one another,' Peron noted on Maria Island. He wrote that

We are seeing these men at a time when all the faculties of their being are magnified. Our ships, the noise of our guns and their terrible effect, the colour of our skin, our clothing, our form, our gifts, everything we possess, everything that surrounds us, our gait, our actions, all are such marvels to them.[6]

At his first meeting with the Tasmanians in 1793 D'Hesmivy d'Auribeau tried to learn some of the words of their language but felt thwarted by what he termed their 'constant agitation at the sight of so many different objects that were so new to them'.[7] The sheer quantity of things the Europeans had in their possession must have amazed the Tasmanians. Almost everything was new to them – shapes, colours, textures. The large numbers of men who came forth from the ships must have been surprising, as were the domestic animals carried on board. And there were the fundamental mysteries of where the white men had come from and why they had suddenly appeared. These questions must have been the subject of endless, anxious debate around 100 campfires, as Peron appreciated:

Moreover, they do not know what our intentions may be towards them or what perhaps is the object of our visit, and they can form no idea of these matters. They can only think that our intentions are hostile. Our presents, our kindness towards them, our protestations of friendship, all are suspect for them. They seek to interpret our looks. They observe us closely. Everything they see us do they suppose to be something mysterious, and always their suspicions of us are unfavourable.[8]

Of all the white men's innumerable possessions guns were the most frightening and perplexing. Their power and destructiveness were apparent from the arrival of Marion du Fresne's expedition in March 1772. As so often happened conflict was born of misunderstanding. There was a brief meeting on the beach at Marion Bay between the local clan and a party from the French ships. All went well until du Fresne himself landed from a second longboat. What followed was recorded by Julien Crozet, who wrote:

One savage left the group and presented him, as the others had, with a firebrand to light a small pile of wood. The captain, imagining this was a ceremony necessary to prove that he had come with pacific intentions, [did not] hesitate to light the pile, but immediately it seemed that this was quite to the contrary, and that the acceptance of the brand was an acceptance of defiance, or a declaration of war. As soon as the pile was lighted, the savages withdrew hastily onto a hillock, from which they threw a shower of stones, by which M. Marion, as well as an officer who was with him, was wounded. We immediately fired several shots and everyone re-embarked.

When the Frenchmen tried to land farther along the bay they were met by a shower of spears, one of which slightly wounded an African servant. They responded with a 'fusillade', which wounded several and killed one. The Tasmanians fled into the trees 'howling fearfully' carrying their wounded countrymen.[9]

News of the encounter and of the white men's weapons spread quickly and soon became common knowledge among the Tasmanian clans. Fear of guns influenced every aspect of future encounters around the Tasmanian coast. The sight, and more especially the sound, of them often precipitated panicked flight. Such a reaction was observed by James Cook at Adventure Bay in January 1777. During an apparently friendly encounter Cook asked one of the Tasmanians to show him how he threw his spears. Eventually, the Polynesian Omai fired his musket 'to show them how superior our weapons were to theirs'. With that, despite the best endeavours of Cook's party to persuade them to stay, all the Tasmanians ran into the bush, dropping all their recently acquired presents. The same thing happened a short time later when a watering party, surprised by the appearance of 'the Indians', fired into the air. The Tasmanians fled 'holding their fingers in their ears'.[10]

In 1793 d'Auribeau recorded a similar incident in Recherche Bay. To the intense interest of a group of Tasmanians he had been lighting gunpowder in shells to produce explosions. But the mood changed dramatically when a gun was produced. 'I had a double-barrelled gun brought to me', the Frenchman wrote:

But the moment they saw it, they fearfully gave me to understand that they were afraid of it. They lay down with their eyes shut, wishing to show me that this weapon caused death. However, I remained in their midst and had two shots fired a little way off in the opposite direction. The noise frightened them greatly, and I perceived that I should be offending them if I did it again.[11]

The Europeans' use of guns was monitored more closely by the watchful Tasmanians than any other aspect of the strangers' behaviour. The presence of firearms among a party was immediately noted. A slight movement of the weapons could raise alarm. The constant noise of guns being used for hunting and for collecting specimens kept tensions high. It wasn't just that guns were known to kill and injure; the mystery of how they actually worked intensified the terror. The problem for the Tasmanians, as for their counterparts on mainland Australia, was that it was impossible to see the death-dealing projectile. It was obvious that the white men pointed their guns towards their chosen targets, that there was a flash of light followed soon after by a loud noise and that a bird, animal or a man could, almost instantly, fall down dead. And although the resulting external wound would be obvious, the offending ball would, in all probability, remain hidden deep in the damaged body.

So many facts about guns remained mysterious until the Tasmanians began to live in close proximity with resident settlers. Only then were their secrets slowly revealed. Initially, it was impossible to know the limitations of the muskets: that they had only a limited range, that they were inaccurate, often misfired and took some time to reload.

Until these things were appreciated the white men appeared to have weapons with magical powers against which there was no defence. Discovery of the secrets of the white men's guns was one of the great intellectual achievements of Aborigines everywhere.

European clothing was another source of wonder and curiosity. Initially, it was not obvious where the covering ended and the body began. The strangers carried about with them so many things, which to the Tasmanians seemed superfluous. When uncovered the whiteness of their skin was another cause for surprise and exclamation. Peron described the reaction of the first Tasmanian he met in the D'Entrecasteaux Channel:

What seemed to impress him at first was the whiteness of our skins, and perhaps wishing to make sure this colour was the same all over our bodies he opened in turn our waistcoats and our shirts; and he showed his astonishment with loud cries of surprise, and above all by stamping his feet very briskly.[12]

As if to show the strangers that their colour was seen as a distinct handicap the Tasmanian women remedied the situation by blackening the Frenchmen's faces with powdered charcoal. Peron observed that he and his equally blackened colleague 'seemed to become the subject of great admiration to the women' and they appeared to congratulate them on the new charms they had acquired. 'This European Whiteness,' Peron wrote, 'of which people were so proud, was in distant regions, no more than an actual deficiency, a sort of deformity.'[13]

Another puzzle presented by the European explorers was the absence of women, despite each ship containing as many as 100 men. It must have caused endless speculation around the camp-fires and debate about whether the white men had normal sex lives. D'Auribeau wrote that it was hard to escape the Tasmanians' eager-ness 'to discover our sex'. It appeared to him that they were aston-ished at not finding a woman among the Europeans and that they were much 'occupied by this idea'.[14] Ten years later the men of Baudin's expedition had similar experiences. Peron explained that on Maria Island the Tasmanians wanted to examine the Frenchmen's legs and chests, which examination was accepted but it was not long before they demanded to extend their researches further and persisted with 'obstinacy and fervour'.[15] Peron provided a graphic account of how the matter was resolved, writing that,

they showed an extreme desire to examine our genital organs, but as this examination was equally displeasing to us all, they insisted on it only in the case of Citizen Michel, one of our sailors, who by his slight build and lack of beard seemed he must be more likely to set their minds at rest. But Citizen Michel, whom I begged to submit to their entreaties, suddenly exhibited such striking proof of his virility that they all uttered loud cries of surprise mingled with loud roars of laughter which were repeated again and again.

With an exquisite display of Gallic vanity Peron concluded that the Tasmanians did not experience Citizen Michel's condition as often as the virile Frenchmen.[16]

It may have been vanity too that persuaded the French explor-ers that the Tasmanian women were flirting with them. Jacques Hamelin recorded that two of the women he met on Bruny Island made 'suggestive signs which in Paris would not be ambiguous'.[17] Peron and two colleagues met another party of women on the island and were, as he put it, 'bombarded with pleasantries and flirtations' to which they responded 'in the most expressive manner of which we were capable'.[18] A young woman of the D'Entrecasteaux Channel was sitting next to Henri Freycinet when she applied her makeup of powdered charcoal. In no time, Peron reported, she was 'frighten-ingly black'. What intrigued the Frenchmen was 'the complacency with which the girl looked at us after this operation and the air of self-assurance this new ornament had contributed to her features'.[19]

Labillardière reported in 1793 that several of the French sailors followed two young girls along 'the different windings' of a beach in Recherche Bay and 'availed themselves of one of the most retired places to behave to them in a manner much too free'. But they were 'received far differently than what they expected'. The young women fled to the nearby rocks and made it clear that if pursued they would dive into the water and swim away.[20] The French explorers repeatedly stressed how they found the Tasmanian women sexually unattractive. These feelings may well have been mutual.

James Cook recorded a similar incident during his 1777 stay in Adventure Bay, recording in his journal:

> Some of the Gentlemen belonging to the *Discovery* I was told, paid their addresses and made them large offers which were rejected with great disdain whether from a sence of Vertue or from fear of displeasing the men I shall not pretend to determine.[21]

The Tasmanians were curious about the Europeans' many possessions, which they either sought out or had thrust upon them by the visitors seeking to signify their benign intentions. E. P. de Rossel described the scene on the shore of Recherche Bay on Shrove Tuesday 1793. 'Almost everybody' from the two ships went ashore to meet the Tasmanians. It was, he observed, a competition to see who could give the most clothes to our 'new friends' who were, as a result, covered with 'materials of every kind, hanging medals round their neck, little bells, mirrors, necklaces and so on'. They were, he declared, 'truly carnival figures!'[22] But what the visitors also discovered was that the Tasmanians, having examined the many objects given or taken, abandoned them, as they found no use for them. Peron noticed, abandoned around a deserted camp-fire, all the objects that the Frenchmen had given away or had been stolen.[23] Glass bottles, which were broken to provide sharp cutting and scraping tools, were among the only European presents that the Tasmanians valued.

Each party to the encounters around the southeast coast found the other unpredictable and volatile. But the Europeans were cosmopolitans who had travelled across the world, and knew at first or second hand about many other tribes and nations. The more sophisticated subscribed to ethnological theories that enabled them to classify and compare what they learnt about the Tasmanians. They found them interesting and exotic but they could not personally experience the awe and wonder that their presence evoked. Nor did they always appreciate the courage that was required of the Tasmanians who advanced to meet them, and then spent time in their company. The supreme test of bravery must have been exhibited by the individuals who were willing to go aboard the great and mysterious ships anchored offshore.

The French sailors invited a party of Recherche Bay men to go on board their flagship and allowed them to inspect the vessel through the telescope. But when the party reached the longboat only one man was willing to go on board. He walked all over the *Recherche* looking closely at everything he came across. The commander of the expedition, Bruni D'Entrecasteaux, was impressed by a man who had 'dared to surrender himself on his own, and without defence, at the mercy of men whose dispositions were unknown to him'.[24] The US whaler Amaso Delano reported on a similar event 10 years later when in Storm Bay. Seeing a party of Tasmanians on the shore he sent a longboat to engage with them; they returned with an old man who thoroughly inspected the ship and 'shewed no signs of fear whatever'.[25]

By the time Delano was in the Derwent the British had already established two settlements on the river although the party under the command of David Collins had only been at Sullivans Cove for a few weeks and the American reported that they had not had 'any interview with the natives'.[26] We have no way of knowing when the Tasmanians who had briefly engaged with Delano and his crew, and the other clans who lived around the southeast coast, came to realise that the two parties camped on the banks of the Derwent had come to stay. They had experienced many visiting expeditions over half a lifetime and had no doubt heard about those with which they had no personal contact. Baudin's ships had been off the coast for six weeks and John Hayes had been in the Derwent for the same period in 1793.

The Tasmanians no doubt wondered why the Europeans came to their shores, but they eventually disappeared over the horizon as mysteriously as they had appeared. The thought that the white men would change their behaviour and stay would have presented an even greater challenge to their understanding of the world. In conversations with Robinson in 1831, Woorrady, who had grown up on Bruny Island, provided some memory of his people's realisation that the parties on the Derwent were much more than brief, exotic sojourners. He recalled that 'when the first people settled they cut down trees, built houses, dug the ground and planted; that by and by more ships came, then at last plenty of ships'.[27]

There can be no doubt that the Tasmanians carefully and continually watched the white men and news of their activities was widely reported among related clan groups. There was so much activity around the two settlement sites on either side of the Derwent. The party led by John Bowen, which arrived from Sydney in two ships in September 1803, was relatively small, made up of 49 officials, soldiers and convicts. But from an Aboriginal perspective it was a large body of people to be in one place for any length of time. Before long these Europeans began to act in ways that differed from the behaviour of the earlier parties of explorers. As Woorrady had noted, they cut down trees, dug up the ground and constructed huts. By the end of November 1803 there were 40 structures of one sort or another on the sloping ground at the head of Risdon Cove. Unlike the Frenchmen, who had been in Tasmania the year before, the party on the Derwent showed no desire to make contact with the resident clans. Bowen reported to Governor King in Sydney in September 1803 that while a few Tasmanians had been seen he was 'not apprehending they would be of any use to us'.

Consequently, he had not made 'any search after them, thinking myself well off if I never see them again'.[28] Parties began to venture further into Aboriginal territory, hunting, exploring and surveying, an activity that must have perplexed Tasmanian onlookers. In February 1804 surveyor James Meehan was confronted by an Aboriginal hunting party. When they pulled out one of his surveying pegs he was, he reported, 'obliged to fire on them'.[29]

By the autumn of 1804 the revolutionary nature of the changes that were taking place in their world must have been apparent to all the Tasmanian clans in the southeast of the island. During February two further ships, the *Ocean* and the *Lady Nelson*, which carried Collins and his party from the abortive settlement at Port Phillip Bay, arrived in the Derwent. By the end of the month they had established their camp on the western side of the estuary at Sullivans Cove. With 262 men, women and children the party was five times larger than the group in the now faltering settlement on the opposite side of the Derwent. Chaplain and diarist Robert Knopwood recorded in the first week in March that 'many of the natives' were seen about the camp but kept their distance. He was in 'no doubt but they see us'.[30]

And what a whirlwind of activity they witnessed. Vast quantities of stores and equipment were unloaded from the two vessels anchored just off shore. The bush was cleared and burnt, stone was quarried, shells collected and burnt for lime, trees cut down, dragged to the saw pits and cut into posts and planks, gardens were hoed, trenched and fenced, the blacksmith set up his forge. Within a few weeks of arrival the governor's wooden house was built and many of the convicts had constructed for themselves wattle and daub huts with thatched grass roofs. By the end of the year, 30 000 bricks had been produced from local clay. The soldiers and officials fanned out into the hinterland, hunting with guns and hounds, collecting specimens and exploring their new surroundings. Knopwood frequently went 'out a shooting' and brought home kangaroo, emu, swans and a large variety of birds.[31] In June the settlement was augmented with the arrival of 160 people who had remained behind at the camp on Port Phillip Bay. By then, the European population at the two camps had already reached 500 souls, almost certainly outnumbering the Aborigines in the immediate vicinity. Ships arrived from Britain and Sydney and English and American whalers hunted their prey in the Derwent. In August Knopwood reported that the *Alexander* was taking whales in Sandy Bay.

By the end of the year the Tasmanians of the Tamar Valley were forced to confront the reality of European settlement with much less prior experience than their counterparts in the southeast. The Tamar Valley had been known to the settlers only from the brief visit of Bass and Flinders in 1798. The party spent several days on the river, saw evidence of Aboriginal presence but had no contact with the resident clans. In January 1804 an exploring party arrived in the Tamar from the settlement on the far side of Bass Strait. A series of confrontations with local clans followed and a number of them were shot. Geologist A. W. H. Humphrey recorded the details of one such incident. Having gone ashore the Europeans suddenly found themselves 'nearly surrounded by fire'. They managed to avoid the flames but, as Humphrey wrote:

We soon, however, had a number of the natives running after us, shouting and crying out. One of them threw a spear at us but did not hurt. We stopped and put down our guns and made signs of friendship but they beat the trees with the short sticks they had in their hands and talked very quick and loud.[32]

We have very little idea of how much contact there was traditionally between the widely separated language groups. The people of the Tamar Valley may have heard reports about the appearance of white men in large ships far to the south but even if that was the case they were totally unprepared to understand what was happening to their world with the sudden and unexpected arrival in November of four ships carrying 146 officials, soldiers and convicts and all their equipment along with sheep, cattle, pigs and one mule. On 11 November a formal ceremony culminated with a salute from the cannon on board the *HMS Buffalo* and a volley of musketry from the soldiers of the New South Wales Corps. The ships were unloaded, tents pitched and land cleared. The following day there was what Commandant William Patterson called 'an affray' with the natives.[33]

A large party of Tasmanians, Patterson thought 'about 80', tentatively approached the camp. The Europeans offered trinkets, but then spurned attempts by the Tasmanians to take other more useful objects. The Tasmanians retreated but returned shortly after and came into conflict with several soldiers. A scuffle escalated until the guard was 'under the unpleasant alternative of defending themselves, and fired upon them, killing one and Wounded another'. The Tasmanians retaliated with spears and stones, with little effect. Patterson feared the affray would be the cause of 'much mischief hereafter' and suggested that on future 'excursions inland' the parties would have to be well armed.[34] Still, the process of settlement progressed relentlessly; parties advanced to the south along the estuary, where they discovered the good land on the banks of the North Esk River, which, in 1806, became the final site of the fledgling community. A small advance party, seeking out a suitable route to move the cattle to the south, was confronted by a large group of Aborigines, members of which made it clear that they did not want the white men to proceed any further into their country. Alexander Riley walked towards the hostile party and 'a mutual interchange of notice took place'. But Riley and his companion, the soldier Richard Bent, pressed on and were eventually both speared. Bent then fired at the Aborigines with unknown effect and the two wounded men managed an agonising walk to the river where they were picked up by an accompanying boat.[35]

By the end of 1806 the foundations had been laid for Tasmania's two major cities, Hobart and Launceston. Both settlements still faced serious problems. Food was often scarce and they were still dependent on supplies sent from Sydney or carried on ships arriving from other overseas ports. In Hobart there were serious cases of scurvy and the lack of food limited the amount of work that could be demanded from the convicts. In both settlements recourse was had to the massive hunting of kangaroo, which required men and their dogs to venture farther and farther into the interior.

The line of demarcation between hunter and escaped convicts who went out hunting and remained in the bush for varying periods of time blurred; many of these men came to know the back country and how to survive there well. Quite suddenly a problem with bushrangers confronted both Patterson and Collins. Patterson explained to his superiors in London how the colony had come to exist 'entirely on the precarious chance of the chase, and Kangaroo was the only food they depended on'. As a result the 'Inhabitants became a set of Wood-Rangers'.[36] A few months later Patterson's fears were borne out, as he explained in another report to London, describing how

Not less than ten prisoners have absconded with their Masters' Dogs, firearms etc., and are living in the woods and mountains, where (from their knowledge of the country) there is little chance their being apprehended; and it is much to be dreaded that they will become a desperate and dangerous Banditti.[37]

Yet for all their problems Collins and Patterson were optimistic about their tiny settlements. As more land came into production, each harvest was an improvement on the last. European crops flourished and by the end of 1806 Knopwood was picking the first green peas and strawberries from his garden. In both settlements the domestic animals thrived, the increase beyond expectations. Collins looked outward down the Derwent estuary and beyond and hoped for a future that involved whaling and sealing. The first bay whaling stations were established in 1806. Patterson, while hoping that the Tamar would become an important port, directed his greatest attention inland to the fertile soils that had been discovered along the North Esk and which were only a foretaste of the rich agricultural land soon to be discovered in the hinterland.

The Europeans were still confined to two small enclaves and they had little real idea of what lay beyond the island's typically close, high horizons. After a five day journey in February 1807 a party led by Lieutenant Thomas Laycock crossed the island from the Tamar to the Derwent and returned by the end of the month. He apparently saw no Aborigines on the way but the settlers at both ends of the island were keenly aware of their presence, particularly when they were burning the country. Knopwood recorded in his diary that on several days in high summer of 1806–07 the country was 'all on fire by the natives'.[38]

While the settlers knew little about the hinterland and its inhabitants the Tasmanians were equally uniformed about the Europeans. We have no idea if knowledge of the white men had spread right across the island. It seems possible that the clans living along the Tamar had no prior knowledge about the settlers' guns. Those living even farther away from the two settlements may have learnt even less about the European intrusion. But the Narra clans of the D'Entrecasteaux Channel and Bruny Island had learnt a great deal about the invaders and probably knew more about the Europeans than the whitefellas knew about them. They may have been much more curious than the settlers and must have had innumerable discussions about them, discussions that would have continued for a generation. But what the Tasmanians could not know was where the white men came from. Nor could they have any idea of the vast population in their distant homeland. They certainly observed carefully what was going on around Sullivans Cove and reported widely what they had seen and heard. Individuals and small groups made cautious forays into the settlement, as Knopwood recorded in his diary on Good Friday 1806:

At 8 a.m, a native girl about 17 was in my garden, the first that I ever see near me. She ran away some small distance and then stopd. I went to see her, she wanted some fire which I got for her, and some fish and bread, but returning to get some more fire she ran off. I see no more of her.[39]

Knopwood gave no hint as to how he had communicated with the young woman. It may have all been done by mime and sign but it is also quite possible that she already had a smattering of English. Knopwood and his fellow settlers had not learnt anything of the languages of the country and showed little interest in doing so.

We have little direct evidence of what happened between the escapees and bushrangers, and the Tasmanians. They may have often avoided each other. Those parties without guns had every reason to do so. They would have been no match for the Tasmanian men in hand to hand conflict. But the gun toting parties who escaped from the Tamar were another matter altogether. Two bushrangers, John Brown and Richard Lemon, were at large in the bush for over two years, during which time they murdered three soldiers and a convict. There would seem to be a very high likelihood that such men attempted to get access to Aboriginal women and would have used violence to achieve their objective. In his 1810 report on the southern settlement John Oxley reported that some of the bushrangers had 'forced the native women after murdering their protectors to live with them and have families'.[40] There was a general consensus among the officers and officials in Hobart and Launceston that the convict bushrangers were guilty of great brutality towards the Aborigines. Writing about the settlement on the Tamar, Oxley observed that, as a consequence of 'the many atrocious cruelties practised upon them by the Convict Bush Rangers, they avoid as much as possible the appearance of a White Man'.[41] In a letter home to his family in 1808 Surveyor George Prideaux Harris explained that the escapees had

wantonly murdered the poor wretches and taken their women from them and they naturally in revenge, making no distinction have killed some of our servants whilst hunting and it is now dangerous to go in the bush but 3 or 4 together well armed.[42]

But the most significant assault on the Tasmanians was not the work of escapees and renegades, but that of the soldiers of the New South Wales Corps at Risdon in May 1804.

Even at the time it was a controversial event and has remained so ever since. Contemporary Aboriginal Tasmanians regard it as the defining event of the white invasion after which nothing could ever be the same again. No one doubts that on 3 May there was a confrontation between a large group of Mairremmener people and settlers. The contention has been about what actually occurred and how many Aborigines were killed.

There also is no agreement about the number of Aborigines who suddenly appeared before the camp at Risdon. The party was large, certainly in the hundreds, and included men, women and children. It is likely that it represented a collection of bands from across a wide area of Mairremmener territory. It seems that the well-organised drive to take kangaroo was carried out to feed the unusually large gathering, that is, the Aborigines were hunting to remain together rather than gathering for the hunt. There must have been ritual or ceremonial business to attend to. Given the time of year it seems possible that the bands from the high country on Central Plateau had just arrived to spend the winter with their coastal kinfolk. Various writers have suggested that the Tasmanians must have been unaware of the European presence, but that seems unlikely given their occupation of the site at Risdon for more than six months. The presence of women and children would suggest that they were not intending to attack the camp. Three eye witnesses left accounts of what happened. Surgeon Jacob Mountgarret wrote to Knopwood telling him that 'not less than 5 or 6 hundred' had made a premeditated attack on the camp. The officer in charge, Lieutenant William Moore, wrote to Governor Collins, explaining that the design of the Tasmanians was 'to attack us, given their numbers and the spears with which they were armed'. Moore also reported that prior to the direct confrontation, the Aborigines had harassed two of the settlers on outlying allotments. With a large number already in the camp one of the cannon was fired 'to intimidate them'. A party of soldiers and prisoners then followed the retreating Aborigines up the valley firing as they went.[43]

A quite different story was told by the convict Edward White, which was given in evidence before an official committee in 1830. He recalled that he was hoeing new ground near the creek when he saw '300 of the Natives coming down in a circular form, and a flock of Kangaroos hemmed in between them'. They looked at him, he explained, 'with all their eyes'. White said that not only was he not scared but also that the Aborigines neither attacked the outlying settlers nor the soldiers; nor did he think they would have molested them. The firing commenced at about 11 o'clock and 'there were a great many of the natives slaughtered and wounded; I don't know how many'.[44]

With two such differing accounts there has been much room for conflicting interpretations. Much depends on whether the cannon was loaded. We will never be sure about this. But one problem has not been fully examined and that is the time it took for the drama to unfold. White recalled that the firing began at 11 o'clock but we know from Knopwood that the cannon was heard on the other side of the Derwent at 2 o'clock in the afternoon. So the confrontation lasted for three hours, or more if we include the pursuit up the valley. This presents us with an intriguing question. What happened during that time? It seems clear that the conflict began when the large hunting party approached the camp and was met by the soldiers' musket fire. If the most common pattern of behaviour had followed, the Aborigines would have fled the scene in great fear and not returned. Had that been the case the incident would have been over in half an hour or so. Despite much having been written about the incident over 200 years, few writers have addressed what seems to be the most important question of all: What happened after the original confrontation? James Boyce realised that there was a question to be answered and wrote in his recent book *Van Diemen's Land: A history*:

The fact that the assault went on for so long is the most difficult and terrible aspect of the tragedy to understand. In later violent encounters the Aborigines invariably fled for cover when shooting began. Were the Aborigines fighting back at Risdon? Or did the volleys of the still unfamiliar musket engender such chaos that the group – which included young children, the frail and the elderly – did not know where to run?[45]

It seems highly unlikely that the Aborigines would not know where to run or that they would stand around in range of the muskets for over two hours. Indeed, Boyce's first alternative appears to provide a much better the answer to our problem.

If, as Moore attested, the Aborigines were still in the camp at the end of the attack, it suggests that they were not intimidated by earlier musket fire and had returned. At the end of the three hour confrontation they would have been far from friendly. In fact, what may have happened was that the Aborigines returned without their women and children, re-armed with spears and bent on revenge. White reported that the original hunting party 'had no spears with them: only waddies'. But Moore made the intriguing remark that during the 'time they were in camp, a number of old men were perceived at the foot of the hill, near the valley, employed in preparing spears'. He also referred to spears in his letter to Collins. So what may well have happened was that the Aborigines, emboldened by their unusually large numbers, returned to the camp having collected their spears and made new ones as well. If Moore and his soldiers had been intimidated enough to start firing at the beginning of the affray their alarm must surely have been all the greater three hours later, enough to resort to their ultimate weapon, the loaded canon. If the Mairremmener had already withstood volleys of musket fire, why would the frightened soldiers think that the mere noise of the canon would effect the relief they clearly needed? Their situation may have been more perilous than most historians have supposed. If they had depended on their muskets alone they may well have been overwhelmed; given the probable size of the attacking party, their lives may have been in serious danger.

Such an interpretation casts a very different light on the behaviour of both settlers and Aborigines. At the start the Aborigines were hunting kangaroo, but later that was probably far from the case. They may have attempted the most serious frontal assault on settlers in Tasmanian history. The soldiers did not, then, fire the cannon without reason on a peaceful hunting party but on a large group of men whose spears presented a serious threat to them.

It became popular wisdom among the settlers that the attack at Risdon permanently damaged all future prospect for peaceful relations with the Aborigines. This almost certainly contained an element of the truth. While reflecting on the causes of frontier conflict in 1829, after visiting a hospital patient who had been speared, Robinson wrote in his journal:

In tracing causes to their primary source an indubitable fact presents itself which occurred upon the first colonisation of this dependency, the circumstances of which are too well known to be adverted to. It is very certain that the natives to this hour foster in their minds a remembrance of this wanton massacre of their fellow beings, and are anxious to atone for this aggression by the blood of their enemies.[46]

Tasmania's colonial historians were equally certain that the affray at Risdon had long term and deleterious effects on relations between the Tasmanians and the settlers. Writing in 1852 John West argued that the 'consequence of these events were lamentable', creating among the Aborigines 'irremediable distrust'.[47] In 1888 J. B. Walker observed that had it not been for 'Lieut. Moore's error at Risdon, a war of extermination, with all its attendant horrors, might have been averted.' The 'unhappy event' of 3 May 1804 'sowed the seeds of hostility on the part of the blacks, which . . . filled the colony with deeds of outrage and horror'.[48]

There is no doubt that the Mairremmener were greatly affected by the affray and were probably never reconciled with the Europeans. Their resistance was at the very heart of the Black War. But we can not be sure that the other language groups even knew the attack had taken place. Within a generation all had been engulfed by the overwhelming tide of settlement.

2

Van Diemen's Land: Settling in the enviable island

The often turbulent water of Bass Strait has played as important a role in the history of Tasmania as any part of the island itself. The final proof that Tasmania was an island came with the circumnavigating voyage of Bass and Flinders, which concluded in January 1799. The advantage of the new passage for ships travelling from Britain and India was immediately apparent. It shortened the voyage by at least a week and avoided the notoriously stormy passage around the south of Tasmania. But problems of a different kind immediately presented themselves. The British assertion of sovereignty over the whole eastern half of the continent by both Cook in 1770 and Phillip in 1788 was, in international law, highly dubious, even after the establishment of the settlement at Sydney. The realisation that Tasmania was an island created even greater uncertainty. A problem, which might have been ignored in other circumstances, assumed an urgency due to the presence in Australian waters during 1802 of the French expedition of Baudin and Peron. Suspicion of French intentions and awareness of Britain's tenuous claims to Tasmania led, as we have seen, to expeditions launching from both London and Sydney to secure the island and guard the sea route through Bass Strait.

It was, then, a new beginning for British settlement. But was there any change in attitudes towards the Aborigines as a result of experience in New South Wales since 1788? The leading members of the First Fleet arrived in Port Jackson with the mistaken belief that New South Wales was largely uninhabited, which was the advice given to British officials by Sir Joseph Banks. But this assumption was never made about Tasmania. Almost every expedition visiting the island between 1772 and 1803 reported the presence on the coast of considerable numbers of Aborigines, even if their assessments were often based on the large number of fires seen at night from the quarterdeck. British uncertainty about their claims of sovereignty and the related rights of the Aborigines were illustrated by the instructions given by the government to the commander of the *Lady Nelson* in March 1801. He was instructed to prosecute 'the discovery and survey of the unknown parts of the coast of New Holland'. Among the large number of instructions about the tasks to be fulfilled was a passage relating to promising locations that might be 'of importance to Great Britain'. In such regions the commander was to

take possession in His Majesty's name, with the consent of the inhabitants, if any, under a discharge of musquetry and artillery, and to record the whole proceedings at length both in his logbook and his journal, and, if uninhabited, set up some proper description as first discoverer and possessor.[1]

This passage presents us with a number of important and intriguing questions. The words are certainly formulaic. They had been repeated many times in the instructions given to expeditions venturing overseas. But perhaps more significantly they had not been used in any of the documents given to Arthur Phillip before the embarkation of the First Fleet. Does this confirm the suspicion that in 1786 Australia was thought to be uninhabited and therefore that the British were the first discoverers and possessors?

By 1801 this had become an open question and the correct procedure under international law was to seek the consent of the local inhabitants in order to establish a settlement. But in the following year the instructions given to David Collins avoided any mention of seeking consent or any implicit recognition of Indigenous land ownership and sovereignty. There was a return to the words that had been used in Arthur Phillip's instructions that exhorted the new settlers to treat the Aborigines with 'amity and kindness'. Collins was urged to 'open an intercourse' with them and to 'conciliate their affections.'[2]

When he arrived in the Derwent in 1804, Collins was already a man with much Australian experience, having been a senior official in New South Wales between 1788 and 1796. He had spent time studying the Aborigines living in areas adjacent to the fledgling settlement. His book, *An Account of the English Colony in New South Wales*, published in 1802, summarised much of what the British had learnt about the people they were displacing. A number of Collins' observations were particularly important. He appreciated that the different tribes (his term) lived in quite specific areas. He understood that the Aborigines had strong attachment to particular places and that land was central to the conflict with the settlers. 'While they entertained the idea of our having dispossessed them of their residences,' he declared, 'they must always consider us as enemies; and upon this principle they made a point of attacking the white people whenever opportunity and safety concurred.' By the end of his sojourn in New South Wales Collins had become disillusioned about the possibility of achieving reconciliations with the Aborigines. He began to sound like a colonist, one whose original idealism had been overwhelmed and replaced with tough minded realism and a tendency, increasingly common, to blame the Aborigines for the fate that had befallen them. Writing near the end of his term in New South Wales, he reflected on the increasing conflict along the Hawkesbury River and what he believed was the failed policy of reconciliation:

Could it have been foreseen, that this was their natural temper it would have been wiser to have kept them at a distance, and in fear, which might have been effected without so much of the severity which their conduct had compelled us to exercise towards them? But the kindness which had been shown them and the familiar intercourse with the white people in which they had been indulged, tended only to make them acquainted with those concerns in which they were most vulnerable, and brought on all the evils which they have suffered from them.[3]

There was something new in the instructions given to Collins as he embarked for the southern hemisphere. He was directed to 'place the Native Inhabitants of whatever place, he should settle at, in the King's peace' and to afford their 'Persons and Property' the protection of the British laws.[4] Collins had some difficulty with this instruction. He decided not to make it public while at Port Phillip and waited until a year after the establishment of Hobart to issue it as a general order, explaining to his superior, Governor King, in September 1804 that he would delay the matter until his 'Numbers' were increased.[5] The wording of the order is interesting in that it included a reference to property. What was meant by this? If it referred to moveable property it would have been more common to talk about possessions. Could the British government have been referring to landed property? It seems possible but as there was never any official follow-up it is unlikely. There was, then, a contradiction at the heart of British policy. The Aborigines were to be regarded as subjects of the king whose rights were protected by the introduced legal system. But their property rights were omitted from the bargain. And this under the aegis of a legal system that put protection of property before everything, before even life itself. The whole convict system, even the settlement of Australia, were monuments to the sanctity of property and the savage penal code that enforced it. The hypocrisy at the heart of policy towards the Aborigines was more understandable, and excusable, at Sydney in 1788. But Collins himself, and anyone who read his book, knew that the Aborigines owned, defended and cherished their ancestral homelands. All the while the magistrates, such as Knopwood, roamed freely while out 'ahunting' over Aboriginal land and had convicts flogged, their backs flayed for petty theft.

In Hobart Collins showed none of the ethnographic curiosity he had displayed in New South Wales. It was as though he felt he knew as much as he needed to know. He clearly wanted as little contact as possible. The lack of communication in the early months of settlement he did 'not much regret'.[6] Even when contact increased he made no attempt to study the Tasmanians or to encourage anyone to learn their languages. While he worried about the possible consequences of the affray at Risdon it meant that the Mairremmener people were, in his words, kept at a distance and in fear. And while Collins and his successors Davy and Sorell were clearly concerned about ill treatment of the Aborigines in the interior they made no serious attempt to bring them within 'the King's Peace'.

Policy shifted dramatically late in 1825 with the arrival in the Derwent of General Ralph Darling, en route to Sydney, to assume his role as governor of New South Wales. He handed Tasmania's

Image 2.1:   Colonel George Arthur, Lieutenant-Governor.
(*Source:* Archives Office of Tasmania.)

own new governor, Colonel George Arthur, the latest instructions
from Secretary of State for the Colonies Lord Bathurst.

They were concerned about what was seen as the appropriate
response to Aboriginal resistance, or the manner in which the

'Native Inhabitants' were to be treated when engaged in making 'hostile incursions for the purpose of plunder': The two governors were informed that they should 'understand it to be their duty, when such disturbances cannot be prevented or allayed by less vigorous measures, to oppose force by force, and to repel such Aggressions in the same manner, as if they proceeded from subjects of an accredited State'.[7]

The language was a little archaic but the meaning was clear: Aborigines who resisted were to be treated not as criminals or rebels, but as enemies of the state. Conflict was to be regarded not as riot or rebellion but warfare. Although these instructions were originally a response to Aboriginal resistance to European settlement beyond the Blue Mountains, they applied just as much to Tasmania. Arthur may have wondered what all the fuss was about. At the time there was little conflict with the island's Aborigines. But within a year or two he, too, was engaged in violent confrontation that came to dominate the attention of his government. Under the influence of the humanitarians British policy changed again in the 1830s but by then the remnant Aboriginal populations was living, and dying, in exile on Flinders Island in Bass Strait.

Fluctuating policy paralleled and was casually related to the great variety of ideas about the Aborigines that the settlers brought with them from Europe. The most prominent characteristic of settler ethnography was the common conviction of visitors and sojourners that they knew in advance all that it was necessary to know about those they chose to call savages. This was not only true of the educated elite who received their knowledge from books and journals. The folk ethnography of the British Isles was replete with sayings, stories and assumed wisdom about distant and exotic peoples. People who settled in Tasmania displayed comparatively little curiosity about the Aborigines. The attitudes of David Collins were characteristic. Much less ethnographic investigation was carried out in the first generation of settlement in Tasmania than had been the case in New South Wales or was to be so in the 1830s in Western Australia. The failure to employ any Aboriginal place names on early maps, in strong contrast to policy in the Swan River colony, was a telling sign of the lack of cultural engagement. The journals of George Augustus Robinson, which contained the most important observations of Aboriginal life and culture, were not publically available until the 1960s. Much more study went into the birds, animals and plants and even the rocks of the island. As a matter of course the British authorities sent geologists and naturalists to Tasmania to collect and classify; their specimens were carefully gathered and dispatched back to Britain. The bones and hair of dead Aborigines elicited more interest than the customs and beliefs of the living.

The late 18th and early 19th centuries witnessed an upsurge of ethnographic theorising in Europe stimulated, in part, by the proliferating reports from exploring expeditions. The 18th century's obsession with classification of species in the natural world was being directed to descriptions of the races of mankind and placing of them in hierarchical sequence in descending order down what was known as the Great Chain of Being. The Australian Aborigines were invariably placed on or near the lowest point of the chain, adjacent to the animals. From the middle of the 18th century, social theorists such as Adam Smith and Jean-Jacques Rousseau had propounded ideas about the course of human development and progress through a series of evolutionary economic changes – from hunting and gathering to herding, agriculture, and then to commerce and industry. Hunters and gatherers represented the earliest and most primitive stage of human progress. By the 1820s theories had been developed to explain the diversity of humankind and the presumed inequality of races. Anatomy was called into use: the angle of the forehead, the shape, configuration and size of the skull were used to explain the bodily manifestations of inferiority and to anchor prejudice in empirical and apparently scientific investigations. The weight of evolving opinion was towards the obsessive and hard-edged definition of races, the assumed superiority of Europeans and the inferiority of hunting and tribal societies wherever they were or whatever their objective circumstances.

But the intellectual traffic was not all in the one direction. Indigenous people always had their champions and currents in European thought sometimes ran counter to the gathering consensus about racial hierarchies and unchangeable inferiority. The members of the French expedition of Bruni D'Entrecasteaux who arrived off the far south coast of Tasmania in 1792–3 were imbued with Jean-Jacques

Rousseau's ideas and the romantic image of the noble savage. Their friendly meetings in 1793 confirmed their views, leading to their lyrical praise of 'such kind people', of these 'simple and kind men', who presented an image that, 'differed so much from the reports on all the savages by different travellers'. The Tasmanians behaved with 'sincere cordiality' and never showed 'a trace of bad temper'; neither in their behaviour nor their customs could the Frenchmen notice anything that weakened 'the good opinion we held them in'. Living so close to nature their candour and kindness contrasted 'so much with the vices of civilisation'. Admiring observation led to Rousseau-inspired speculation in D'Entrecasteaux's journal:

This tribe seems to offer the most perfect image of pristine society, in which men have not yet been stirred by passion, or corrupted by the vices caused by civilisation. Composed of several family groups, without property other than their wives and children, there must exist no cause for dissent, as the only chiefs are those designated by nature itself: the fathers and the old men. A mutual affection must exist between the members of the group, whose links are further strengthened by the marriages which must take place within the small number of families living together. Secure in finding their means of subsistence these men enjoy peace and contentment. Thus, their open and smiling expression reveals a happiness that has never been troubled by intrusive thoughts and unattainable desires.[8]

But such praise for the Tasmanians, or for the life of the hunter-gatherer, rarely appeared again in the writings of European observers. The idea of the noble savage was already falling out of fashion in Europe at the end of the 18th century. When the Baudin expedition visited Tasmania in 1802 Peron's ethnography was directed at questioning his predecessor's admiration for the life of peoples such as the Tasmanians. Primitive man still had lessons to teach the European savant but the text now was about the great advantages of progress and civilisation. This message had irresistable appeal to settlers who, in one way or another, saw their task as recreating the Old World in the new and who welcomed, often with uncritical zeal, any measure of progress. The life of the original people was not to be praised but replaced and surpassed. Pioneer colonisation saw a return to a simpler manner of living with small rudimentary settlements, limited technology, and rough and ready housing. The universally accepted measure of progress was the

PÊCHE DES SAUVAGES DU CAP DE DIEMEN.

Image 2.2: *Pêche des Sauvages du Cap de Diemen*.
(*Source:* National Library of Australia, an8953974a-v.)

improvement of material conditions: buildings in stone and brick,
paved roads and fenced fields. It was harder to see virtue in the life
of the Aborigines on the frontier of settlement than in London or
Paris.

Christianity was another critical measure of the perceived difference between civilisation and savagery. Early annunciation was an
urgent official requirement. Preaching, prayer and the sacraments
were to be introduced within days of arrival, all the more important
for a congregation of convicts. Guilt in life and fear of unprepared
death were seen as valuable coadjutors to the chain and the lash.
Even the casual Christian was aware of a great gulf between themselves and pagans, their faith shaping not only existence on earth
but also prospects for life after death. The Tasmanian settlers learnt
very little about Aboriginal spiritual belief and there was no obvious sense of regret about their ignorance. Simple material culture
was equated with superstition and devil worship, the less known
about the better. For those who cared, the overriding task was to
reveal to the savage the doctrines of the true and revealed religion

and to prepare them for the promised salvation available to all who opened their hearts to the message of Jesus Christ. To know the way was to be possessed of unquestioned power and irresistible, if often understated, power. Cultural change was only possible, only thinkable, in one direction.

The Bible itself was an endless source of ideas, aphorisms, precepts and ever-potent texts readily accessible to the literate and, to the unlettered, through sermons and reiterated quotation. It was also a fountainhead of implied ethnography all the more influential because it was unimpeachable and more widely known than any other text. The scriptures gave comfort to the colonist in ways foreign to the normal reassurances of theology. Perhaps the most widely used text in Tasmania, as in other settler societies, was the injunction of God in Genesis for humankind to go forth and multiply, to subdue and replenish the earth. This was seen as confirming the imperative of agriculture, of planting, sowing and reaping and, above all, of that ever-present, inescapable Christian image of the bountiful harvest. It was a divinely inspired licence to dispossess. Having no crops, no cultivated fields, the Aborigines did not use their land properly. Theirs was not a legitimate use of the land. They had ignored the divine injunction, albeit through ignorance, by ranging over the land rather than settling upon it. They did not possess it and therefore they held no title over it. What in other situations would have been thought of as theft could be seen as necessary appropriation of wasteland. International law was at hand to justify the pioneer, already fortified by theology. The most celebrated and widely read jurist at the time of Tasmanian settlement was Emerich de Vattel, whose major work, *The Law of Nations*, was published in English in 1758. The book, or at least extracts from it, were quoted in public debate in Hobart in the 1820s. The passage favoured in all settler colonies ran:

There is another celebrated question to which the discovery of the New World has principally given rise. It is asked if a nation may lawfully take possession of a part of a vast country, in which are found none but erratic nations, incapable, by the smallness of their numbers to people the whole? We have already observed in establishing the obligation to cultivate the earth, that these nations cannot exclusively appropriate to themselves more land than they have occasion for, and which they are unable to settle and cultivate. Their removing their habitations through these immense regions, cannot be taken for a true and legal possession, and the people of Europe, too closely pent up, finding the land of which these nations are in no particular want, and of which they make no actual and constant use, may lawfully possess it, and establish colonies there.[9]

Scripture and international law eased the colonial conscience, but there were simpler and more robust ways to justify land theft and murder. If the Aborigines were not fully human they could be treated more like animals than people. When New South Wales and Tasmania were settled, slavery was still practised throughout the British empire although increasingly questioned. The enslavement of millions of Africans was justified by their putative racial inferiority seen as being related to the colour of their skins. The emerging theories about racial hierarchies placed the Tasmanians on the same level as Africans, even below them. The savant's speculation could easily become murderous doctrines, on turbulent frontiers. If the Aborigines were beneath the reach of the European conscience, then anything was possible; atrocity had automatic and prospective legitimation.

But the Bible had other stories to tell. The message regarding racial equality was hard to miss. All of humanity was 'of one blood', made in the image of God, with equal capacity for salvation. That simple but profound message fortified the colonial humanitarians. They held it high, carrying it, standard-like, into disputation and debate. The injunction could be ignored or slyly circumvented. But it was hard to ridicule the word of God. However, it was not a text that colonists wanted to be reminded of, let alone lecture about. What to the virtuous appeared to be moral certainty was seen by others as puffed-up importance and self-righteousness. There was, too, the critical question of whether killing blacks was murder, which was a capital crime and a mortal sin. It was often discussed in public and doubtless worried about in private. Declarations about the equality of man were far more troubling in settler societies than any random text taken from political philosophy. All the contention surrounding these questions provided intimations of an uneasy, collective conscience, usually undeclared and gingerly scouted.

But the colonial humanitarians faced one, often unanswerable, riposte. If the colonial venture was morally unsustainable, then the only possible response was to board the first available ship and return to Europe. Debate about the morality of colonisation and expropriation was always complicated in Tasmania because a large majority of the early settlers were convicts who had no choice about their voyage to the antipodes and enforced residence on Aboriginal land. They were the unwilling, indeed, the compelled agents of the dispossession. The rapid growth of a Tasmanian-born population with no other home than their cherished island further muddied the crystal waters of moral certainty.

Running parallel with, and closely related to, the intellectual and moral struggle to ease the colonial conscience about relations with the Indigenous peoples was the more vigorous, more popular and contemporaneous process that transformed the isolated island, as far from Europe as it was possible to be, into a homeland. It was a development common to European settler colonies. But it had everywhere inimitable trajectories and this was clearly the case in Tasmania where the rise of a distinctive island patriotism occurred in a particular way and with remarkable, surprising celerity. It came about because of the nature of Tasmania itself, the way in which settlement unfolded, and the ideas and preferences that the sojourners and settlers carried with them from the other side of the world.

Among the most important was the aesthetic appreciation of landforms and vistas common in Tasmania. The generation educated in the late 18th century and early 19th century had been prepared in Europe to find Tasmania beautiful. Their eyes were attuned in advance to appreciate what they saw. The last years of the 18th century had witnessed the fashionable pursuit and worship of the picturesque, of rugged mountain scenery, wild rivers, plunging waterfalls and the evanescent effects of cloud and mist.

Travellers interested in the picturesque visited the Lake District, north Wales, the Scottish Highlands and eventually the Alps to experience the frisson induced by nature at its most awesome and exhilarating. At the same time popular taste came to prefer landscape painting over epic scenes of historical importance and both men and women dabbled in the new hobby of sketching and painting with watercolours.

The picturesque potential of Tasmania was recognised by the earliest visitors. While sailing along the rugged south coast in 1798 George Bass was moved to lyrical praise of the land:

THE FRENCHMAN'S CAP.

Image 2.3:   A. Hayman's wood engraving, *The Frenchman's Cap*, which appeared in the *Picturesque Atlas of Australasia*, volume II, depicts the Central Highlands of Tasmania. (*Source:* Archives Office of Tasmania.)

To a very unusual elevation is added an irregularity of form, that justly entitles it to rank among the foremost of the grand and wildly magnificent scenes of nature. It abounds with peaks, and ridges, gaps and fissures, that not only disdain the smallest uniformity of figure, but are ever-changing shape, as the point of view shifts.[10]

A few years later the French officers and scientists were equally awed by the coastal scenery. Francois Peron described how 'everyone was gazing at the land'; they vied with each other 'in our admiration of the lofty mountains' and marvelled at the 'huge tablelands of the interior'. Overwhelmed by the scenery, they surrendered 'to the sweet dreamings which such picturesque sights had aroused in our hearts'.[11]

The land also cast its spell on those who were the first to venture inland. Surveyor Harris wrote home to his family about the land around the Tamar. It was, he declared, 'the finest country in the world, as beautiful a country in appearance as I ever saw'.[12] The gorge of the South Esk elicited further superlatives. It was, Governor Patterson believed, 'picturesque beyond description'.[13] Another surveyor, William Collins, thought the beauty of the scene was 'probably not surpass'd in the world'.[14] New arrivals recapitulated these pioneer enthusiasms. In one of the first books about Tasmania, Charles Jeffreys captured the common reaction of visitors arriving in the Derwent. The scenery along the whole course of the river, he wrote, 'is exquisitely beautiful, and in some places highly romantic and picturesque'.[15] The gorge on the North Esk at Corra Lynn inspired further lyricism:

The overhanging rocks, and the apparently pendant trees, nodding over the vale below, fill the mind of the traveller with sentiments of awe and admiration, the whole scene is indeed indescribably grand and majestic.[16]

The lakes on the Central Plateau became favourite locations for those seeking romantic vistas. The first traveller to reach Lake Echo, Dr James Ross, found a scene 'of enchanting serenity', a charm of nature 'so supreme, so eloquent'. The party, he wrote, 'satiated our eyes with the heavenly prospect'. The pleasure produced by the beautiful sight was 'enhanced by conceiving ourselves the first discoverers of it among Europeans'. The overall effect was sublime and we exulted in a sort of rhapsody'. 'We stood,' he wrote, 'upon the beach, forgetting all the fatigue of the day, and fancying ourselves the lords and masters of the scene before us.'[17] It is a striking image that provokes many questions about the pursuit of the picturesque in settler colonies and the extent to which appreciation accompanied and enhanced appropriation. What was, in Britain, a harmless, mildly eccentric pastime, became in the New World part of the process of displacement and dispossession. Clearly, the affectionate and enthusiastic engagement with the landscape eased the colonists into their new life and helped appease an inescapable sense of exile. It was through their appreciation that they augmented their sense of moral right to the new land. It was as if the Aborigines did not deserve to keep their homeland in the face of such admiring, aesthetically refined rivals. Visiting agricultural expert Henry Widowson wrote of his experience on the Jordon River, which found its way

through the immense ravines of rocks and mountains among which I was once for some time enlabrynthed; but the pleasure I derived in surveying the immense precipices, many of which were 200 feet in height, amply compensated for the fears I at first entertained of being out all night in a country surrounded by natives.[18]

A correspondent wrote to the *Launceston Advertiser* in 1830 at the time of the Black Line, observing that, with the Aborigines removed, 'We will then be able to enjoy the sublime scenes presented by the interior ... without being massacred by savages'.[19]

Settler sensibilities responded to more than the wild vistas of mountain and torrent. The English landscape had been transformed during the 18th century by the creation of the great parks designed by Capability Brown, Humphrey Repton and their imitators and associates. The overriding purpose of these English gardens was to create an image of open grassland with carefully clustered bands of trees planted in such a way as to appear entirely natural. Success was measured by the extent to which the observer of the completed project was unaware of the careful design and often elaborate earthworks.

For quite different reasons and in distinctive ways the Aboriginal bands had created a landscape that looked very similar to the work of Capability Brown. Their constant use of fire kept the country open, suppressed the otherwise vigorous undergrowth, enhanced the growth of indigenous grasses and provided optimum conditions that favoured the browsing marsupials such as wallabies and emus, and facilitated their hunting.

The settlers discovered this country in the earliest years of their occupation, initially because they hunted wallaby themselves for food in large numbers, and then because it was ideal grazing land for their sheep and cattle. As early as 1806 William Patterson was celebrating the 'excellent walks' where the sheep were thriving.[20] Again and again the open grassland of the Midlands was compared with the grand estates in England. 'In very many places,' one settler wrote, 'there are no more trees than would be considered ornamental in a gentleman's park', while wattles grew in small and picturesque clumps, 'as if so placed by the hand of man'.[21] The plains in the centre of the island, another visitor wrote, were 'moderately wooded by small clumps of trees, and as if planted by the hand of man to ornament an estate'.[22] Charles Jeffreys explained to his putative English readers how there was ample evidence of 'the thinly wooded nature of the country',

which without any aid of artificial means, is capable of being traversed on horseback with almost as much facility as if the island had been in a state of civilisation and cultivation for centuries.[23]

The appeal of this country was as much economic as aesthetic, a visiting farm overseer noting that

The emigrant has not to wage hopeless and ruinous war with interminable forests, and impregnable jungle; as he finds prepared by the hand of nature, extensive plains ready for the ploughshare, and capable of repaying manifold in the first season.[24]

Like their stay at home relatives the Tasmanian settlers were able to appreciate, at one and the same time, the picturesque and the pastoral, characteristic scenes of those two great contemporary painters, Turner and Constable. But in the New World the contrast was more potent and resonant of deeper ideological currents. While the colonists might be enthusiasts for picturesque wilderness, they preferred it at a distance. Their transfer to the antipodes had not been effected to refine the sensibility but to establish or restore family fortunes. Material progress was the central

obsession in all settler colonies. It was the measure of individual
and collective success. A prospering colony reassured the settler
that the momentous decision to remove to the far corner of the
earth had been vindicated. So every improvement in farming, housing, industry or transport was an occasion for collective congratula-
tion. While on his way to his jubilant discovery of picturesque Lake
Echo, Dr Ross found another, quite different, scene to celebrate. On
the outer fringe of the settlement he walked past a pioneering farm
that had a small flock of sheep, a cottage with stockyard and 'other
rural accompaniments', and in a small neat enclosure evidence of
the 'first operations of the plough'. Ross turned back to look at the
farm through a natural rock arch and thought the scene was equal,
'in triumphal glory to Napoleon's boasted monument in Paris'.[25]
Writing of his own farming endeavours Ross asked himself why he
had 'felt such joy' when he cut down his first tree for shingles.[26]
It was a question addressed in the two most significant cultural
achievements of the fledgling society; the painting of John Glover
and the history of Tasmania by John West. Glover's famous canvas,
My Harvest Home, is one of the greatest artefacts celebrating settler
colonialism to be found anywhere in the world.

For his part West declared: 'No man can witness the triumph
of colonisation, when cities rise in the desert, and the wilderness
blossoms as the rose, without being gladdened by the change.'[27]

While only a minority could emulate Glover and take up land
for farming, many more established small gardens; admiring visitors noted familiar English flowers growing in profusion around
humble cottages. Discussion of local gardens occasionally took on
a political character as settlers sought a distinctive form of colonial
garden. A writer in the *Hobart Town Courier* in 1829 urged his
readers to eschew the well-known pattern of English gardens with
the lawns running right up to the house and all utilitarian features
such as orchards and vegetable patches hidden away at the back.
It was a fashion that seemed 'quite out of keeping with the present
state of this country'. Gardens should be brought back from hidden
corners and planted to surround the house in order to 'prove the
triumph we are obtaining over the wilderness'. Fences, too, should
be featured instead of the 'hahas and other concealments in vogue
in home'. They should be 'distinctly seen and the design traced, not

Image 2.4: *My Harvest Home* by John Glover.
(*Source:* Archives Office of Tasmania.)

obtrusively, but yet so as to excite in the mind of the observer a consciousness of control and power'.[28]

Appreciation of the landscape was surpassed by that lavished on the island's climate. While it was familiar to anyone from the British Isles, and enough to feel homely, it was warmer and brighter, with a shorter, milder winter and more abundant sunshine. From the very earliest years of European intrusion the climate had its admirers. The island was blessed with a 'salubrity of climate which no country can surpass'.[29] 'Nothing can exceed the salubrity of the climate', another admirer wrote, 'the atmosphere is clear and elastic'. G. W. Evans, an official in the colony from 1812 to 1825, declared that the climate was 'perhaps the most salubrious of any on the globe for an European'.[30] The rapid change of weather, its daily variability and unpredictability provided Tasmanians then, as it does now, with an ever-present topic of communal conversation. Writing of his 10 year residence in the colony John Dixon declared:

Although the seasons perform the same revolution as in England, yet their effect upon ourselves is quite different; for instead of that quiet, undeviating return of weather which we experience at home; in Van Diemen's Land there is nothing but capricious variability. The seasons, with respect to their temperature, seem to be confounded; and the cold in summer is sometimes as keen as in winter. But the most fickle months are those of summer. Then the weather changes day after day; and often, hour after hour; not only by slight degrees, but frequently, to great extremes. Those changes are at times so sudden in Hobart Town, as that, in going up one street, you could throw off you your coat, and in coming down the next, you might put on an additional one . . . From what I have said respecting the variability of the climate, perhaps it might be thought by my reader to be unhealthy. But such it is not. In spite of its uncertainty, no climate in the world is more healthy . . . and on the whole, from many years experience, I can aver, that few climates in the world are finer, in every respect than that of Van Diemen's Land.[31]

The climate promised early economic advantage. William Patterson reported to his superiors in London in 1806 that it was 'highly favourable for all purposes of Agriculture' and most particularly for the 'Stile followed in Great Britain'. It was far more temperate than New South Wales with none of those 'severe months of snow and frost' experienced in Britain itself.[32]

The weather was not only a constant subject of conversation but also a source of pride and the focus for incipient island patriotism that enabled Tasmanians to assume an air of superiority over the older and larger sister colony of New South Wales. While visiting the island, Widowson noted the 'spirit of rivalry' between the two colonies, while Tasmanians felt New South Wales looked down 'upon her sister as a tender stripling'.[33] In an 1825 editorial that compared Sydney and Hobart, the *Colonial Times* declared:

On a candid review of both we can discover no advantage which Sydney has over us, excepting certain half tropical productions of little value; while we enjoy an atmosphere and climate the best suited to the health and constitution of an English man of any in the world.[34]

The *Hobart Town Courier* contrasted the English lifestyle of the island with the 'broiling heat of a West Indian sugar plantation', found in New South Wales where the colonists would eventually 'mellow into Asian softness'.[35] Islanders boasted that their wheat was superior, their horses hardier, their sheep more productive, their increase 'being much greater than in any country we know of'.[36] Even the military potential of the colony was proclaimed, the *Colonial Times* declaring in 1829 that the island enjoyed

A climate so genial, temperate, and so admirably calculated to infuse vigour and health into both mind and body, that we feel little hesitation in hazarding an opinion, that the inhabitants of New South Wales must fall far short of the physical powers of those reared in this Colony; and more, in less than half a century, we will exceed, if not in numbers, at least in Military prowess (if necessary), and active exertion.[37]

By the 1820s the colonists began to remark on distinctive customs that were developing in their fledgling society. New words were coming into currency, old ones put to new uses. In an article on 'The Vocabulary of Van Diemen's Land', published in the *Hobart Town Courier* in 1827, the writer noted that the original emigrants 'carried their mother tongue along with them', but 'the peculiarities of a new country soon loaded it with new terms and new acceptations to old words'.[38] John Dixon observed that the many accents brought from the British Isles were being 'lost in the general admixture of dialects'.[39]

As in any other settler colony the bestowal of place names was an abiding aspect of the process of possessions and dispossession. Naming was a way to claim ownership and to replace the detailed, if largely unknown, Indigenous nomenclature. There was no attempt in Tasmania to employ Aboriginal names, although it was a common practice in early Western Australia. The radical Sydney cleric, J. D. Lang, observed in 1838 that when he had visited Tasmania some years earlier, 'he enquired the native names of various places, but none were known. Not a single native name remains'.[40] But there was constant tension between the official names bestowed by explorers, surveyors and other officials and the demotic ones that emerged from the community. The official names, as often as not, referred to places in the British Isles or to important people who resided there. They rarely had any real relationship with the New World. The demotic names referred to local experience and shared understandings and were the work of the poor and the convicted. They were, as a result, frowned upon by embarrassed, educated settlers. They were 'ridiculous and uncouth names', many of the 'lowest description'.[41] The *Colonial Times* declared in 1827 that 'the appellations given to some of the places in Van Diemen's Land are detestable, and show great want of taste'. The writer listed such 'odious names' as 'Dick Brown's River, Devil's Backbone, and Kitty's Rivulet'. He believed that, as a result, the colony was, 'laughed at in the Sydney papers'.[42] In his 1824 book, *An Account of the Colony of Van Diemen's Land*, Edward Curr observed how the poorer settlers were wedded to the local names, which reflected their experience and their own way of coming to terms with their exile in the New World. There was, he observed, 'already a degree of nationality' in the island, referring to the fact that

people began to talk of the good times with which the old names are connected, and a Governor might as well abolish the English language by proclamation, as the names which are associated with former days. We still talk of the Fat Doe River, Gallow's Hill, Murderer's Plain and Hell's Corners. These names were bestowed on them by bushrangers and the hunters of the kangaroo, who in fact have been the discoverers of all the good districts in the island.[43]

Curr's observation provides us with a passing insight into the world of the poor, largely convict and emancipist working class, members of which did not write articles in newspapers, or even read them, and who did not address public meetings or send letters home to relatives in England. Boyce's *Van Diemen's Land* enables us to learn even more about the first generation of humble and often illiterate settlers.[44] Despite the inescapable rigours of pioneer communities and the harshness of the penal regime, Tasmania provided a benign environment where it was possible to live off the land in the bush for extended periods and experience a freedom from the inquisitorial attention of squire, parson and overseer unthinkable in the British Isles of the early 19th century.

But Curr's 'degree of nationality' was equally apparent among the educated elite. They too went through the process of transferring their allegiance and emotional engagement from the Old World to the new. It was described by Deputy Surveyor-General George Frankland in an address to the 1830 inaugural meeting of the scientific and cultural Van Diemen's Land Society in Hobart.

We all remember, said he, that melancholy day, when standing upon the poop of the good ship, that danced beneath our feet, we strained our eyes to catch a last glimpse of our native land; and not less so the many succeeding hours, which were occupied in looking over the bulwarks, and recalling the many joys from which we were sailing away. Our hearts filled with these recollection, we then thought it impossible, that we could ever feel a permanent interest in any land but that of our early love. But these fears were changed to hopes, when we came and saw the richness and beauty of the country for which we had left our home, we found the soil productive of abundant harvests, the climate most congenial to our constitutions, the scenery magnificent and new, and the land altogether full of the most interesting curiosities. Who will deny, that his sensations, in making these discoveries, were joyous, and at the same time preparatory to those of permanent interest in the place of his new residence? Such, I believe, are the feelings of all who hear me, and I propose to them a toast, which they will joyfully pledge, 'Prosperity to the land we live in'.[45]

All settler societies showed an interest in the first generation of native-born children and all expressed anxiety about their physique, health and character. Parents who had made the often momentous decision to emigrate worried about the impact of their removal on the next generation. This common concern was greatly accentuated in Tasmania and New South Wales where so many children had one or both parents who had been transported and where free settlers were dependent on convict servants. In both colonies there was a constant debate about the competing influences of heredity and the environment, or what we now call nature or nurture.

The native-born Tasmanians exceeded the most sanguine expectations and in a small society many adults closely watched their growth and development. John Pascoe Fawkner, who arrived with Collins in 1804 in the company of his convict father, recalled in later life that not one of the children of the free settlers or the marines and only two of those of the prisoners 'came to an untimely end, for any crime; or were sentenced to transportation for felony'.[46] Observers discerned distinctive physical characteristics among the Tasmanian-born youth. They were 'proverbially of tall and elegant stature'.[47] Newspaper editor and author Henry Melville thought the rising generation 'a very superior race, the boys tall and well made, the girls, handsome and interesting'.[48] They showed great prowess as oarsmen and whalers. Melville thought that on the water they were not to be surpassed by any other people. They regularly challenged and beat teams from visiting British and American ships.[49] Many began working at an early age, their parents

> being in the habit of employing them, both girls and boys, as soon as they can lift their legs high enough to walk over a tuft of grass, either to mind pigs, poultry or sheep; and the boys, when a little older, first to take charge of and then learn to drive the bullocks.[50]

The acerbic senior official G. T. W. B. Boyes described the native youth in a letter home to Britain in October 1831:

> They are such beauties, you cannot imagine such a beautiful race as the rising generation in this Colony. As they grow up they think nothing of England and can't bear the idea of going there. It is extraordinary the passionate love they have for the country of their birth, but I believe it is remarked that the natives of a Mountain Land feel stronger attachment for their birthplace than the Natives of the Plains. There is a degree of liberty here which you can hardly imagine at your side of the Equator. The whole country round, Mountains and Valleys, Rocks Glens, Rivers and Brooks seem to be their own domain; they shoot, ride, fish, bathe, go bivouacking in the woods – hunt 'possum and Kangaroos, catch and train parrots, Wombats, Kangaroo Rats etc etc. They are in short as free as the Birds of the Air and the Aboriginal Natives of the Forests.[51]

There was a terrible irony in Boyes' observations. The young European children were able to 'bivouac' safely in the woods because there were no longer any Aboriginal natives in the forests close to Hobart or Launceston and those left in the remote parts of the island were being exiled to islands in Bass Strait. In just 30 years the settler population had grown to be at least three times larger than the Indigenous population had been on the eve of the arrival of the French and English ships. Most of them were certainly 'gladdened by the change', although there was also regret and remorse about what had happened. But we have no record of anyone leaving the island because of revulsion at the brutal consequences of colonisation. The colonists felt themselves at home and congratulated themselves as they settled in to what many of them now regarded as their enviable island.

3

The Black War

The tragic fate of the Tasmanian Aborigines

It was an event of global significance and is more widely known than anything else that has happened on the island since the arrival of Europeans. The similar fate which befell other Aboriginal nations in early contact with Europeans has often been obscured by the size and scale of continental Australia. No such attenuation was possible in Tasmania. Settlement of the 'enviable island' was invasion and usurpation, partnered with violence, atrocity and the death of all but a small handful of survivors who escaped the overwhelming fate of their kin almost by chance, aided by the isolation of the islands of Bass Strait. While the Tasmanian story is not exceptional when viewed against the backdrop of five centuries of European colonialism, or even the more focused story of Australian settlement, it had an inimitable intensity produced by confined space and compressed time. In just over 30 years the Aboriginal population fell by at least 90 per cent; the survivors were exiled to Flinders Island where deaths accelerated. The greatest of Tasmanian historians, John West, reflected on these tragic events in his history published in 1852. He had arrived in the colony when memories of violence were fresh in the minds of many settlers. 'From Windmill Hill at Launceston,' he wrote, 'whence a wide and beautiful country is visible, the spectator could discern the site of twenty aboriginal murders – settlers, servants, and infants; the aged and the kind had fallen, as well as the base hearted and cruel.' But while welcoming the Indigenous exile from the Tasmanian mainland he was deeply moved as well:

ABORIGINES of TASMANIA

Image 3.1:   Aborigines of Tasmania at Oyster Cove.
(*Source:* Archives Office of Tasmania.)

It was, indeed a mournful spectacle: the last Tasmanian quitting the shores
of his ancestor! Forty years before, the first settler had erected his encampment! A change so rapid in the relations of a people to the soil, will scarcely
find a parallel in this world's history.[1]

The story is quite well known. Since the 1830s it has attracted
many historians and, in more recent times, novelists, poets and

filmmakers. It has been the focus for the most intense controversy that accompanied Australia's so-called history wars. Many themes therefore merit re-examination, not just for their importance in island history but also for their relevance to the wider national story and to questions that trouble us still. In the simplest form they relate to both war and peace. The contemporary reader would clearly like to know about the conflict of the late 1820s and how the Aborigines were able to create such havoc in the whole community. Why were they such effective warriors? What tactics did they develop? Why did the colonial government mobilise the whole community and hundreds of British soldiers in the Black Line? How did the settlers deal with the profound moral questions that became inescapable once Aboriginal resistance had become manifest? Was it seen as warfare at the time? Should we see it that way now and, if so, how do we relate this understanding to Australia's broader military history? Was the fate of the Tasmanians an early example of genocide, as many contemporary writers argue? If so who was primarily responsible – the imperial government or the colonists themselves? Then there are the unresolved questions about the way in which conflict came to an end.

Was there an unwritten treaty, or understanding, negotiated by George Augustus Robinson that was later dishonoured? Was there, in effect, a peace party among the Aborigines, members of which facilitated the exile to Flinders Island? Did the colonial administration of Governor George Arthur expect, and even welcome, the spiralling death toll at the settlement at Wybalenna? Was it, as it became known in the 20th century, a concentration camp?

There are, then, many questions to which the historian needs to respond. We should begin with the Black War of the 1820s, which came as a surprise to the original settlers because up until then there had been only sporadic conflict around the two small settlements on the Tamar and Derwent. The parties venturing into the interior to hunt kangaroo were often harassed, robbed and occasionally killed or wounded. We know little about white aggression towards the Aborigines but it was widely believed at the time that hunters and escapees shot their way out of trouble and took women and children by force. The first two governors, Collins and Davey, issued proclamations that denounced the murders and abominable cruelties practised by white miscreants in the bush. Until the early 1820s the settlers believed that the Aborigines were a mild and peaceful people, a view reflected in the comments of John Dixon, who said that they were 'perfectly harmless' and that 'a man with a single musket will make them run'.[2] The editor of the *Hobart Town Gazette* observed in 1824 that they had 'always been considered the most harmless race of people in the world...the most peaceable creatures in the universe'.[3] There were, no doubt, many settlers who asked the same question as an assigned servant in the troubled district around Oatlands, who wondered: 'What made them so blood thirsty towards us?'[4] The answer must lie in the early period of relatively peaceful contact as well as in the violent times that followed.

The two Tasmanian settlements grew very slowly during the first 20 years, much of the period taken up with the Napoleonic wars and their aftermath. Many Aboriginal groups would have known of the alien presence but had little actual contact with the Europeans. For those whose country had been occupied the large concentration of population in the two towns made any thought of attack seem futile. On the other hand it must have seemed possible to live with the relatively static settlements. The groups living close to the towns picked up enough English to be able to make themselves understood, began to wear assorted items of clothing and had come to appreciate tea, sugar and tobacco. There may have been considerable sexual contact between Aboriginal women and the large, woman-less convict population. This is a contentious question, about which we know very little. As has been stated we do know, from what English and French explorers noted in their journals, that the early explorers were struck by the fact that their crews found it impossible to engage in any sexual activity with the local women. This was quite contrary to their experience in many parts of the Pacific. A generation later all this may have changed. Aboriginal men may have traded their women to eager, importunate white men or the women may have visited them on their own account. In whatever way contact occurred the result was that the Aborigines had come to understand a good deal about the Europeans and perhaps the most significant was knowledge of how guns worked and what their limitations were, which knowledge must have spread far back into the hinterland. In a petition to the government in 1826 settlers from Campbell Town observed that 'the natives are no longer alarmed by the discharge of a musket'.[5] At much the same time the editor of the *Colonial Times* declared: 'We find by everyday experience that the natives are no longer afraid of a white man.'[6]

The increase in conflict coincided with, and was clearly related to, the rapid expansion of settlement between 1820 and 1830. There were only 5400 Europeans in Tasmania in 1820; 10 years later there were over 24 000. Over the same period large areas of land – over 2 million acres – had been granted and by 1830 over 50 000 acres were in cultivation. The sheep flock had grown from 180 000 to over 680 000 and there were over 100 000 cattle competing with them on the increasingly crowded island pastures. The greatest expansion was along the river valleys north from Hobart and south from Launceston. Within a few years the two waves of settlement met in what came to be known as the Midlands. This was the country where Aboriginal land management had created park-like vistas as attractive to the grazier as to the hunter. Much of it was also valuable tribal territory of the Mairremminer people whose most active young men were infants or adolescents at the time of the affray at Risdon. The north–south movement of the settlers crossed the traditional pathways and disrupted the seasonal movement of the Mairremminer east and west from the coast to the Central Plateau. During the 1820s they must have found more settlers and ever-increasing animal numbers each time they moved across their traditional lands. West observed that 'on every reappearance' the native found 'some favourite spot surrounded by new enclosures', and that is was no longer his. Increasingly, he was forced to 'steal across the land he once held in sovereignty'.[7]

Prominent Irish emancipist Richard Dry, who had been in the colony since 1807, provided the most perceptive assessment of the dramatic change in the Aboriginal response to settlement. While there had been violent incidents in the early years those responsible had usually been excited by 'some Temporary Aggression of the Whites'. The action had only involved the aggrieved group and eventually gave way to better feelings. But during the 1820s 'a determined spirit of hostility' had been manifested by the 'whole of the Black population' and 'acts of outrage' were perpetuated in every

settled district in the island. The motivation was no longer individual revenge or reaction to personal injury or affront, but could
be attributed to 'causes whereby they are all equally effected and
aggrieved'. The principal reason, Dry was convinced, was

the Rapid increase of Settlers who now occupy the Best portions of the
Land, extensive plains and fine tracts, where formerly Emu and Kangaroo
fed in such numbers, that procuring subsistence was pastime to a Black
Native, and not as it is now, attended with Toil and uncertainty. From this
land they are excluded and daily witness our encroachment in the extensive
Fences erected by the Settlers. The circumstances tho' inseparable from the
Nature of Settlement must impress the Blacks with unfavourable ideas of
our intentions towards them.

Dry concluded that the Aborigines had come to look 'on the whole
of the white population as enemies' and they were 'not sensible of
any benefit they might derive from living with [them] on friendly
terms'.[8]

The Black War was carefully documented at the time and incidents were extensively reported in the Hobart and Launceston newspapers. It has been much discussed by historians in the 19th and
20th centuries. In 1992 eminent Tasmanian ethnographer N. J. B.
Plomley published his detailed study, *The Aboriginal/Settler Clash
in Van Diemen's Land, 1803–1831*, which was based on a careful
study of the main sources. He determined that between 1803 and
1824 Aboriginal attacks on the settlers were uncommon although
he believed they were certainly underreported. The average for this
early period was only 1.7 attacks a year; in some years there were
none at all. But from 1824 there was a rapid escalation in conflict.
Attacks averaged 18 a year between 1824 and 1826, and then spiralled upwards from 72 in 1827 to 144 in 1828 to 148 in 1829,
and reached a peak of 222 in 1830 before falling back again to 68
in 1831. In all there were 706 incidents during which the Aborigines attacked the settlers or their property. During the seven years
170 settlers were killed, 200 were wounded and a further 225 were
harassed or threatened in one way or another. Three hundred and
forty-seven houses or huts were plundered or burnt.[9] Surveyor-
historian J. E. Calder, who had studied the Black War, observed in
1875 that in many publications the island Aborigines were depicted
as an inferior, cowardly, albeit inoffensive, race. It was, he wrote,

a very false description of them for they were not deficient of pluck, and their so-called harmlessness seems to have consisted in their making at least a thousand attacks on the colonists and fighting them as long as one of them was left on the mainland.[10]

Ethnographer H. L. Roth made similar comments a few years later. That the Tasmanian Aborigines were 'more successful in their struggles with Europeans than other races better provided for, was hardly to have been expected'.[11]

The statistics were indeed striking. They emphasised the dramatic impact of Aboriginal resistance on Tasmanian settler society and not just on those killed or wounded but also on the whole community. Conflict raged a short distance from the two major towns, as John West's reflections on Launceston's Windmill Hill showed. It was not something that was happening on a vast inland frontier, remote in space and distant in imagination. Because of its proximity incidents were graphically reported soon after they had occurred. Few people could feel detached from what was happening. Almost everyone, bond and free alike, felt emotionally, if not physically, engaged in the conflict. The turmoil created by the Aboriginal bands was all the more surprising because by the late 1820s there were so few of them left. Probably no more than 100 young, fit men were actively involved in attacks on the Europeans and their ranks rapidly thinned as the conflict continued. Commenting on his own research, Plomley observed that

until about 1824 or thereabouts the takeover of lands useful to the settler in Tasmania proceeded without much hindrance from the Aborigines but thereafter there developed a state of war, virtual or actual, a Seven Years War, which was waged by both sides with increasing bitterness.[12]

The success of Aboriginal resistance can be attributed to characteristics of traditional society and adaptations forced on that society by contact with the settlers.

Like tribal people all over the world the island Aborigines had deep and detailed knowledge of their own country. They understood its flora and fauna, knew where to locate food and water, could find their way across country, understood its characteristically complex tangle of intersecting hills and valleys and knew the location of every pass and ford. They could move across country at a speed that often amazed the normally clumsy, encumbered colonists.

The young men who had grown up after 1803 had absorbed the knowledge and acquired the skills of the successful hunter. Their sight, smell and hearing had been sharpened by the daily food quest and the sporadic skirmishing with tribal enemies, equally talented in pursuit and attack, evasion and escape. Robinson, who spent many months travelling with Aboriginal parties in the bush, appreciated that all too often the settlers had been at a great disadvantage when attempting to 'come up with the blacks. The natives,' he wrote,

have the advantage in every respect in their sight, hearing, nay all their senses; Their sense of smelling also. They can smell smoke at a long distance, especially if the wind sets towards them. I have known instances of their scenting a kangaroo roasting by hostile natives... They can perceive the smallest traces, much less the plain footmarks of white men.[13]

The well-known Danish convict Jorgen Jorgenson led one of the so-called roving parties tasked with pursuing the Aborigines through the bush. During 14 months of endeavour the group had little success, Jorgenson ruefully admitting that 'the vigilance of the Native Tribes... proved an overmatch for all our most strenuous exertions'. He realised that his party was watched throughout their frustrating, daily travails.[14] The settlers again and again complained of the difficulty of finding Aboriginal parties in the 'almost inaccessible vastnesses' and British soldiers were even less use in the bush than experienced colonists. 'The whole country,' Robinson observed, 'affords them concealment.'[15]

Men such as Robinson and Jorgenson realised that the Aborigines were supremely confident of their ability in the bush and contemptuous of the settlers who, with some exceptions, lacked the skills that they themselves valued. Jorgenson concluded that they 'consider themselves our superiors in the art of warfare, save their fear of our firearms'. The problem was to find ways of 'humbling their savage pride'.[16] Robinson said similar things on numerous occasions, arguing that it was essential to find ways to convince them that they 'were not invincible'.[17] On another occasion he wrote that 'They have great confidence in their own strength more particularly as they conceive their concealment in the fastnesses of the

Mountains affords them great confidence and security'.[18] The Aborigines ridiculed the 'idea of white men following them in the woods' and told many stories of how they had got the better of parties lumbering in pursuit.[19]

There were many interesting comments from settlers who appreciated the effectiveness of traditional skills when employed in frontier conflict. This was apparent to the old soldier Governor Arthur, who, while writing to an officer out in the field, warned that he must recognise that his troops would be dealing with a people who 'always in the most adroit manner, reconnoitre the ground on which they propose passing'.[20] The editor of the *Hobart Town Courier* observed that the Aborigine had adopted the 'natural tactics of war with which providence had provided him'.[21] In his 1875 book, *Some Account of the Wars, Extirpation, Habits, etc, of the Native Tribes of Tasmania*, J. E. Calder noted that the raiding parties 'never attacked at a disadvantage' and invariably 'retired directly when overmastered'. It was, therefore extremely difficult to 'put down such an enemy' who was neither to be 'easily met with in flight, nor overtaken in pursuit'. Calder remarked that if it had been possible to 'bring the savage into fair and open fight', the story would have been quite different but the 'black assailants' were far too 'acute and crafty an enemy' to be betrayed 'into this style of contest, and never fought his opponent at a disadvantage to himself'.[22] It was not just that the Europeans found it very difficult to pursue the raiding parties into the bush but also that there was almost nothing for them to do when they got there. There were no villages to sack, forts to raze, crops to destroy, livestock to kill or run off or wells to poison. There was just the rugged, empty bush. But the Aborigines could patiently watch the huts of frontier settlers without being seen or heard, swoop down at a propitious moment and carry away anything that might prove useful. A military officer given the task of protecting the settlers wrote that the houses were easy prey to the 'insidious depredators' who would,

for days and weeks, watch a house that they have marked out for plunder, till they find the whole of the males absent, they then pounce upon the dwelling, and with a celerity incredible plunder it of every article they consider valuable.[23]

By the 1820s the Aborigines had already learnt a good deal about the settlers, if only from observing them from afar. They understood enough about the pattern of farming life to know how and when to attack and how to make their getaway. They knew that muskets, while lethal at close range, had marked deficiencies. They missed their target as often as they hit it and they took time to reload once the first charge had been delivered, which allowed time for an attack on distracted gunmen who had to reload with fumbling, frightened hands. The Aborigines had at a very early stage in the colonisation, adopted dogs, some domestic stolen from the Europeans, others already feral, captured and tamed. Whatever the provenance, they were quickly incorporated into tribal life and used for hunting and for their role as watchdogs and de facto sentries. It was a remarkable example of rapid, creative acculturation. There is much evidence, too, that the Aborigines learnt to appreciate and use such European commodities as flour, tea and sugar, and tobacco, which were frequently stolen in large quantities. As the pressure from the settlers increased European food became increasingly important, particularly as hunting exposed the hunters to long periods of vulnerability in the open ground that was contested with shepherds and cattle herders and progressively being fenced. Blankets, too, became increasingly important because nighttime fires solicited the serious threat of nocturnal attack.

While the Aboriginal bands had distinct advantages in their conflict with the settlers there were other ways in which they were particularly vulnerable. Increasingly, experienced immigrant and native-born bushmen were learning how to travel lightly and quietly, and to live off the land; they had also come to understand the seasonal patterns of Aboriginal cross-country migration. They learnt, too, as bushmen did all over the continent, that Aborigines, who were superbly elusive during the day, were sedentary at night, were likely to be collected together and, above all, that the fires they would normally have for warmth and cooking could be seen from a distance. As night attacks increased the Aborigines were forced to do away with fires altogether, to hide them behind screens of leaves or to create small smokeless blazes that would be left or extinguished before sleeping. But the greatest danger for the bands was the appearance of horsemen. Most Europeans they were contending with – shepherds, timber getters, soldiers and members of the roving parties – were on foot. Horses were expensive in Tasmania, weren't essential for work on the small island properties and, above all, were not thought appropriate for felons, who could use them to evade salutary surveillance. But on the outer fringes of settlement, and on rugged foothills, some of the larger landowners ran herds of half-wild cattle and they required mounted stockmen who were also able to threaten travelling bands, once seen, with the prospect of frantic but often futile flight.

As the Black War intensified, the pressure on the Aboriginal bands must have progressively increased. More and more Europeans crowded into their traditional lands. Many of the Europeans – soldiers, roving parties, vigilantes and bounty hunters – had hostile intent. Some had murder in their hearts. But every white man was suspect. None could be trusted. Constant, endless movement was imperative. The need for instant flight was ever-present. Normal life must have become impossible. Young children and the elderly would have found it harder and harder to keep up with the young and the fit. All were endlessly harassed. The police magistrate in the troubled Bothwell region believed that the local bands had

suffered but little from our exertions, yet the constant state of alarm they must be left in, and the frequent change of position rendered necessary to avoid the parties, must be very harassing to themselves and their families.[24]

We have no clear idea of how many Aborigines were killed in the Black War. There are many accounts in official reports and newspapers of settlers shooting their adversaries, but no one tried to keep an accurate account and many skirmishes were probably unreported. We also have no idea of how many men were wounded and escaped, only to die of their wounds. Perhaps the most authoritative estimate of the Aboriginal death rate in the 1820s was that of Plomley who believed that the overall population fell from 1500 in 1824 to 350 in 1831. The figure for 1831 is accurate; that for 1824 speculative. He was only able to speculate about the major causes of death. He doubted that disease played a major role during the 1820s, there being little evidence to support a contrary conclusion. Traditional tribal enmities persisted and intertribal fighting, which probably continued even during the Black War, resulted in bloodshed and the capture of women. So we are left with armed conflict and the chronic disruption of normal life as the major causes of death. The 19th century historian, James Bonwick, provided an imaginative, albeit moving, account of the vanquished band members who came to terms with Robinson in 1831:

They had fought for the soil and were vanquished. They had lost fathers, brothers, sons in war. Their mothers, wives, and daughters, harassed by the continued alarms, worn by perpetual marches, enfeebled by want and of cold, hunger and fatigue.[25]

The intensity of the Black War came as a surprise to settler and official alike. Governor George Arthur, who arrived in May 1824, had served in Honduras where he gained a reputation among humanitarians for his support of the local Indians and his insistence that they must not be enslaved. He had the best of intentions. Within a few weeks of his assumption of office he issued a proclamation addressed to the fact that he had learnt that settlers were 'in the habit of maliciously and wantonly firing at, injuring and destroying the defenceless Natives and Aborigines of this island'. The whole settler community was exhorted to treat them on all occasions with the 'utmost kindness and compassion'.[26] At the end of 1824 a large party of Narra people unaccountably walked into Hobart. Arthur rushed out to meet them, offering them food, shelter and protection. He attempted, without success, to establish a local missionary organisation – an Institution for the Civilisation and Instruction of the Aborigines – on the island, but even vice-regal patronage failed to overcome local indifference to the cause. Further, government attention was, at the time, devoted to the violence and plunder of bushranging gangs, which were so great in 1825 that settlers were abandoning isolated properties and resorting into the two towns. Arthur feared the ravages of the armed bandits would threaten the future of the colony.

By the end of 1826, when the leading gang members had been shot down in the bush or strung up in town, the 'defenceless Natives' were putting far more pressure on settler society than the bushrangers had ever done. 'A Gentleman in the Interior' wrote to the Hobart papers complaining that the Aborigines were 'much worse than the late banditti of bushrangers'.[27] John West captured the resurgent fears of the settlers in a memorable passage in his history:

The fierce robbers, of European origin, who had infested the land were not half so terrible: these were at least restrained by early association and national sympathies: often by conscience, and even by each other. But the Natives now united the antipathy of a national foe, and the rapacity of a banditti, with the spite of individual revenge: they were at once a people in arms, and a distributed band of assassins.[28]

By the end of 1826 the colonial government was forced into action. A proclamation called on the settlers to act in their own defence. Given the determination of 'one or more of the Native tribes to attack, rob, or murder the White inhabitants', any settler was permitted to take up arms and, 'joining themselves to the military', drive them by force to a safe distance, 'treating them as open Enemies'.[29] Neither government exhortation nor settler anxiety reduced the tempo of conflict. Aboriginal attacks spiralled during the summer of 1827–8. Prominent settlers met in rural areas and sent alarmed petitions to Hobart. The newspapers carried constant accounts of robbery, assault and violent death. Fear spread like fire through remote districts. While out in the bush, settlers ached with anxiety. Travelling was the occasion for intensified fears. West explained how the traveller would 'often pause, to listen; the moving of a leaf would terrify him'. To appear in safety at the end of a journey 'was a new though daily deliverance'.[30]

It was clear to the governor and his officials that the settlers alone were unable to counter the Aboriginal onslaught, which seemed now to 'indicate a plan of offensive operations resulting from deliberation and concerted schemes of attack'.[31] More troops were ordered into the interior. There were 450 there from early in 1828. Not that they had much effect. They were easy to see and thus to avoid. During the summer there were 48 attacks on settler property, during which 16 settlers were killed and 12 wounded. Arthur declared that the Aborigines were daily 'evincing a growing spirit of hatred, outrage and enmity' against the settlers.[32] His response was 'to bring about a temporary separation of the coloured from the British population of this territory'. It was the Aborigines who would have to move, not the settlers. They should be 'induced by peaceful means to depart, or should otherwise be expelled by force'.[33]

The plan had no effect on the course of the conflict. The last months of 1828 saw a new level of violence. The deaths of two women and two infants in October further alarmed the colonists, the executive council noting that 'great and well founded alarm generally prevails'. The next step in the escalating campaign was the November 1828 declaration of martial law. The Aborigines in the disputed districts were placed outside the law as enemies of the king. It was in effect a declaration of war; Solicitor-General Alfred Stephen declared that the effect of the proclamation was to place the Aborigines 'on the footing of open enemies of the King; in a state of actual warfare against him'.[34]

In explaining their actions the governor and his senior officials displayed mixed emotions and conflicting motives. The prime aim was to repress the insurgency. Though they expressed the 'deepest regret' about their decision, the clear objective, as the minutes of the crucial executive council meeting indicated, was 'To inspire them with terror, the council fear, will be found the only effectual means of security for the future'.[35]

There were other considerations. With the growing insecurity many landowners found it necessary to arm their convict servants who increasingly objected to working in isolated districts without weapons. The governor feared that there would be a growth of vigilante action, a war of 'private persons', as he termed it. In such a situation control would pass out of the hands of officials, magistrates and army officers, an alarming prospect in a penal colony. The result would be 'lawless and cruel warfare' that would lead ultimately to the 'annihilation of Aboriginal tribes'.[36]

The violence reached a crescendo in 1830. The executive council was called together for crisis meetings four times during the third week of February. Governor Arthur expressed the 'utmost perplexity with regard to measures to be taken for the protection of the settlers'. Both old and new measures were sanctioned – more soldiers and roving parties and advice to the settlers to arm every male above the age of 14 in their establishment. Aborigines were to be recruited in Sydney to act as guides and cash awards were to be offered to bounty hunters – £5 per adult and £2 per child brought in from the bush. None of the measures, new or old, had any noticeable effect on the violence, and the coming of spring pre-saged increased attacks on the beleaguered settlers. That August there were more attacks than ever before. Arthur felt it essential to take decisive action. The executive council meeting on 27 August approved his proposal to rally the whole community and to drive the Aborigines from the settled districts southward into the two peninsulas in the far southeast of the island. It was, by any measure, a massive and desperate undertaking. The hope was to bring the conflict to an end once and for all, or, as the council explained, it was a measure 'calculated to bring to a decisive issue a state of warfare which there seems no happy ending by any other means'.[37] The 19th century historian James Fenton captured the essence of the proposal. Arthur, he wrote, had planned a 'coup-de-main on a gigantic scale, by which he hoped the native difficulty would be disposed of once and for ever'.[38]

Arthur was principally responding to the repeated calls from the settlers for greater protection. But there were questions of a more general kind. By 1830 the conflict was beginning to impact on the whole economy. Settlers were abandoning remote farms, servants refusing to venture away from the homesteads. But the great fear was that the Aborigines would begin to burn the grain crops on which the colony depended. The population was by then far too large to be fed by supplies shipped in from overseas. If the harvest failed, the situation would have been perilous. The Aborigines did begin to burn crops more systematically in 1830 but by then it was too late. They may not have fully appreciated just how powerful a weapon the firebrand might have been. But settler concern for the future of the colony itself was more than alarmist fantasy. Colonial Auditor Boyes had spent his career as an officer in the commissariat. He understood better than anyone in the colony the problems asso-ciated with feeding the community. At the time of the Line he wrote in a letter to relatives in England:

Our papers are filled weekly with the atrocities of the Blacks and it has become apparent that unless means are devised for making them prisoners . . . in some well adapted part of this county, or, otherwise exter-minating the race, that the country must be abandoned.[39]

The story of the Black Line has been told many times. It was an extraordinary operation. Two thousand two hundred men, including 550 soldiers from several regiments, moved across the island for six weeks between 7 October and 24 November. It was planned with the care and attention to detail of a military campaign. Each day's march was carefully plotted. Rations of meat, flour, tea sugar and salt were ferried by fleets of carts to the many depots. Hundreds of pairs of shoes and trousers, along with jackets, haversacks and blankets, were provided to the participants. Hundreds of muskets, pistols and bayonets as well as shot, powder and flint and tomahawks were drawn from the government stores or bought for inflated prices from jubilant gunsmiths in Hobart and Launceston. The Line cost the government £30 000, an enormous sum at the time and equal to one-half of the colony's annual budget. The indirect cost in lost production must have been correspondingly high. Yet it completely failed in its objective: only two Aborigines were captured.

There has been much speculation about the government's motivation. Sensational accounts have often assumed that the intention was to assassinate the hostile bands. There is no doubt that any Aborigine who resisted arrest or took action against the Linesmen would have been shot; that was implicit in the manner of the operation and the equipment provided. It is equally clear that the governor would have preferred that the removal be effected without bloodshed, that the massive show of force would intimidate the hostile bands, forcing them to flee in advance of the Line, which broadcast its progress during daylight hours with random gunfire and bugle calls, at night by a coruscating line of large bonfires. Such a result would have been far more palatable to his superiors in London than what would have become a well-publicised massacre. There is no doubt that Arthur was aware of this and the potential it would have in determining his future career prospects. It is also clear that the settlers greatly exaggerated the number of Aborigines still at large in the central districts of the island and greatly underestimated the determined task. But the whole operation must have alarmed the Aboriginal bands, who had never been confronted by any more than sporadic, sluggish pursuit by small parties of soldiers and settlers. They were probably unable to appreciate that the Line was a one-off operation that would never be repeated. They may have assumed that the settlers had dramatically changed their method of attack and that the murderous multitude might reappear at any time.

Arthur found one source of comfort in the debacle. The convicts had behaved with discipline and decorum. Indeed, the whole community had been drawn together, united by the common foe. The participants returned home, 'their shoes worn out, their garments tattered, their hair long and shaggy, their arms tarnished'. The events of the Line, West wrote, though not very glorious, passed into the island's nascent folklore: on almost every evening in the year, 'some settler's fireside is enlivened by a story of the fatigues and frolics of the Black War. But collective, jocular, reminiscing did not disguise the seriousness of the Line, 'the first military lesson given to the colonists.[40] It was everywhere regarded in that light. The House of Commons paper on the situation in the colony, published in 1831, was unequivocal. The title was *Military Operations lately carried on against the Aboriginal Inhabitants of Van Diemen's Land*. The colonial officials continually referred to the conflict with the Aborigines as warfare. Even in 1825, before the violence had begun, Arthur had received instructions from London to treat insurgent Aborigines as enemies rather than as rebels. In his first official response to the burgeoning conflict in November 1826 he called on the settlers to treat their adversaries as open enemies. He referred to warfare many times in his official correspondence and though the phrasing changed, the meaning remained constant. It was, variously, 'lawless and cruel warfare', 'lawless warfare', 'our continued warfare', 'our unpleasant warfare', 'the warfare with the natives', 'this lamented and protracted warfare', 'the species of warfare ... which is of the most distressing nature; a war of the most dreadful kind'. It must be remembered that Arthur was a professional soldier who was often writing to other military officers who recognised a war when they saw one. The treatment of Aborigines who were caught or surrendered differed quite distinctly from the fate meted out to captured bushrangers, who were brought in from the bush in chains, quickly tried and invariably hung. Members of the remnant band of the Mairremminer people who came to Hobart with Robinson in 1831 were unrestrained; they carried their spears with them when they were taken to meet the governor at his official residence They were treated as prisoners of war rather than criminals or rebels and while they had killed many settlers, there was no suggestion that they stand trial for their actions.

The debate around the council table and in the officers' mess about the nature of the conflict was echoed in the community. There was no consensus. The measure of empathy for the Aborigines varied widely. Many wished them dead or driven into remote corners of the land and attributed the violence to their savage natures. The official Aborigines Committee declared that Aboriginal violence had its source in a 'wanton and savage spirit inherent in them, and impelling them to mischief and cruelty when it appeared probable they might be perpetrated with impunity'.[41] Other settlers told a very different story and saw the Aborigines as patriots defending their homeland against a ruthless invader. Such views were openly and forcefully articulated although not widely applauded.

A correspondent wrote to the *Hobart Town Gazette* in 1824 arguing that the settlers 'ought to feel that we have invaded a domain from which our invasion has expelled those who were born, bred and providentially supplied in it'.[42] 'A Border Settler', writing to the *Tasmanian* in December 1827, observed that while the papers were full of accounts of Aboriginal aggression little attention was given to the other side of the story, to a 'race of people whose crime is that of repelling the invaders of their country' and seeking to 'preserve that liberty of hunting and acting', which the colonists were daily circumscribing.[43] Another sympathiser, R. M. Ayton, wrote to the government arguing that the Aborigines were no more deserving of censure than the colonists would be in similar circumstances if they set out to 'expel or extirpate an invading enemy who stripped them of their property; forcibly imposed strange laws and customs upon them and wantonly robbed them of existence'. But those who kill us, he observed, 'are execrated as murderers whilst those who kill for us are celebrated as patriots'.[44] The most searching examination of the moral and legal questions associated with colonisation was provided by a correspondent, 'J. E.', who wrote to the *Launceston Advertiser* in 1831. It was a long letter and should be quoted at length. 'Are these unhappy creatures,' he demanded, addressing the governor,

the subjects of our king, in a state of rebellion? Or are they an injured people, whom we have invaded and with whom we are at war? Are they within the reach of our laws; or are they to be judged by the law of nations? Are they to be viewed in the light of murderers or as prisoners of war?

Have they been guilty of any crime under the law of nations which is punishable by death, or have they been carrying on war in their way?

Are they British subjects at all, or a foreign enemy who has never yet been subdued, and which resists our usurped authority and dominion?

The British colonists have taken their country from them by force; they have persecuted them, wantonly sacrificed them, and taught them to hate the whites... They consider themselves, and justly so, ill-used. They seek to avenge the deaths of their relatives. We are at war with them : they look upon us as enemies – as invaders as their oppressors and persecutors – they resist our invasion.

They have never been subdued, therefore they are not rebellious subjects, but an injured nation, defending in their own way, their rightful possessions, which have been torn from them by force... What we call their crime is what in a white man we should call patriotism. Where is the man among ourselves who would not avenge the murder of his parents, the ill-usage of his wife and daughter, and the spoliation of all his earthly goods, by a foreign enemy if he had an opportunity? He who would not do so, would be scouted, execrated, nay executed as a coward and a traitor; while he who did would be immortalised as a patriot. Why then deny the same feelings of the Blacks? How can we condemn as a crime in these savages what we would esteem a virtue in ourselves? Why punish a black man with death for doing that which a white man would be executed for not doing? Is there such an effect produced on the soul by wearing a black skin, that it converts into vices those acts and feelings which are virtuous when done or entertained under a white one.[45]

These were provocative, challenging questions in 1831. What is more unsettling is that they remain so today. There is little recognition of the Aborigines as patriots and even less inclination to celebrate their heroism. Even more central to the question at hand is the inability to recognise the conflict of 1824–31 as warfare. This might matter less if Australia did not put so much effort into commemorating war, the imperative to do so having intensified in recent years. The sacred, ubiquitous phrase, 'Lest we forget', seems more potent than ever. New brass plaques placed on war memorials in towns across the country in recent years refer to every overseas military engagement since the beginning of the 20th century, even for such forgotten ventures as the minor involvement in the repression of the Boxer Rebellion. Involvement in war, any war it seems, regardless of where or why it was fought, bestows an aura of memorable heroism on the participants. The central question then becomes why conflict between colonists and Aborigines has never been accorded the same status as even minor overseas engagements. The reasoning seems less than persuasive. As we have seen above, contemporaries, from the governor down, constantly referred to the conflict as warfare. It overshadowed life in Tasmania for seven years and the issues in contention were of fundamental political importance. The future of the colony was at stake in a way that was not true of any of Australia's 20th century wars with the exception of the conflict in the Pacific between 1941 and 1945.

The death toll in the 1820s was significant even when measured by 20th century standards. The emphasis on the numbers who 'fell' in Australia's martial iconography illustrates how important the body count has become in calibrating the relative significance of diverse conflicts. The Black War of the 1820s measures up in this ghoulish league table. As we have seen, at least 170 settlers died. At least that number of Aborigines were also victims of direct violence; the actual death toll may have been much higher. But there is more to the question than that. Servicemen and women who died of disease in time of war are counted among the fallen and accorded the same status as those who were killed in conflict. Their sacrifice is not diminished by the recorded cause of death. If we apply that standard to the Black War, then we have to revise upward our death toll to the point where it was almost certainly higher than the 323 casualties in the Korean War or the 523 in Vietnam.

At the war memorial in Launceston there is a plaque that does recognise Aboriginal involvement in war. It reads: 'In recognition of Tasmanian Aborigines Who Served or Fell in Defence of their Country: 1901–1999'. It was an appropriate and well-meant gesture but it actually compounds the problem of who is publicly remembered and why, and, concomitantly, who is forgotten and thereby retrospectively disdained. Why begin the story in 1901? Federation perhaps, but the focus was on Tasmania not the Commonwealth. The implications are significant. Is it a matter of forgetting or a deliberate refusal to recognise that the Tasmanian Aborigines had fallen in defence of their country in a desperate attempt to retain their freedom and independence against units of the British army and assorted groups of armed settlers? Are contemporary Tasmanians less able to see than their ancestors that they were patriots defending their ancestral homeland against an overwhelming invasion? Measured by the standards of heroism applied to Australia's armed forces their resistance was impressive and more effective than any other Aboriginal group in Australia. In a tribute to the Tasmanian tribesmen, and in particular the bands of the Mairremminer people, 19th century historian James Bonwick wrote regarding their surrender to Robinson:

With a knowledge of the mischief done by these few, their wonderful marches and their widespread aggressions, their enemies cannot deny to them the attributes of courage and military tact. A Wallace might harass a large army with a small and determined band; but the contending parties were at least equal in arms and civilisation. The Caffres who fought us in Africa, the Maories in New Zealand, the Indians in America, were far better provided with weapons, more advanced in the science of war, and considerably more numerous, than the naked Tasmanians. Governor Arthur rightly called them a noble race.[46]

J. E. Calder, who spent more time studying the records of the Black War than any other Tasmanian settler, reached a similar conclusion, observing in 1875 that whatever the future historian might write about the island Aborigines, he would do them an injustice if he failed to record that 'as a body they held their ground bravely for 30 years against the invaders of their beautiful domains'.[47]

4

An Indelible Stain?

Aboriginal resistance came to dominate the attention of Governor Arthur's administration. His response to this challenge has had more influence on the way history has judged his administration than anything else he did during an industrious 12 years in Tasmania. Arthur himself regretted the way it had all turned out and wrote remorseful reflections about the experience. In an 1833 letter to the Colonial Office he declared that he found it distressing to recall the 'injuries that the Government [was] unwillingly and unavoidably made the instrument of inflicting' and of 'driving a simple but warlike, and, it now appears, noble-minded race, from their hunting grounds'.[1] In a similar official letter he declared that when he first arrived in the colony he was influenced by popular opinion and as a result, 'fell into some very wrong notions ... from which very injurious consequences followed'.[2] It may have been genuine regret on Arthur's part or a clever appeal to superiors in Britain who were increasingly influenced by humanitarian zeal. It could have been both. Of greater consequence was Arthur's reflection on the need for treaties when dealing with Indigenous peoples. 'It was,' he wrote in 1832, 'a fatal error in the first settlement of Van Diemen's Land that a treaty was not entered into with the natives, of which the savages well comprehend the nature ... ' Had they received compensation and been adequately protected the colonisation could have been effected 'without the injurious consequences which have followed our occupation, and which would forever remain a stain upon the settlement of the island'.[3] He returned to the subject three years later in another letter to the Colonial Office in which he wrote:

On the first occupation of the Colony it was a great oversight that a treaty was not, at that time, made with the natives, and such compensation given to the chiefs as they would have deemed a fair equivalent for what they surrendered.[4]

Arthur informed the Colonial Office that he had discussed the matter of treaties 'at great length with Mr. Robinson'.[5] Arthur's views may have been openly discussed in the colony in the early 1830s and were certainly known to the group of entrepreneurs of the Port Phillip Association, the syndicate of which Arthur's nephew Henry was a member, and which planned John Batman's voyage to Port Phillip in May 1835, which resulted in his famous treaty with the local Aborigines. Of wider consequence was Arthur's presence in London in 1837 when the Colonial Office was deciding what to do about New Zealand. It seems highly probable that he was influential in helping shape the decision to negotiate the Treaty of Waitangi as a prelude to colonisation.

There was much discussion about the need to come to terms with the Aborigines during the course of the Black War. In several of his official documents Arthur referred to his hope for a negotiated settlement with the 'chiefs of Aboriginal tribes'.[6] In December 1827 Arthur asked his police magistrates to seek out anyone willing to 'incur the hazard of attempting to open a conciliatory communication with the Aborigines'.[7] No one came forward. Writing to Governor Darling in New South Wales a few months later Arthur lamented his failure to 'induce them to listen to any specific terms of accommodation'.[8] There was much discussion within the government about the possibility of assigning part of the island for the exclusive use of the Aborigines. In his dispatches to London Arthur referred to his plan to 'allot and assign certain specified tracts of land for their exclusive benefit and continued occupation'. This division of the island was, he declared, to 'form part of the intended negotiation with certain chiefs of aboriginal tribes'.[9] The editor of the *Colonial Times* observed in April 1830 that the government had divided the colony into 'two parts'; one to belong to the English inhabitants, the other to the Aborigines. He explained to his readers that

The British inhabitants of Van Diemen's Land do not claim an exclusive property in the soil; the Government has taken care to fix certain boundaries, beyond which the Aborigines are perfectly secure, and furnishing them an ample extent for all purposes of that precarious subsistence to which they are accustomed.[10]

Even during the Line the plan was to force the most hostile bands into exile in the southern peninsulas. A map of the colony issued in September 1830 had the words 'Establishment for the Aborigines' printed across the land in question. The assumption at the time was that the Aboriginal language groups in the more remote parts of the colony would remain in their own land even if the Line had been successful. The idea of banishment to the offshore islands had been discussed at various times during the 1820s but was initially opposed by the government. With the intensification of conflict it became an increasingly attractive objective, the official Aborigines Committee declaring in 1831 that after the most 'deliberate attention' it had been decided that the hostile natives should be 'collected by every possible means' and removed to Flinders Island.[11] The committee members had no idea of how the exile could be achieved, but at the time of their meeting Robinson had already been out in the bush for two years on what Arthur termed 'an embassy of conciliation' that had begun on Bruny Island, south of Hobart, in 1829.

After a visit to the town by the Aborigines of the area the governor decided to create a small establishment to provide them with rations in an attempt to develop close relations with them. He appointed George Augustus Robinson to the position, thereby beginning his 10 year intense and tragic association with the Aborigines. Robinson was a 41 year old self-educated, London-born building contractor who had been in the colony since 1824. It did not appear to be a good career move but Robinson was hungry for recognition, acutely aware of his relative lack of status and possessed of a religious zeal that predisposed him to evangelical crusading. During the early decades of the 19th century men of his mould were working for the great British Missionary organisations in all corners of the world.

Robinson subsequently jotted down the reasons for his acceptance of the position on Bruny Island. They were:

1st: A missionary desire to benefit this portion of the human race.

2nd: To benefit this land of my adoption, by an endeavour to stay the effusion of human blood which had and was still carrying on between the Black and White inhabitants with such bitterness and rancour.

3rd: To become better acquainted with the history, manners, and language of this interesting portion of the human race, particularly as very little or nothing was known of them now especially as I had entertained an impression that this race would ultimately and at no distant period become extinct.[12]

Robinson's initial plans would have been familiar to any missionary working in the field. He set about learning the local language, tried to inculcate the need for labour, sought to gain control over the children and preached, as best he could, the promise of salvation. But many frustrations arose. He had trouble with his convict assistants, the Aborigines would not do as he wanted and were attracted to pre-existing camps of white men in the region who were timber getting or bay whaling. Members of what he liked to think of as his congregation sickened and died of respiratory diseases. It might have ended in conspicuous failure, as had many such endeavours in early colonial Australia. But within a few months Robinson suggested to the governor that he undertake an expedition to the colony's west coast in order to make known Arthur's 'humane intentions' towards the Aborigines. In a meeting with Robinson in June 1829 the governor gave his approval. The stated purpose was to endeavour to effect 'an amicable understanding with the Aborigines of that quarter and through them with the tribes of the interior'.[13] The land party of six convicts and a dozen Aborigines set off in January, supported by an accompanying schooner and whaleboat.

Robinson remained out in the bush until he arrived in Launceston nine months later.

Given the importance of what became known as the 'Friendly Mission' it is necessary to look more closely at the origin of the west coast expedition. The Aborigines on Bruny Island at the time of Robinson's arrival came from a number of places around the south coast, including Port Davey on the west coast. The same language was spoken from the west side of the Derwent estuary right around to the southern shore of Macquarie Harbour. There was almost certainly constant travel back and forth along well-marked tracks. On 9 July Robinson recorded how the whole community was in happy turmoil with the arrival of a party of nine men, women and children who had come from the west coast. 'The joy exhibited on both sides,' Robinson wrote, 'was unbounded and fully indicative of the affection they felt towards to each other.'[14] Robinson's clerk, Charles Stirling, concluded that the party had arrived to accompany the Bruny Islanders back to the west coast but the planned departure date was put forward because of the number of people who were sick. The Aborigines' decision changed Robinson's timetable. In August the governor met Robinson and expressed surprise that he had not already left for the west coast. Robinson replied that the tribe had been sick. The picture, then, is clear: the Aborigines were planning to make a traditional journey back to the west coast and agreed that Robinson could accompany them. His decision to go was courageous but opportunistic. It was not a case, as he presented it, that the expedition was his idea and that the Aborigines cheerfully acquiesced in it. Its nature and progress accords with this interpretation. Robinson and the other Europeans were totally inexperienced in the bush and were venturing into some of the most rugged and inhospitable country in Australia. Without their Aboriginal guides the expedition would have failed and the Europeans may have died in the bush.

Robinson was fully aware of his dependence. The party survived for days on the bush food provided by the Aborigines. They were, he wrote, well-acquainted with the resources of the country and would not allow him to starve. The young Bruny Island woman Trugannini recalled later in life:

We walked hundreds of miles in that time and had to take a little flour with us and some salt to make the roots and the kangaroos, wombats and possums we lived on taste better.[15]

Although Robinson carried a compass he followed the line of march chosen by the Aborigines. He was, he wrote, 'entirely governed' by their advice as to 'routes I may be induced to take while travelling in the interior'. The Bruny Islanders were of 'immense service as guides'. Their superior local knowledge of the country enabled him 'to traverse a huge tract in a very short time'.[16]

Robinson learnt a lot about the bush while engaged on the Friendly Mission but the patterns established in those first few weeks were constantly recapitulated during all six expeditions, which took place between January 1830 and August 1834. Twenty-seven Aborigines participated in the Friendly Mission. On every expedition there were more Aborigines than Europeans, the number ranging from eight to 14.

Trugannini, her husband Woorrady and another woman, Pagerly, from the Bruny Island – d'Entrecasteaux Channel country, were involved in the mission from the start. Aborigines from other parts of the island, including Dray, Kickerterpoller, Manalargenna and Tanleeboneyer, were also important partners in the venture. While the bushcraft and food gathering skills were of irreplaceable value to the mission, the knowledge of various languages and local customs, protocols and diplomatic niceties were even more important. 'I cannot effect anything without these people', Robinson confessed in a moment of modesty.[17] He had appreciated this from the start of his venture, writing to the Colonial Secretary before his departure from the west coast that the accompanying Aborigines could

be employed as messengers to the tribes of natives I may be employed to visit – would make known the purport of my mission – bear testimony as to the sincerity of my intentions, and consequently would be the best auxiliary that could accompany me.[18]

Much of the negotiation associated with the mission was carried out by the Aborigines themselves. In the 14 important meetings held in various parts of the island between November 1830 and April 1834 the Aborigines either prepared the way for Robinson to talk with the strangers or, more commonly, conducted the negotiations themselves. They invariably found the tracks of the bands they were seeking or saw their fires. When they were in striking distance Robinson and any other Europeans made camp while a small delegation of Aborigines went forward to meet the strangers. They approached them and negotiated with them for periods ranging from a few hours to a day or more in their own languages and in their own way. Robinson may not have known on many of these occasions what discussion had actually taken place.

This is important for any interpretation of the highly contentious events resulting from the mission. All the later expeditions were carried out to gather up the remaining bands and transfer them to the islands in Bass Strait and eventually to the settlement of Wybalenna on Flinders Island. By the end of 1834 only one small family group remained at large on mainland Tasmania. This was seen as an extraordinary and unexpected outcome at the time and has been the subject of much speculation ever since. In some accounts the Black Line and the mission have been conflated and the assumption that followed was that the Aborigines were forced at gunpoint from their ancestral lands. In the last years of the mission Robinson was more inclined to threaten the use of force than had been the case earlier. He was totally vulnerable throughout the mission and could have been killed at almost any moment; for many months he slept every night within reach of Aborigines. In a speech he gave in Sydney in 1838 he dismissed the idea of a forced removal, declaring that

In effecting these removals he made use of no compulsion, it was done with their own free consent; in fact it was not possible to subject them by force – he went so far as to say, that the whole British Army could not have effected it; at any rate the military force in the colony could not.[19]

Given the spectacular and well-known failure of the Line it was a persuasive argument.

Contemporaries attributed the success of the mission to unique and almost magical powers possessed by Robinson. Even that shrewd manager of men, George Arthur, was persuaded, telling his superiors in London that the Aborigines had been 'by some means taught to venerate him'. Others wrote of magical powers or, as West saw it, 'some species of animal enchantment'. Calder believed that Robinson subdued the tribes to his will because he was 'no ordinary man'.[20]

Such explanations can still be found in recent studies. In her 1988 biography of Robinson, Vivien Rae-Ellis declared that the secret to Robinson's putative power was that he was able to hypnotise his Aboriginal associates. He possessed 'latent power as a mesmerist'. Indeed, the 'hypnotic influence he exerted over the tribes . . . was the secret of his success'.[21] Robinson did little to disown the special powers attributed to him or the celebrity status he had acquired. Undoubtedly, his own view was that he was doing God's work and that divine intervention was at the heart of his achievement. This accords with accounts in much missionary literature of the time when conversion awaited the all powerful hand of God.

The fundamental problem with this long stream of interpretation is that it has never allowed the Aborigines to have minds or objectives of their own. If there was a coalition of intent it was because the white man had imposed his will on the weak minded savages who didn't realise that they were victims of incessant manipulation in order to get them do things that were against their own best interests. It allows for no discernment and political awareness among the Aboriginal members of the mission. Their contemptible belittling has been magnified in relation to the pivotal role played by the young Bruny Island woman Trugannini, who has been volubly accused of betraying her people out of girlish impulsiveness or out of sexual attachment to Robinson. She has rarely been considered to have been engaged in politics or diplomacy. It is an important corrective to consider the reasons she articulated herself for her role in a discussion later in life with J. E. Calder. She explained that she had come to the conclusion that Robinson was a good man, could speak her language and was very different from the rough frontiersmen then living in her tribal territory. She decided to go on the mission in the hope that 'we would save all my people that were left'. She had been to Hobart and 'knew it was no use my people trying to kill all the white people now, there were so many of them always coming in big boats'. When she negotiated with her kin members at Port Davey she told them, 'why we have come and that our people were all being killed and it was no use fighting anymore, and Mr. Robinson was our friend, and would take us to a good place'.[22]

By any measure this was a realistic assessment of the situation as seen from the perspective of Bruny Island in the late 1820s. The clans in the region had been in contact with the Europeans long before Trugannini was born in about 1812. Her people had often been to Hobart or had heard all about it from those who had ventured into the settlement. Many of them spoke some English, wore clothing and were used to using tea, sugar, flour, potatoes and tobacco. They had suffered from a good deal of casual violence and equally casual intimacy from whalers, timber getters and seamen off passing ships. But there had been little organised resistance. From Bruny Island or the opposite coast there was a clear view of all the ships that passed up the channel on their way to Hobart. It is not unreasonable to conclude that Trugannini's views were commonly held among her kin, that they were the members of what might quite fairly be called the peace party, who, unlike the Mairrimmenar, had decided that it was futile to attack the Europeans and that the most promising option was to use Robinson to achieve the best peace agreement possible. They had every reason to think that Robinson came cloaked in the authority of the government. He announced this in his self-important way at every turn and was forever asserting it over his convict servants. In March 1831 he was appointed as a special constable with authority over the whole colony, but Trugannini and Dray, two key members of the mission, had been to Hobart with Robinson in July 1829 where, dressed for the occasion, they met the governor who may well have discussed the forthcoming journey to the west coast.

The message of the peace party was undoubtedly enhanced by the Black Line, which would have strengthened the arguments of the Bruny Island people that there were now too many Europeans for there to be any hope for effective resistance. It was probably this message, combined with the terms offered by Robinson, that allowed for the mission's successful diplomacy. Besides, what Robinson offered must have been attractive after years of conflict. We have the clearest account of what he was proposing from a journal entry recording his discussion with Mannalargenna, the leading man of the northeastern language group, in August 1831.

This morning I developed my plans to the chief Mannalargenna and explained to him the benevolent views of the government towards himself and his people. He cordially acquiesced and his entire approbation of the salutary measure, and promised his utmost aid and assistance. I informed him in the presence of Kickerterpoller that I was commissioned by the Governor to inform him that, if the natives would desist from their wonted outrages upon the whites, they would be allowed to remain in their respective districts and would have flour, tea and sugar, clothes etc. given them; that a good white man would dwell with them who would take care of them and would not allow any bad white men to shoot them, and he would go with them about the bush like myself and they then could hunt. He was much delighted.[23]

Robinson made a similar promise to Umarrah, a senior man of the so-called Stony Creek tribe, a few weeks later.

Several points need emphasis here. Robinson knew that 'the chief', as he called Mannalargenna, was a man of power and authority in Aboriginal society. He assured him that he was commissioned by the chief of the white men to offer the terms of a peace deal. The Tasmanian Aboriginal nations had their own system of intergroup relations: agreements or treaties, necessarily verbal, were negotiated, and then honoured or became the subject of disputation. Mannarlagenna had reason to accept Robinson's word and it explains why he became an important member of the mission during its last expeditions. Robinson realised that the Aborigines 'look for and expect a fulfilment of such promises as are made to them'. Indeed, he admitted that they relied 'with implicit faith on the fulfilment of the promises I made to them on the part of the Government'.[24]

Robinson clearly persuaded the Aborigines that they would go to the Bass Strait islands for a short period before returning to their homelands. This was absolutely fundamental to his success in effecting the removal. He admitted as much in an official report written in 1838 when he explained that 'it was guaranteed by me on behalf of the government' that the Aborigines on Flinders Island would be permitted to return to their own country during the summer months. Another key promise formed part of the agreement, clearly demanded by the Aborigines and it was that 'their customs were to be respected, and not broken into by any rash or misguided interference'.[25] It is not clear if Robinson believed, during his negotiations, that there would be a return from exile. We don't know if the governor commissioned him to make the promises he did. There is nothing on paper to suggest that Arthur had sanctioned such an agreement. But that is not in itself proof that he didn't give verbal approval to the terms that Robinson offered to Mannalargenna and other leading Aborigines.

Then there is the meeting between Arthur and the last surviving band of the Mairremminer, the members of which came to Hobart with Robinson in January 1832. They were taken to Government House where they had a meeting with Arthur. Despite its importance, which was fully recognised at the time, and the fact that the visit to Government House was widely reported in the newspapers of the time, Arthur himself made no record of what he said or what was promised to the Aboriginal leaders. He was a meticulous administrator and the lack of any record was unlikely due to negligence or incompetence. We can only assume he deliberately chose not to leave any written evidence of promises made that the Colonial Office or London's powerful missionary societies might decide to hold him to. The fact that the Mairrimmener went willingly to Flinders Island strongly suggests that he, too, promised that they would be able to return to their home territories. He also had many unrecorded conversations with Robinson; the absence of any account of what he said on such occasions leaves the matter uncertain. The lack of any record may indicate that Robinson offered terms in good faith but which Arthur knew he could disown once the Aborigines were safely in exile. Robinson could be left to bear the burden of betrayal and bad faith at the time and in retrospect.

Robinson was clearly uneasy about his betrayal, and the difficulty he had in explaining his failure to carry out the conditions of what he called 'the compact' made to the Aborigines. J. E. Calder declared that he was often heard to express regret that the promises 'made to them on which they surrendered their liberties were so faithlessly kept'.[26]

For their part the Aborigines had every reason to believe that Robinson spoke for the government and that his promises would be honoured. In a letter to the colonial secretary Robinson explained that the Aborigine 'considered me as the ostensible agent on the part of the government'.[27] They had every reason to believe that they had a formal agreement and that the terms had not been met. This sentiment was expressed in a petition sent by a group of Flinders Island residents to the queen in February 1846, which stated:

Your petitioners humbly state to your Majesty that Mr. Robinson made for us with Colonel Arthur an agreement which we have not lost from our minds since and we made our part of it good.[28]

Was there, then, a treaty? There is no doubt that the agreement negotiated by Robinson was similar to treaties signed with North American Indians in the early years of the 19th century. If the terms had been written down the situation would have been much clearer and if leading Aborigines had known enough about the European way of doing things to ask for a written document they may have received one. The relevant jurisprudence in the USA puts the emphasis on the indigenous viewpoint when deciding the existence or validity of relevant historical documents. In a recent and pertinent case the Canadian Supreme Court had to decide if an agreement between a British army officer and a Native American tribe dating from the middle of the 18th century was, in fact, a treaty. The critical point was whether the Native Americans had reason to believe the agreement was a treaty: The threshold issue, the Court decided,

in determining whether or not [a document] was a treaty was to determine the question the capacity of the parties involved. The question of capacity must, however, be seen from the point of view of the Indians at that time and the court must ask whether it was reasonable for them to have assumed that the other party they were dealing with had the authority to enter into a valid treaty with them.[29]

It is weighty authority to support the view of the Tasmanian Aborigines that they had, indeed, negotiated a treaty with the government of George Arthur, the main terms of which were never met.

The short, tragic history of Wybalenna, the Aboriginal settlement on Flinders Island, has been told many times before. The main outlines of the story are clear. It was occupied from February 1833 until October 1847. About 220 Aborigines arrived there, but by the time it was abandoned only 46 remained. The settlement has an evil reputation as a place of death, as a prison or concentration camp, where the survivors of the Black War were systematically stripped of their culture and had Christianity and British culture thrust upon them in a brutal, insensitive manner. Many accounts of Wybalenna have pointed an accusing finger at the colonial government, accusing it, at best, of indifference and neglect. Some writers have gone further arguing that the authorities had from the start seen the settlement as a site where their genocidal intentions could be relentlessly played out far from investigative eyes.

It is here that Wybalenna is thought to have contemporary res-
onance as a forerunner of the gulags and death camps of the 20th
century. In his international best seller, *The Fatal Shore*, Robert
Hughes declared that Flinders Island was a 'concentration camp
where genocide was committed'.[30] Many other writers, historians, jurists and anthropologists have echoed this judgement. The
overwhelming feature of the settlement was the constant, pressing presence of death: between 1832 and 1847, 132 died. There
were periods of high mortality interspersed with months of relative
good health. Twenty-three Aborigines died between 5 June and 24
August 1833, 13 died during the first three months of 1837 and eight
succumbed in five days early in 1838. The main cause of death was
respiratory disease, commonly pneumonia, following in the wake
of influenza or colds. We can catch something of the horror and
fear that stalked the stricken community in a Christmas Day, 1833
entry in Robinson's journal. It was far from festive:

It is an appalling sight to view the mounds of earth now before us where
the people are buried, as they are in single graves. Each one reminds us
that the body of a native lies there. This is their repository of the dead – no
white man lies there. These are the remains of persons once animated as
we are but now the crimson fluid ceases to circulate in their veins … of all
ages and sexes, of all ranks and degrees of the aboriginal inhabitants, but
also no mixture of colour. These numerous graves contain only the bodies
of aborigines.[31]

Very few children were born in the community; ever fewer survived
their first year.

Many issues spring to mind. The mortality rate at Wybalenna
was probably no higher than that in comparable mission stations
set up for Aborigines in other parts of Australia during the 19th
century. These missions had the advantage of having larger ambient
populations to make up for the loss through high death rates. The
combination of low resistance to introduced disease and enforced
concentration of settlement was a fatal combination everywhere.
Even though Flinders Island was almost certainly the only Aboriginal institution in Australia to have resident surgeons, their methods
did little to deter the irresistible tide of mortality. They bled and
cupped and fretted, but they were of little use, though their numerous autopsies were professional. Indeed, their work on dead bodies

was more proficient than their attempts to ameliorate the suffering of the sick.

Robinson's observation about the ravages of disease affecting only the Aboriginal community presents us with further means to investigate the calamity. What is often not understood is that Wybalenna was also home to a considerable convict population. Between September 1833 and May 1837, 70 convicts worked at the settlement, where they shared with the Aborigines the same physical environment and public health arrangements. Their rations were, if anything, more frugal and they were unable to hunt for bush food or even to gather shellfish along the shore, which was the common experience of the Aborigines. Convicts' general conditions were harsher, they worked long hours and were often punished by chain or lash. And yet their health was remarkably good. Over a four year period only one convict died of disease whereas 40 Aborigines – men, women and children – were interred over that period in the island's increasingly cluttered cemetery.

The contrast with the convicts is instructive in other ways as well. The Aborigines were sharply aware that they were not treated like the convicts and, even more to the point, they did not regard themselves as prisoners. They were only too well aware that they were exiles but that was a different matter altogether. In the petition of 1846 this message was clear. It was a plea from 'the free Aborigines of Van Diemen's Land now living upon Flinders Island', who were not taken prisoners but came to the island as the result of an agreement. This declaration would matter less if the embodied sentiments had not infused almost everything that happened on the island.

The Aborigines made it clear on many occasions that they believed that their rations and clothes were theirs by right and that these items were part of the terms that they had agreed to in the bush. Robinson wrote to the colonial secretary to explain that while they were 'grateful for the favours conferred upon them, they considered them more a matter of right rather than debt or obligation'. A colleague, Peter Fisher (Commandant, 1841–42), observed that they were aware that the government had 'to keep them without any labour on their behalf'.[32]

The question of labour was another point of contention. Almost all the work on the settlement was performed by convicts. Robinson

and the other officials believed that one of the central objectives of
the mission, to impart civilisation, was to teach the Aborigines to
work with persistence and regularity. Henry Nickolls, who was the
commandant from 1834 to 1835, believed it was essential to show
the Aborigines 'the use and value of labour by leading them to work
in their gardens'. But he soon found that they evinced a 'determined
hostility to anything like work', declaring, 'white men work not
they'. Senior men complained to Fisher a few years later: 'Why do
you make us work like prisoners?' The Aborigines usually got the
better of the argument. They believed that the white men owed them
a very large debt for the homelands they had lost. Fisher reported
that they often declared that 'white man has no right to make them
work as he has got their land'.33

Another source of struggle between officials and Aborigines was
the matter of freedom of movement. A sedentary lifestyle in the
village was seen as a necessary prelude to the acceptance of civilisation. For most of the time during the settlement's history the
Aborigines came and went as they pleased. They spent long periods out in the bush, hunting and gathering and no doubt attending
to ceremony. It seems that the different language groups may have
divided up the island into separate territories and they may have
developed procedures to assert their spiritual claim on the new land
that had not been occupied for thousands of years. A 1839 board
of inquiry found that as many as half the total population was 'frequently absent on hunting excursions for weeks together'.34 During
the previous year as many as one-quarter of the population was continually absent. Threats, bribes and entreaties made little difference.
Fisher remarked, 'I may solemnly declare they will not be prevented
from going to the bush occasionally, with all the luxuries, and the
firmness in the world, unless a Bayonet is fixed before them'.35

The convicts were not allowed to leave the settlement. If they did
they were flogged and placed in irons. There were occasions when
Aboriginal parties tracked the straying felons and brought them
back to meet their fate.

Wybalenna was, then, a very distinctive institution. It was a
place of exile but hardly prison or concentration camp, and the
inmates believed it belonged to them, along with all the stores and
equipment, which were their compensation, to the extent that they

resented the fact that the convicts were supplied from their store. It made management a very difficult task and forces us to significantly redraw the traditional picture of powerless and dispirited Aborigines dominated by masterful white men bent on extinguishing their traditional culture and practices. Not that men such as Robinson didn't have aspirations to turn the Aborigines into village dwelling, God-fearing, monogamous peasants. He not only aspired to engineer significant acculturation, but he also wrote long reports announcing his successes, though they were little more than empty posturing.

The Aborigines adopted some aspects of European culture as they had been doing in parts of Tasmania for a generation or more. They wore clothes when it pleased them but threw them off when dancing or out in the bush. They appreciated European foods but still hunted and gathered at will. At times they persuaded the officials to lend them guns to go hunting. Many people attended the regular church services and it was generally conceded that they were sensitive to the seriousness and solemnity of white people. A few of the younger Aborigines did become Christians or at least found ways to place the new faith alongside the old. Many more learnt a few prayers by heart and were happy to perform for admiring white visitors. The music was perhaps the feature of Christianity that had the greatest impact. The words may not have meant much but the melodies were pleasing. Resident clergyman Thomas Dove noted 'they were manifestly gratified with singing hymns' even if they did not associate them with Christian doctrine.[36] Robinson reported that the Aborigines were becoming 'passionately fond of the vocal melody and seem to regard with much interest its scientific arrangements'.[37] The outstanding characteristic of the settlement was that despite living in exile and facing the terrible sense of doom cast by the relentless progress of death the Aborigines showed a capacity to adapt to their new circumstances and to continue to assert their demand to be treated as a free people with political grievances and rights.

The banishment of the Aborigines was greeted with jubilation among the settlers. It had immediate economic benefits, confidence in the future returned, investment increased and the value of land rapidly rose. The anxiety and insecurity of those years dissipated, although they were remembered for many years to come. Like many of the settlers Governor Arthur believed that the success of the Friendly Mission had redeemed the honour of his administration and the colony at large. And what may have been even more important, the settlement on Flinders Island soothed his conscience as his continued interest in its success indicated.

As he prepared to leave the colony in the middle of 1836 Arthur was greatly encouraged by Robinson's highly optimistic but essentially fanciful reports about progress on Flinders Island. In May, during one of his last interviews with Robinson, he declared that the Aborigines were 'not to want for anything'. According to Robinson the governor 'begged and entreated that I would use every endeavour to prevent the race from becoming extinct'. In a second interview a fortnight later, one that lasted four hours, Arthur complimented Robinson on his recent reports. Robinson recorded in his journal that the governor seemed 'deeply interested' in the settlement, had granted all the assistance he had applied for and 'begged I would omit nothing I conceived necessary for the comfort and good of the Aborigines'.[38]

But sceptical colonists were not willing to accept Robinson's fanciful accounts of the settlement, which were reprinted in the local papers. *Bent's News* reported in April 1836 that several people from Flinders Island had stated that the Aborigines had 'become quite sensible as to their having been captured and forced from their native soil, and consequently express themselves in the strongest terms of revenge to those who were instrumental in affecting the same'.[39] While visiting Hobart in February 1836 the young Charles Darwin heard that the Aborigines were 'very far from being contented'. Some of his informants believed that the race 'would soon become extinct'. In reflections that prefigured his later momentous works on evolution Darwin observed that he did not know 'a more striking instance of the comparative rate of increase of a civilised over a savage people'.[40]

At the height of the Black War Arthur feared that the destruction of Aboriginal society would leave an indelible stain on the reputation of his administration and on the colony itself. Tasmania has ever since been burdened with what happened on the island in the 1820s and on Flinders in the following decade. It is often one of the few things that people in the wider world know about island history. Opinion about those tragic events has always been divided, as it was at the time. Some colonists raged against the brutality and atrocities and believed that the whole society had been morally tainted by the manner in which the Europeans had acquired their new homeland. But settler societies find it hard to maintain a stance that questions the very right of their continued existence. And that is why George Augustus Robinson was so fulsomely rewarded with land and money and miscellaneous valuable gifts: he lifted the burden of acute insecurity from the shoulders of people in the rural districts. Colonists everywhere felt their consciences ease. Guilt was banished from the island.

The most sensitive chronicler of the great tragedy was the congregational clergyman John West, a near contemporary to the events he related (he arrived in Tasmania in 1838) and an assiduous researcher who read widely among the records and talked extensively with participants. In his history of Tasmania he showed as much concern for the fate of the Aborigines and compassion for their suffering as any writer in the whole of colonial Australia. Reflecting on the departure of the Aborigines for Flinders Island he wrote:

It was indeed a mournful spectacle: the last Tasmanians quitting the shores of his ancestors! Forty years before, the first settler had erected his encampment! A change so rapid in the relations of a people to the soil, will scarcely find a parallel in this world's history; but that banishment which if originally contrived, had been an atrocious crime, was at last an act of mercy – the tardy humanity of Englishmen which rescued a remnant, extenuated the dishonour of their cruelty to the race.[41]

But even without the apparent humanity of the friendly mission West's moral balance was weighted heavily in the favour of the colonists. In a well-known passage he observed:

The original occupation of this country necessarily involved most of the consequences which followed: was that occupation, then, just? The right of wandering hordes to engross vast regions – for ever to retain exclusive property in the soil, and which would feed millions where hundreds are scattered can never be maintained.

Then, in one of his most memorable sentences in which he expressed a classic apotheosis of colonisation, he wrote: 'No man can witness the triumph of colonisation, where cities rise in the desert, and the wilderness blossoms as the rose, without being gladdened by the change.'[42]

The settlement on Flinders Island was abandoned in 1847; the survivors were returned to mainland Tasmania and housed in a disused convict station at Oyster Cove south of Hobart. This was done partly to reduce the expense of maintaining the remote Wybalenna despite considerable opposition from settlers with memories of the Black War. An equally important reason for the repatriation was the political activism of a group of the residents who came into conflict with an unpopular superintendant, Dr Henry Jeanneret, and who submitted a petition to Queen Victoria signed by eight men seeking redress for their numerous grievances. It was a remarkable document. The petitioners asked for the assistance of European residents in the settlement but there is no doubt it was an Aboriginal initiative and one of the most important documents in the history of Aboriginal politics in 19th century Australia. The leading figure in the campaign against Jeanneret was a young man, Walter George Arthur, who had grown up since the European occupation and spent some time in the Boys Orphan School at New Town. He was a Christian and could read and write, a protégé of Robinson. The most striking aspect of Arthur's petition and numerous letters he wrote to the government was his sense of his political rights as a free-born British subject. He argued that the Aborigines had gone to Flinders Island after an agreement with Governor Arthur, that they were not prisoners and therefore had all the rights of citizens. His main complaint against Jeanneret was that he treated the residents as slaves and indeed he himself had been imprisoned by the superintendant. The petition was forwarded to Britain and was taken seriously in the Colonial Office where there was a keen sense that the question could possibly lead to embarrassment in the House of Commons. Eventually, Jeanneret was replaced and the settlement closed down. Walter and his wife Mary Anne began farming in the vicinity of Oyster Cove, and then with several of the young men Walter went on a whaling voyage. He died in a boating accident on the Derwent soon after his return.

The remaining residents received basic rations from the government. They went on several hunting expeditions into the southwest.

But a pall of death hung over the decaying buildings. The residents aged and no children were born. White visitors took a ghoulish interest in the remnants of the race, confirming the increasingly fashionable ideas of evolution. Eventually, only Trugannini remained and she spent her last years in Hobart, a celebrity often seen about the street until her death in 1876.[43]

5

The Triumph of Colonisation

The opening of the Ross Bridge, which spanned the Macquarie River, in October 1836 was one of Governor George Arthur's last official appearances prior to his departure from the colony a week later. It was a notable occasion. In a procession following the vice-regal party 37 carriages of different descriptions crossed the new carriageway to gather for a celebratory picnic. The reporter from the *Hobart Town Courier* observed that the 'wines from Champagne to humble port were excellent' and that ample justice was done to them.[1] Local Police Magistrate Benjamin Horne told his festive audience that he had arrived in the district 13 years before when the only structure apparent was one mud hut, but now:

A trackless inhospitable wilderness that had but a few years ago acknowledged no other Lord but the wily savage, has been made to yield to the industry of civilized man. Its plains reduced to a state of high fertility, amply supply the wants of a numerous and rapidly increasing population. The forests and mountains, formerly the haunt of the wild native and the lawless, are now the peaceful abode of the shepherd, and his flocks secure from every danger, whilst the unsightly sod hut, the emblem of our infancy, has everywhere vanished, to make room for substantial, comfortable dwellings.[2]

It was a speech that would have pleased the governor. As he reflected on his 12 years in the colony he was able to put aside his remorse about the fate of the Aborigines and to celebrate what historian John West was later to term 'the triumph of colonisation'.

The progress of Van Diemen's Land, Arthur believed, had been exceptional. There was, he reported to the Colonial Office, no parallel of such rapid success in 'any former instance of Colonization'. Never in so short a space of time 'did the first possessors of any territory pass 'from a state of comparative poverty, into one, not of abundance, but of absolute wealth'. The island's rapid transition, which could be matched only by that of New South Wales, involved within the experience 'of a single life' such a series of progressive changes 'as are in Old Countries, the result, not of years, but of centuries of effort'.[3] Pride in development was not confined to the vice-regal drawing room. An aspiring Launceston poet contributed some lines on Van Diemen's Land to the *Cornwall Chronicle* in September 1836, which ran, in part:

> What late was barren soil which nothing yields
> Is now rich land and cultivated fields;
> For emigration free so great has been
> Now beauteous villas ornament the scene
> Churches and buildings upwards rear their head
> And all around as if by magic spread[4]

While Arthur was confident about his own contribution to the colony's rapid expansion he accurately assessed the circumstances that spurred the development. Rapid population increase, from convict transportation and free immigration, underpinned economic growth and met one of the abiding problems of New World societies – a shortage, and consequent high cost, of labour. In 1825 there had been just under 15 000 people in the colony; by 1835 there were over 40 000. The owners of large land holdings, who had almost universally received free grants of land from Arthur or his predecessor William Sorell, benefited from the cheap labour of assigned convict servants on field and in farmhouse. By the time of Arthur's departure from the colony many of the grand Georgian houses with brick or sandstone outbuildings, which still characterise the areas of early settlement, had been built, fields fenced, and gardens and orchards established. Arthur favoured the island's new gentry with patronage, legislation and regulation because they were essential assistants in the convict system and they provided the leadership and high status necessary to cap the hierarchical society so eminently desired and modelled on rural Britain. Never,

Image 5.1: *View on the Macquarie River, Van Diemen's Land, near the ford at Argyle Plains.* (*Source:* State Library of New South Wales.)

Arthur declared, did the primary landholders, in any territory, 'having overcome the first difficulties of settling' advance from comparative poverty, towards the enjoyment, not of comfort merely, but of affluence. The gentry could now 'aspire to the possession of every luxury'.[5] They were, indeed, sitting pretty. Compared with the holdings that were to become common on mainland Australia their properties were small, but they were fertile, well watered and held without encumbrance. With the adequate, if often unwilling, workforce they could afford to develop mixed farms that supplied most of the food necessary for their own establishments, which became like small, largely self-contained villages.

The greatest concentration of thriving large estates was along the fertile, sinuous banks of the South Esk, Meander and Macquarie Rivers and all of the were within a day's ride of Launceston.

Youthful widow Jane Williams travelled with her young sister from her home near Bothwell to spend six weeks staying at several of the grand houses in the northern Midlands in 1836. She reported her activities in chatty letters to her parents. She was struck by the evident prosperity of the northern gentry. 'This is a wealthy & gay looking district', she observed, and in a following letter declared, that 'The people here are very gay looking – they dress in great style & their houses are so large & and so handsomely furnished that really it does not seem as if we were in this country'. She told her father that the local families employed gardeners and that, as a result, the grounds near their houses were 'so clean, so nice, so tidy'.[6]

A serious-minded and pious woman Jane enjoyed the church services at Christ Church, Longford, noting in her diary:[7]

Sunday went to church – very pretty church, & the service altogether conducted in a superior style; well filled, with many carriages at the door; the Organ such a delightful assistance to the singing.[8]

Her sister enjoyed dancing quadrilles to the music of a harp at 'Woolmers', the homestead of the Archer family. Annie Baxter, the young wife of an army officer stationed at Launceston, also enjoyed herself among the younger members of the northern gentry families, dancing till dawn, going on excursions into the bush and flirting outrageously with the future political leader Richard Dry. The matriarch of the Archer family scolded her and they argued about the decency of the waltz, as Annie detailed in her diary:

We had a long debate today on the propriety (or rather the impropriety) of waltzing – I have found this dance delightful – but never until the last two dances have I found it entrancing! – to be held by one you love, you adore – Oh! There's no describing a waltz in such a situation.[9]

At recently formed, gentry dominated agricultural societies, discussion focused on improvements to husbandry and prizes were offered for the development of local bloodstock. At a meeting of the Richmond Agricultural Society in January 1836, local landowner and political activist, T. G. Gregson spoke of the difficulties and the advantages inherent in New World agriculture:

The best and most practical agriculturist will here find many difficulties which taken conjointly, no one person has ever experienced at home, and there it would take a lifetime to surmount; but where many persons from various soils, climates and districts meet, it will seldom happen that each has not met some one and conquered it; thus the knowledge of all will be united to overcome the united difficulty.[10]

Land sales records for 1836 enable us to appreciate the condition of the larger properties. A 1000 acre property at Broadmarsh had 100 acres in cultivation and 4 miles of fencing, a nine room house with a cellar, dairy, stable, barn, cow sheds, outhouses of all descriptions and a large garden 'in the best state of cultivation'.[11] In the north of the colony a genteel residence on the South Esk River was offered for sale. Included among the attractions was a dressing room with 'water closet attached', an excellent kitchen fitted with every convenience, storeroom, wash house, a dairy flagged and fitted with stone dressers, poultry house, pigsty, men's lodge, wine and beer cellar, stockyards and milking sheds. There were 18 acres of wheat, 6 acres of oats, 6 acres of English grasses and 2 acres of potatoes.[12]

During the 1830s the gentry was buoyed by the rapid rise in the prices they received on the English wool market. At the local end, the flock masters progressively improved their flocks, while attendant shipping and financial services grew in efficiency and sophistication. Between 1830 and 1835 the price of wool in Britain doubled, pushing up the local return for livestock and for meat sold domestically. Governor Arthur explained the local impact in a 1836 report to London. A flock of 1000 ewes, which, in 1830, would have cost £300 would now fetch (£)1000.[13]

Arthur's enthusiasm was backed by impressive statistics. Between 1830 and 1836 wool production more than trebled from 990 000 pounds weight to 2920 500. The financial return to the colony rose even more steeply, from £29 000 to £171 000. The local sheep flock doubled during the 1830s and reached 1.2 million in 1837 where it remained for the next decade.

Painter John Glover's family members were celebrating the successful pioneering efforts to establish their property Patterdale to the southeast of Launceston in 1836. Writing home to his brother in London in January, John junior explained that he had just finished planning and planting out a garden on his own land grant. He had recently completed the first washing of his sheep and the family's wool clip had been dispatched to Launceston for shipment to Britain. He was about to pack a consignment of 35 of his father's pictures for exhibition in London, including his now famous *My Harvest Home*, which he began on 19 March 1835, the 'day the harvest was all got in'.[14]

A few settlers worried about the costs of rapid rural development and its impact on the environment. Jane Williams noted that the richness of the native grasslands declined with the coming of European animals. Many of the indigenous flowers disappeared within a few years. She recalled that when she first arrived in the Bothwell district the grassland presented 'as beautiful a floral sight as the imagination can conceive', but with the introduction of large numbers of sheep and cattle the flowers had become 'comparatively rare: for here as elsewhere beauty is sacrificed to utility'.[15] The police magistrate and amateur botanist Robert Campbell Gunn wrote to Sir William Hooker at Kew Gardens in 1836 lamenting that so little had been done to study or preserve the indigenous fauna, and he observed that

Emus are now extremely rare – and in a few years will be quite gone, and no means has been taken in the Colony to domesticate or breed them. Kangaroo have been killed in tens of thousands for the sake of their skins, & people may live in V. D. L. for months without seeing one.[16]

The establishment of the new colonies in Western Australia, South Australia and at Port Phillip between 1829 and 1837 boosted prices for sheep, cattle and horses and provided local entrepreneurs with promising, if fickle, markets for the assorted articles needed in rudimentary settlements. Launceston became the essential entrepot for the settlement on the shores of Port Phillip Bay, providing the pioneer settlers much of the capital and most of the livestock and other essential supplies. Local newspapers reported on the great profits possible in sheep farming over the Strait with an incessant demand for ever more sheep. Reports emphasised the apparently endless expanse of open, rolling grassland without Tasmania's ever-present, all-embracing hills. A settler returning from the new colony reported that on climbing a tree, 'you can stretch the eye to boundless limits, for few mountains are to be seen in any direction'.[17] In March 1836 Port Phillip was 'now the great subject of conversation'. There were references to Port Phillip 'mania', to the 'Phillippians'. In Launceston not a day passed without flocks of sheep being driven through the town for 'exportation to this new colony – which may be made to and from in four or five days'.[18]

There was considerable debate about the long-term consequences of the establishment of Tasmania's colony on the opposite shore of Bass Strait. The optimistic believed that with its precocious development Tasmania would continue to be the older more sophisticated society that provided leadership to the new, callow colonies of southern Australia. Others worried that the fresh and wider pastures would draw away labour and capital and reduce the value of local farms. No one writing in 1836 could have predicted the explosive growth triggered by the squatting rush just then underway, which saw sheep farmers occupying pastures over the whole of southeastern Australia. It was even less likely that they could have foreseen the discovery of Victoria's rich goldfields 15 years later. Victorian growth far surpassed anything seen in Tasmania in the 1830s. Its population had passed that of Tasmania by 1851 and by 1861 was five times larger.

Tasmanians argued about the best way to prolong the growth of the colony. The policy of encouraging a prosperous local gentry was often attacked because little encouragement was given to small farmers, who were usually denied access to assigned convict servants, could only borrow money at ruinous rates and whose traditional use of wasteland for grazing their animals was restricted by the Impounding Act, which gave the police power to place any stray animals in public pounds, a measure that a correspondent to the *Cornwall Chronicle* declared would ultimately lead to the 'complete annihilation of a peasantry', who alone were the 'bulwark and support of a country'.[19] The editor of the paper had much the same view. The policies pursued by Governor Arthur would prevent the possibility 'of a peasantry ever existing in this country'.[20] A flourishing trade in stolen sheep was ruthlessly suppressed by the extensive use of capital punishment. Even the unexplained possession of a sheepskin could lead one to the gallows.

While governors, magistrates and poets enthused about rural development it was the two major port towns, Hobart and Launceston, that displayed the most obvious signs of colonial progress.

At the end of 1836 Hobart had just under 14 000 people of whom 25 per cent were convicts under sentence. It represented just over 36 per cent of the colony's total population. Then as now the town was dominated by its physical environment with Mount Wellington providing what by common opinion was a uniquely picturesque backdrop across the face of which was enacted the drama of each day's weather. Mount Direction and Mount Nelson further enclosed the town, blocking views of the hinterland and directing the eye across Sullivan's Cove and down the wide Derwent estuary. While visitors and locals alike praised the picturesque landscape, the town itself evoked varied responses. Arriving on the *Beagle* in February 1836 Charles Darwin thought that the first aspect of the town was 'very inferior to that of Sydney; the latter might be called a city, this only a town'. The growth of small houses was 'most abundant'. The vast number of little red brick dwellings scattered on the hill destroyed its picturesque appearance.[21] But local newspaper editor and political activist Henry Melville saw it differently, noticing not the mean little cottages, but rather the 'handsome villas and enclosures occupying ground in every direction'.[22]

Like most of his contemporaries Melville took pride in the harbour, observing that the cove afforded 'one of the best and most secure anchorages in the world, for any number of vessels, and of any burthen'. No wind could affect them 'to their injury' and the nature of the anchorage was 'equally excellent'.[23] Most people in the town lived close to the Derwent. They could smell the ocean and shivered when the sea breezes whipped up the estuary. The masts of the tall ships clustered around the cove created a permanent, if ever-changing thicket that reached higher than the town's tallest buildings. Everyone was attuned to the arrival and departure of ships, whose movements were reported in the local papers. Polyglot crews roistering around the cove after weeks at sea were the most obvious reminder of the colony's dependence on the ocean. Townsmen and women waited impatiently for letters from families abroad and for the latest batch of newspapers from Sydney and Britain, as well as from the USA, the Cape Colony and Mauritius. The ships also brought visitors, immigrants and additional batches of convicts along with the innumerable articles ordered from overseas months before or brought in by merchants and shopkeepers to be advertised in the local papers with the cachet of being the very latest arrival from the Old World. The ships also picked up the colony's exports of wool, whale oil and bones, the hides and wattle bark increasingly used in tanning and brought back impatiently awaited payment for prior shipments.

The volume of shipping was also an obvious measure of colonial progress. In a speech to his Legislative Council Governor Arthur explained that between 1834 and 1835 the number of ships arriving in Hobart had increased from 150 to 169.[24] The greatest number had come from New South Wales but there was a constant presence in the port of ships from many parts of the world. During the first four months of 1836, 61 ships arrived in Hobart. Ten had come from Mauritius, five from London, four from Liverpool, three each from China and the Cape of Good Hope, two each from Portsmouth and Sourabaya and single vessels from Leith, Cork, Boston and Calcutta. Travel by sailing ship may have been slow, often uncomfortable and sometimes dangerous, but the striking thing about Hobart's ties with the outside world was the ready and constant availability of passenger births to Sydney, Britain, Mauritius, South Africa and India. At any one time there were at least two or three ships offering passage to Britain although the cost put it out of the reach of most people.

With the ships came visitors, information and innumerable commodities. Although one of the world's remotest ports, Hobart was on one of the great sea routes marked out by the prevailing winds in the era before the opening of the Suez Canal. It was probably more in touch with the wider world and therefore less parochial than many comparably sized land-locked towns in the interior of Europe or the Americas.

When the latest newspapers arrived the local press often carried long and serious summaries of events in Britain and Europe and, less commonly, about the affairs of the USA, South Africa and Mauritius. Hobart's public reading rooms offered subscribers access to many overseas papers and journals. Davis' Reading Rooms held files of seven London papers, three from Ireland and two from Scotland, as well as eight of the English-speaking world's leading reviews. Interested readers could keep up with what was happening in the world although their news was always three and a half to four months out of date. How they must have wondered and speculated about what was going on and how eagerly they awaited the next ship to arrive with the latest episode in the great drama of the world.

Visitors were often surprised by the sophistication of Hobart's leading shops, which offered the latest Paris fashions, and clothes and fabrics of all descriptions from Europe, India and China. French wines and English ales were always available along with cheaper, less favoured wines from the Cape. The town's 'Connoisseurs in Snuff', which included the chief justice, were tempted with pound and half-pound jars of such concoctions as Violet Strasburgh, Genuine Lundy Foot, Dr Ruddleman's Mixture and Finest Scented Rapee. The music shops offered instruments of all descriptions and sheet music of popular melodies, waltzes and quadrilles, as well as the more serious works of leading European composers. The bookshops were equally ecumenical in their offerings. Derwent House had on offer the complete works of Sir Walter Scott and Lord Byron, and a 15 volume collection of the works of Shakespeare. The local nurserymen were equally entrepreneurial. In gardens and greenhouses they had propagated literally hundreds of plants – flowers, vegetables, fruit trees and ornamental shrubs from Europe, South Africa and Asia. Local gardeners were able to scan column after column in the local papers to look for a desired specimen, familiar and exotic. Daniel Bunce of Denmark Hill provided readers with a list of 400 plants that were available at his gardens at New Town.

The port was more than a conduit for people and goods coming and going. Trades and industries developed to service and supply the visiting ships. At great expense the government developed, with a large convict workforce, the so-called New Wharf on the sheltered southern side of the cove, which led to the extensive building of stone warehouses, workshops and hotels along Salamanca Place. The wharf impressed locals and visitors alike. Even that stern critic of Arthur's administration, Henry Melville, thought it 'a noble wharf' and a 'stupendous undertaking'.[25]

By the 1830s the sealing industry had gone into catastrophic decline as a result of reckless over-exploitation. But local merchants developed shore-based or bay whaling, an industry that needed little fixed investment and enabled small entrepreneurs with limited capital to set up stations to capture the black whales as they ventured

Image 5.2:   *Salamanca Place.* (*Source:* Archives Office of Tasmania.)

into the sheltered bays around the southeast and east coast, which
a contemporary observed:

render it such a place of resort for whales throughout the winter, that
with the equipment of a few boats, and the erection of a boiler or two
upon the shore for rendering down the oil, are nearly sufficient, as the
outfit of what may be considered with tolerable certainty, a profitable
enterprise. The consequence is that each winter, fresh parties...fit out
whaling expeditions...Thus almost at our very door or threshold, we are
provided with the means of becoming rich with little trouble and exertion.[26]

The bay whaling gangs were commonly recruited from among the
young men born in the colony. It was, according to *Bent's News*,
'truly Colonial work'.[27] The industry was, therefore, 'rearing up a
fine and manly race of native youths, in a nursery that would qualify
them to contest the palm of superiority on the water, with any
inhabitants of any country upon the whole face of the globe'.[28] In
1836 there were nine parties working out of Hobart that employed
392 men and one out of Launceston with 50 men. The fisheries
were worth £57 000 in that year and peaked in the following year at
£135 000, which came close to the returns from wool production.

But as fewer and fewer whales were seen in Tasmania's inshore waters, bay whaling slowly followed the earlier downward spiral of sealing.

By the mid 1830s steam technology had arrived in the two leading island ports. There were two small steamships on the Derwent and one in Launceston. One of Hobart's vessels was locally made and therefore an object of considerable pride. On the Derwent the ferries provided passenger services to the eastern shore of the estuary and upstream to New Norfolk. Picnic expeditions on board the 'steamer *Governor Arthur*', were advertised in 1836 for five shillings a head, for which participants could expect to enjoy a day 'of real and rational gratification'.[29] On the Tamar steam power was even more necessary. The long 45 mile voyage from Launceston to Bass Strait was especially frustrating for sailing ships and sometimes took days to complete. Narrow winding channels and attendant mud banks made tacking hazardous, which meant that the cost of the steam tug was often a sensible investment.

Hobart supported an assortment of manufacturing ventures in 1836 – soap and candle making, a distillery, several breweries, tanneries, three windmills and six water mills. Three new windmills were under construction in that year. Local pride helped promote small undertakings. *Bent's News* reported that the best of several pastrycooking establishments was run by a Mr Moses who proudly declared that his articles were all of colonial make, and, as far as possible, composed of colonial ingredients.[30] A local coachmaker built a landau mainly with Tasmanian materials for a client who, being a native of the colony, 'wished to have his carriage Colonial'. Local opinion was that it was 'almost equal to anything out of London'.[31] The *Tasmanian* praised the cordials made in the local distillery, which were 'not only equal, but infinitely superior to any thing which has been imported from Britain'.[32] The editor argued that there could be 'no doubt that it is the first duty of every Colonist to support the manufactures of the Colony in preference to all which come from without'.[33] But the most significant secondary industry in the colony was shipbuilding, which was carried out on the Derwent and the Tamar. Ships of all sizes were made in local shipyards utilising Tasmania's already celebrated and readily accessible timber. The size of the undertakings and the ships constructed

Image 5.3: *Hobart Town (Ile Van Diemen)*, dessine par
LeBreton; lith par A. Mayer et Guiaud, 1841

increased during the 1830s, with numerous vessels built to service
the growing trade across Bass Strait. By the 1840s larger, locally
made ships were traversing the word's great oceans.

The young Charles Darwin may not have been impressed by his
first sight of Hobart from the deck of the *Beagle* but when ashore
he was quite taken with the charm of his hosts and the elegance
of their lifestyle. On one evening he had dinner at 'Stephenville',
the imposing residence of the glamorous attorney-general, Alfred
Stephen. The young scientist described the occasion in a letter to his
sister Catherine:

You would be astonished to know what pleasant society there is here. I
dined yesterday at the Attorneys-General, where, amongst a small party
of his most intimate friends he got up an excellent concert of first rate
Italian music. The house large, beautifully furnished; dinner most elegant
and respectable (although of course all convicts) Servants.[34]

On the occasion of his 27th birthday Darwin had dinner in another
'very pleasant House', in this case the home of Surveyor-General
George Frankland, 'Secheron', an elegant regency mansion on Battery Point with sweeping views from its wide verandahs down the

Derwent. Darwin had what he called the most agreeable evening since leaving England four years before. He heard of a recent event held at the house – a dancing party for 96 – and was told the next night of a grand fancy dress ball at the home of Alfred Stephen for 113 revellers. 'Is this not astonishing in so remote a part of the world?', he wrote somewhat breathlessly to his sister.

Darwin preferred Hobart to Sydney. While it was partly to do with the climate and the greater similarity with England, there was more to it than that. In explaining his choice to his sister he observed that there was 'a better class of society' in the smaller colony. Here there were 'no convicts driving in their carriages and revelling in wealth'.[35] He jotted down similar sentiments in his diary, observing:

I suspect society is here on a pleasanter footing, certainly it is free from the contamination of rich convicts, and the dissensions consequent on the existence of two classes of wealthy residents.[36]

Given Darwin's short stay in Hobart (it was only 10 days) he may have been reflecting the opinions of his smart dinner companions as much as he was responding to personal experience. But his two hosts, Stephen and Frankland, provided a convenient way into an assessment of Hobart society in the 1830s.

The two men were in their 30s and were well connected. Frankland's father was a senior churchman, his mother the daughter of the Earl of Colville. His older brother inherited a title from his grandfather. Stephen was the nephew of the famous colonial official James Stephen and related to members of the famous Clapham sect who were the driving force behind the anti-slavery crusade. Both were senior public servants with handsome salaries. Stephen received £900 a year, Frankland £500. Stephen's salary was almost 20 times greater than the wage received by a tradesman at the time. Stephen was also able to engage in a lucrative private practice. He was well placed in the strictly hierarchical bureaucracy. The governor received £2500, the chief justice £1500 and the colonial secretary £1200. Less senior officers received smaller salaries but all but very junior officers received considerably more than skilled tradesmen and many of them would have been able to have access to convict servants. Arthur worried that his police magistrates in rural areas were finding it difficult to keep up with the increasingly affluent gentry. They had to make 'the best appearance' they could on £300 with £50 for a house and £45 for a horse.[37] There were detachments from two regiments in the colony in 1836, the 21st Fusiliers and the 50th Queen's Own. In all there were 780 soldiers, including 26 commissioned officers.

So who would have made the grade and been invited to the balls at 'Secheron' and 'Stephenville'? We have no way of knowing but guest lists would have been a very clear indication of who was and who wasn't acceptable in colonial society. The commissioned officers of the regiment and their wives would have been there, including the young lieutenants. We know that Annie Baxter was there, having just arrived in the colony with her husband Lieutenant Andrew Baxter. Was there any waltzing that night? The senior public servants and their partners would have made up a significant part of the guest list. The solicitors and surgeons, the bankers and the merchants would have been acceptable, as would any of the rural gentry who happened to be in town. There seems to have been a very clear idea in the colony as to who was and who wasn't a gentleman. Melville's *Van Diemen's Land Annual* was quite definite as to which men were designated with the title 'esquire' and who were not. It is most unlikely that any emancipated convict would have received an invitation no matter how prosperous or respectable; Tasmania was so small that it was impossible to shed one's personal history and invent a new identity.

Government House was the pinnacle of political power and social acceptability. Governor Arthur and his wife Eliza entertained constantly. They gave dinners for 20 guests every Tuesday and much larger balls on special occasions such as the king's birthday and St George's Day. The invitation lists were the subject of earnest thought inside Government House and an equal measure of anxiety outside it. To be invited to one of the governor's weekly dinners was a cachet of unimpeachable respectability. The Arthurs were strong upholders of conventional morality. Any irregularity in lifestyle would preclude the sought after invitation. Emancipists were excluded as a matter of principle, regardless of their success, lifestyle or previous station in life. Even the children of convicts were looked on with disapproval.[38] Arthur assured the officials in the Colonial Office that 'no emancipist or time-expired convict has ever been received at my table, none have been promoted to a higher municipal office than that of a constable'.[39] There was a flinty harshness in Arthur's unforgiving attitude to the emancipists. He declared that 'The time expired convict has still been a Felon, and...he is forever precluded from being the private friend or companion in a Penal Colony'.[40]

Arthur's political opponents, who were never offered hospitality, responded by ridiculing the dinners and balls as dreary and penny-pinching affairs. Yet the food at table appeared to be abundant to the point of excess. One dinner guest described a choice of roast goose, turkey, two ducks, boiled pork and fowls, a round of beef, mutton and pork chops.[41] The anxiety of waiting for a gubernatorial invitation was sometimes apparent in the newspapers. When the Arthurs visited Launceston there was keen expectation in the heart of 'every man who wears a long coat and every woman that wears stays'.[42] The *True Colonist* printed a piece of verse on anxieties in Hobart as the governor's ball approached:

> The Government Ball is soon to take place
> So Charlotte, my love, keep the sun from your face
> By going uncovered you're getting quite brown
> And faces so tinted don't do in a town.[43]

Many of those on the guest list at 'Stephenville' and 'Secheron' would have patronised the local theatre. Alfred Stephen scandalised the more straight-laced members of the town by taking his children to the theatre. There were two venues operating in 1836 just prior to the opening of the famous Theatre Royal, which was completed at the end of 1836 and opened with great ceremony in March 1837. The usual fare was made up of assorted melodramas interspersed with singing and dancing. On 5 January the audience at the elegant Argyle Assembly Rooms was presented with a 'petite comedy', *Kill or Curse*, followed by a romantic pantomimic drama, *Wild Man of the Wood or the Bear of the Ardennes*, a song by Mr Falchon, a dance by Mr Smith and finally the 'much admired and laughable farce', *Two Gregories or Who Wacked the Thieves*. Music was provided by Mr Peck's orchestra which the *Tasmanian* believed was 'certainly superior to any to be found in any of the best constituted provincial theatres' in Britain.[44] The winner of a door prize was presented with a large 12th night cake. In March the captain of a visiting US whaler 'bespoke' one Wednesday night's performance, choosing from among the repertoire a favourite play called *Black Eyed Susan*. Written by Douglas Jerrold, it was one of the most popular British plays of the time. It premiered in London in January 1829 and ran for a record 300 performances. The local production, *Bent's News* reported, was 'played to life, and drew tears from eyes, unaccustomed to weeping'.[45]

The more sporting of Tasmania's gentlemen may not have frequented the theatres but they certainly would have ridden out to the village of New Town just to the north of Hobart to attend the annual racing carnival held over three days in March. The best bred horses in the colony competed for purses ranging from 25 to 100 sovereigns, the higher sum representing well over a year's wages for a skilled worker. The meeting of 1836 was painted in watercolours by Benjamin Duterau, but while the scene attracted the eye of the painter the race meetings were strongly opposed by the governor, who declined his patronage to the turf club because several years before the patrons of the track had hissed and booed as the governor's entourage passed by on the nearby highway. Keen horsemen were able to cross the Derwent and engage in hunting wallaby across the dry open woodland on the eastern shore. T. G. Gregson kept what was regarded as the best pack of hounds in the colony on his estate 'Restdown' and rode red-coated at the head of the hunt. The 73 year old Reverend Robert Knopwood was another regular at both the hunt and the dinners that followed. He recorded in his diary that on Saturday, 16 May, 'This morn T. G. Gregson's hounds went out for the first time this season . . . and had a good run'. A fortnight later he wrote:

This morn the Risdon hounds met at Lyndhurston cottage; soon found a kangaroo and killed; found another and had an excellent run which we killed; the third a capital run and ran him into the Derwent River and was drowned. T. G. Gregson Esqr.; W. Wilson Esqr. and self dined at Mr. Clark's new Inn at Kangaroo Point; Major De Gillon And W. Butcher Esqr. J. P. joined us.[46]

Darwin believed there was less social dissension in Tasmania than in New South Wales. A longer stay might have disabused him. Boyes had other ideas, lamenting in his diary in August 1836 that there was so much disunity and conflict that society was 'in a lamentable state'. He was responding to reports of a fight on Wellington Bridge in the middle of the town between Colonial Surgeon Dr James Scott and a Mr Hackett. It was an event that caused difficulties for Constable William Atkinson, a recently arrived free immigrant, who was charged with neglect of duty for failing to come between the brawling pair. In his defence Atkinson explained that 'he mistook the parties for gentlemen, being unacquainted with the materials of this Colony, and therefore declined to interfere'.[47] Two of the prominent newspaper editors, Dr James Ross and Gilbert Robinson, brawled in the street a few months later. But even more serious were the duels fought by army officers and leading settlers. During 1836, four were reported; there may have been others that were unreported.[48] Andrew Bent observed that 'duels and nothing but duels are the order of day'.[49] Just a week or so before he entertained Darwin, the elegant Alfred Stephen had been engaged in a serious affray with the collector of customs and the governor's nephew, Henry Arthur. A planned duel was apparently prevented at the last minute by the police.

Much of the evident dissension arose from sharp political differences that found few means of productive expression, as we will see below. But there were other features of colonial society that fostered antagonism and rivalry. Practically every adult in the island, bond or free, poor or prosperous, had been uprooted from their familiar world and their extended families. Expectations of success at the antipodes were frequently unrealistically high and just as often disappointed. Social pretensions, exaggerated by migration, flourished in the New World but were easily cut down by a rebuke or even a thoughtless word or gesture. Almost everyone hoped to improve themselves economically and to advance their status. That was the prime motivation for free migration. Success was common enough, and well enough known in the small society, to endlessly revive thwarted expectations. Those who succeeded financially, from the governor down, became money lenders holding both mortgages and ambitions in their hands, earning for themselves profits as well as envious, if shielded, antagonism.

Social turmoil, fuelled by the endless flow of alcohol, was apparent among poor immigrants and emancipated convicts. Gilbert Robertson estimated that there were 114 public houses in Hobart in 1836. About a quarter of them were decent and respectably conducted, the rest, he declared, were 'of the most infamous description'.[50] The *Colonial Times* reported that when the Magistrate's Court opened after the Christmas weekend there were the 'usual appearances of black eyes, scratched faces, bloody noses, broken and aching heads, with other symptoms of the preceding day's carousing'.[51] There was an endless procession of men and women before the courts for drunkenness, or, in the local cant, being 'a little fresh', 'full charged', 'so glorious'. Fighting was equally common and had its own demotic lexicon with expressions such as to 'serve him out', 'pay him off', 'fine draw him', to 'disfigure his title page' or give him 'a lacing'.

But for all the personal conflict at the different levels of society the violence perpetrated by the state was much more relentless, obvious and irresistible. One notorious case of violence had a connection with the annual race meeting at New Town. A young convict called Greenwood escaped from a chain gang and made his way to Hobart. Two policemen saw him picking a pocket at the race meeting and gave chase. When cornered, Greenwood slashed one of his pursuers with a knife. He was convicted of absconding and wounding, for which he received 100 lashes and was hung soon after. When taken to the gallows the spectators could see the wounds from the flogging, some of which burst open when he was pinioned.[52] The Quaker missionary and reformer James Backhouse was horrified when travelling near the small northern village of Perth early in 1837 when he saw a gibbet, 'lately erected', that held the rotting body of a prisoner. He felt the action had failed because popular feeling was strongly against it.[53] Such dramatic acts by the government caused controversy and opposition but the regular imposition of extremely harsh sentences for petty theft seem to have been taken for granted. Such punitive sentencing in Britain is a well-known feature of the convict system, but the colonial use of such a savage penal code is less well understood, even though after almost every session of the Magistrate's Court cruel sentences were reported without comment in the local papers. There were, for instance, many characteristic cases reported in the *Colonial Times* during November 1836, such as that of Benjamin Messenger who stole a quart of gooseberries worth 8 pence and was sentenced to a chain gang for three months. John Harlop, who took a leg of mutton, was sent down to spend 12 months in chains. James Smith stole property worth 2 pence and had his sentence extended by a year. William Williams plucked a cotton handkerchief worth 6 pence from someone else's pocket and had two years added to his sentence. Robert Campbell stole a log of wood and was dispatched to a chain gang for six months. Charles Barnett 'wasted' his master's property in an undisclosed manner, for which he received 25 lashes and was sent to a road party. Sentences at the Launceston Quarter Sessions were even more punitive. In January 1836 Thomas Miller was convicted of stealing three shirts, a hat and waistcoat and was sentenced to seven years at Port Arthur, as was Edward Williams for stealing a waistcoat. William Peko, convicted of stealing 130 pounds of butter, was condemned to hard labour in irons for four years.

We have no way of knowing how the brutality of the system and the casual everyday violence impacted on the ever-growing number of native-born children. It is difficult to determine the exact number in the colony in any one year because the population was often enumerated in the broad categories of bond and free, which included adults and infants. But in 1820 there were 687 children out of a total population of just over 4000, and while the overall population grew rapidly the percentage of largely, but not solely, native-born children increased even faster. There were 1190 children in Hobart in 1830 out of a total town population of 6800. At the more detailed colony-wide census of 1847 just over 26 per cent of the population were locally born; nearly 34 per cent were aged under 21.[54]

Children had been a constant and growing presence since the earliest years of the settlement. Their parents and other adults had a normal human interest in them but there were distinctive features of the colony that prolonged and intensified concern about how the rising generation would turn out.

There was the broad question of what effect the new environment would have in producing children who might, therefore, differ from their British-born parents. The better educated wondered if exile from the great cultural traditions of Europe would lead to intellectual impoverishment and an obsessive focus on the material and the practical. The greater freedom permitted to local children when compared with their stay-at-home contemporaries seemed to presage a future population lacking in discipline and deference. Jane Reid, who arrived with her parents in 1821 and settled near Bothwell, recalled how she and her siblings were pleased when she realised they would not be able to go to school. She wrote in her reminiscences:

But our anticipations of freedom from the bondage of schools were all verified. Much time elapsed before seminaries such as an anxious parent could approve were established, and in the first years of a settler's life there were few spare moments which could be devoted to the culture of their children's minds; consequently they for the most part grew up as wild as the country they dwelt in.[55]

She believed though that there were some advantages flowing from colonial children's desultory mode of education. These children possessed an energy of character 'united to a freedom of mind and freshness of feeling' which, she believed was rarely found, 'except among the inhabitants of a new country'.[56]

The colonial elite provided their children with tutors and kept them under close supervision at home. Jane Williams told her parents about a gentry family she had met who were 'very particular about the associates for their family, I assure you – so much so that the girls never leave home'.[57] The sons of those with sufficient wealth were sent back to Britain for their secondary education. But by 1836 there were numerous fee-paying schools for young gentlemen, and young ladies in Hobart, Launceston and the countryside. There were 15 such 'seminaries' in Hobart in 1835 and 12 in Launceston and the rural areas. The quality of these schools varied widely and some closed after only a short existence. But they offered what appeared to be a rigorous education. The Longford Hall Academy set out its prospectus in January 1836 offering a large number of subjects, including Latin, Greek, French, algebra, geometry, surveying, navigation, dancing and fencing. Mrs Piguenet's Ladies' Seminary in New Town offered to educate young women in every branch of useful and polite learning, with particular reference to the age and taste of each pupil. The subjects included

English grammar, with critical and accurate parsing, composition, geography, French, music and drawing, and needlework in all its branches.

But any discussion about children and their education had to take into account the overriding importance of the convict system and the anxiety about the large number of children with one or more prisoner or ex-prisoner parent. Would the children of convicts inherit their parents' criminal propensities, be irretrievably corrupted as a result of being brought up among scenes of depravity and degradation, or be nurtured in a dangerous tradition of rebellion and defiance? It was a problem that Governor Arthur wrestled with and came to believe that the state itself should be directly responsible for the upbringing of the youth of the colony who possessed 'a peculiar claim to the kind consideration of government', which may, he argued in a dispatch to the Colonial Office, 'be even more emphatically than elsewhere, the common parent and guardian of those who may, not inappropriately, be styled, the "Children of the State"'.[58]

With this ambition in mind Arthur established a system of government schools; by the end of 1836 there were 29 of them in operation, as well as several kindergartens that were assisted with subsidies. Arthur was quite clear what the purpose of education was and the means by which it could be achieved. In an address to the secretaries of the infant schools he argued that even young children should imperceptibly imbibe habits 'of order, of attention, and of submission'. Such a training would prevent them from being 'rendered, by early contamination, intractable'. The teachers and clergymen should commit themselves to

subduing that vice which is the necessary effect of the wild liberty of which so many of the Children of Hobart Town are now permitted to indulge in during years in which much is learned having a tendency to render future admonition at least comparatively inoperative.[59]

Religion was the means by which unruly colonial children would be taught order and submission; it was the 'groundwork of every system of public education'. But for Arthur the truths of religion should be imparted by the rote learning of the catechism, a series of answers given in a sort of chant to a set of often obscure theological questions. In his address to the infant school secretaries he explained that children should

Get by heart a catechism containing a full exposition of scripture truths even though they may be unable at present to understand the full import of many of the questions, and answers, for these would be as a Treasury from which they might derive consolation and instruction in riper years.[60]

Adults, too, required the guidance provided by religion. To this end, during Arthur's governorship the major Christian denominations received assistance in recruiting clergy and in building churches, often in the teeth of opposition from prominent members of the Anglican establishment. He opened Hobart's Presbyterian church on the eve of his departure and lay the foundation stone for St George's on Battery Point. But church building alone was not enough. He wanted proselytising clergy who had the 'energy of character and expression requisite to ensure the deference and anxious attention' of a class of hearers, upon whose minds it was important to urge the truth of religion, just in proportion as they were 'naturally disinclined to receive them'. The active clergyman should be willing to follow a man into his own dwelling 'with advice and instruction' should he be indisposed to receive it in the church. It was the 'lower classes' who were the principal target of Arthur's evangelical crusade, for while they made up the main parts of any society, they were particularly in need of guidance in Van Diemen's Land where 'so peculiar an infelicity attaches to their condition'. As a result their religious instruction 'was a permanent object of care and solicitude'.[61]

But there were other colonists who wanted education to have a much broader purpose, to elevate rather than to hold down. Dr James Ross, editor of the *Hobart Town Courier*, stressed the importance of the arts and sciences in a colony that was 'estranged from home and all its treasures'. It was only with a due regard to higher education that it would be possible to raise the new society 'to its due and proper standing of eminence and renown among other nations'.[62] Ross was concerned about the future if the colonial children were not well enough educated to hold their own in the wider world. 'Are we to have no men of learning in the colony after this generation?', he asked, apart from those who happened to migrate from Britain and 'lord it over our ignorance as they assuredly will'.[63] Ross strongly advocated the establishment of a university and in an address to the Hobart Town Mechanic's Institute he declared:

We could confer degrees, become as learned and have as little occasion to visit European seats of learning as they would have to seek us. We are too remote to depend on the other hemisphere for the immediate rays of science that are to enlighten us in this.

What hindrance, he asked his audience, is there that we could not teach the sciences as well in Hobart as within any college in Oxford or Cambridge? In a peroration he declared:

Look at the beautiful and interesting open, ingenuous countenances of your native youths, staring at you, with dumb but earnest entreaty full in the face; and say if you can refuse them this.[64]

Apart from the obvious presence of a swelling generation of native-born children, the great majority of whom would never leave the Australian colonies, there were other aspects of colonial society that distinguished it from the distant homeland. While homesick colonists might wish to reproduce something like the society they had left behind there were always others who had the opposite intention. And like other New World colonies Van Diemen's Land had, from the earliest years, mixed people up with a speed and finality that was at that time unknown in Britain. After living in the colony for 10 years John Dixon observed:

It must be borne in mind, that the society of Van Diemen's Land is an English society. But as you travel through the United Kingdom you perceive local peculiarities distinguishing the inhabitants of each part of it, which in Van Diemen's Land you do not; for as emigration has flowed from all these parts respectively, those peculiarities are lost in the general admixture of dialects; and therefore no distinctions remain.[65]

But it was in the colony's political life that the two forces of emulation and innovation were most clearly articulated.

6

The Politics of Van Diemen's Land

Soon after *The Elphinstone* dropped anchor in Sullivan's Cove on Tuesday, 24 May 1836, the news spread like wildfire: after 12 years in the colony Governor Arthur had been recalled. Boyes noted in his diary that the news was all over town in half an hour. He believed that it seemed 'to diffuse general joy'.[1] Arthur's enemies were exultant, many claiming, and probably believing, that their incessant agitation had precipitated the recall. In Hobart and Launceston members of the informal political Opposition gathered for celebratory dinners where many speeches were delivered and even more toasts drunk. In the north, the *Cornwall Chronicle* published a special supplement with banner headlines that declared:

REJOICE
For the day of
RETRIBUTION
Has
ARRIVED

The editor declared that

Tomorrow ought to be a day of general THANKSGIVING!
For the deliverance from the iron hand of GOVERNOR ARTHUR.
We have now the prospect of breathing. The accursed gang of blood suckers will be destroyed . . . and a gang of Felons will be no longer permitted to violate the LAWS OF CIVILIZED SOCIETY.[2]

In Hobart the opposition paper, the *Colonial Times*, headed its editorial 'Oh Joyous News', and then went on to declare that it was 'with the utmost satisfaction that the inhabitants of Hobart Town welcomed the happy intelligence...that Colonel Arthur is forthwith to be removed from this Government'.[3]

Bent's News published a piece of doggerel with the heading 'The Fall of Arthur's Dynasty', which ran:

> Over the seas and far away
> Over the seas and far away
> Your Governor is called away
> For twelve long years his wicked clan
> Has persecuted every man
> For he's the cause of all our woes.[4]

The pro-government *Hobart Town Courier* spoke with a very different and deferential voice, announcing the news of the recall with deep regret and asking whether anything could compensate the community for the loss of a man to whom so much was due. The praise mounted as the editorial unfolded.

He has indeed been the father of the people, and the various mementos of his sojourn in Van Diemen's Land, as time advances, will rise more and more in the grateful recollection of its inhabitants. Never did the British Crown possess a more faithful servant, nor were the necessarily confidential affairs of a distant colony more conscientiously administered.[5]

The reactions to news of Arthur's recall illustrated many aspects of the political life of Van Diemen's Land in the 1830s. Supporters and opponents alike were aware of the central importance of the governor to the life of the colony, especially so in the case of Arthur who had been in power for the unusually lengthy term of 12 years. Though advised by a small Executive Council of senior officials and a larger Legislative Council that included appointed colonists, the governor wielded extensive powers. Arthur was a man who understood power, enjoyed using it and had a tidy, efficient and decisive mind. He was sharply aware of the need to keep on good terms with his superiors in the Colonial Office whose favour he successfully courted; to the chagrin of his domestic opponents he left the colony with high official approval. The seven local newspapers were the main vehicle for political comment and they conducted their campaigns with a raw, crude vigour revelling in invective and vituperation. West was no friend of George Arthur but on reading backruns of the local newspapers he was struck by the violence of the writing. The limited field of discussion, he believed, 'huddled all disputes into a squabble'.[6] In the absence of any democratic institutions the papers, along with public meetings, dinners and the drafting of petitions to the British government, were the major avenue for opposition to the government. The press, West argued, 'was the more licentious because nothing else was free'.[7]

Colonial politics reflected international and local developments. The educated settlers were aware of the spread of democratic ideas in Britain, which culminated in the *Reform Act 1832*, and on the continent of Europe as the era of reaction following the wars with revolutionary France ended in the insurrection of 1830. West observed that, 'So lively was the interest in the affairs of Europe, that the tri-colour was mounted by more ardent politicians. The last wave of revolution, which had scattered thrones, rippled on these shores'.[8]

The colonists maintained a close interest in the more democratic political life of the USA, which was constantly renewed by regular contact with crews from visiting whalers. There was also an alert local awareness of the growth of opposition politics in the older and larger sister colony of New South Wales where radical democrats challenged the authoritarian power of Governors Brisbane and Darling. But the focus was principally on the local scene. Colonists and sojourners alike had an interest in the future of the island. As were their counterparts in settler societies elsewhere in the world, they were obsessed not with what had been but what was to come. The fundamental question for almost a generation was what was to happen with the convict system. No other issue approached it in importance. It was for this reason that, notwithstanding knowledge and interest in other issues and other societies, political life was inimitable, focused on local issues and the quite unique nature of island society.

The central and ever-present question was how far the institutions and customs of British society could be transplanted into a colony whose central purpose was the punishment of felons. How normal could this 'peculiarly circumstanced' community become?[9] Both sides in this ubiquitous and persistent debate had cogent, well-entrenched arguments, which in part explains why there was so much contention. The fundamental question related to the very nature of British colonial societies. The legal situation had been stated by William Blackstone in his classic work on the common law, *The Commentaries on the Laws of England*, known at least by repute to most educated settlers. First published in 1776 it was in its 18th edition by 1823. Blackstone explained the legal situation that arose when settlers arrived in the New World. All English laws 'then in being, which are the birth right of every subject' were 'immediately there in force'. However, there was a fundamentally important qualification, as the great jurist explained:

But this must be understood with very many and very great restrictions. Such colonists carry with them only so much of the English law, as is applicable to their own situation and the conditions of the infant colony.[10]

Both sides in the Van Diemen's Land debate could therefore appeal to Blackstone. The opposition demanded that they be granted the rights of 'free born Englishmen'. The government party insisted that they were not applicable in a penal colony and that, by freely choosing to come to Van Diemen's Land, settlers had tacitly accepted the necessary 'very great restrictions' on their freedom.

Governor Arthur forcefully and consistently stated his position. The imperial government had established the colony as a penal settlement and had invested large amounts of money to further that end. All other developments must be subordinated to that objective. He was the servant of the British authorities and he answered to them, not to public opinion in the colony. His unusually long tenure was a tribute to his commitment to imperial policies and to the fact that he was never intimidated by local agitation. Nor did he, as did some colonial governors, become slowly assimilated into the host society and begin to see the world through Creole eyes. Arthur wrote to the Colonial Office soon after his arrival on the island, observing that 'this colony must be considered in the light of a great gaol to the Empire' and the free inhabitants 'whether immigrants or prisoners free by emancipation or servitude should be looked upon as visitors and liable to submit to the rules established for the general peace and order of the colony'.[11] He said exactly the same thing 10 years later in another dispatch. 'Van Diemen's Land,' he observed, 'had been for a very special purpose occupied by Great Britain at a very

large expense', and every other consideration 'must be secondary
to that Grand National Object'.[12] The normal institutions of the
British Isles were inappropriate for such 'a wretched sequestered
spot peopled by the refuse of Newgate', a society 'nourished in
every species of crime', and one where the convicts and emancipists
outnumbered the free settlers.[13]

The governor had spent his whole adult life in the army where as
a senior officer he was used to command and expected obedience.
He had spent little time in Britain itself and was quite unsympathetic
to democratic aspirations, which he associated with revolutionary
France against which he had spent years fighting. He said on a
variety of occasions that if it were not for the convict system he
would warmly advocate the introduction of free institutions. What
is more intriguing is that he did appreciate the nature of colonial
societies, that they were essentially dynamic and innovative and
used to rapid change and dramatic social mobility. In an address to
his Legislative Council in 1836 he observed:

Untrammelled by ancient customs, the Colony is enabled with little delay, to
avail itself of improvements, the introduction of which at a more advanced
period of its history, might have interfered with pre-existing interests, as to
have rendered change, however desirable, in itself, highly inexpedient.[14]

He was clearly quite unable to deal equably with criticism, which
he associated with rebellion. He was also socially conservative and
expected deference as well as obedience from the lower orders.
His refusal to allow emancipated convicts to be received in polite
society was a clear manifestation of his belief in a rigidly stratified
and essentially static society.

Arthur was particularly irritated by attacks in the local newspapers on his administration and he made several attempts to control
them but his exercises in censorship were disallowed, first by Governor Brisbane in New South Wales, and then by the Colonial Office.
Newspaper proprietors Andrew Bent and Gilbert Robertson were
both gaoled for libel. Arthur's aim was to prevent the publication
of material that he believed brought the government 'into hatred
and contempt'. A free press was out of place in Van Diemen's
Land. Indeed, it would be the 'height of imprudence . . . to admit
an unrestricted free Press' within the colony. The privileges enjoyed

in Britain were 'quite inconsistent and unsafe' in a convict colony. There was, he said, 'no stopping half way'. In a dispatch to the Colonial Office he was even more emphatic, arguing that 'in a convict colony no measure could have been devised more mischievous or practically injurious than the introduction of a free press'.[15] He went into greater detail in a 1826 letter to Lord Bathurst in which he explained that while he appreciated that attempts to control the press would arouse fierce opposition, the measures were necessary:

Of all the sources of unpopularity, any attempt to interfere with the liberty of the press is the most odious and the most permanent. This circumstance therefore, coupled with the knowledge of my entertaining sentiments opposed to the exercise of that liberty within this island, has not been without its effect upon the individuals hostile to my administration.

I nevertheless continue to feel that this absolutely unrestrained freedom in a small community composed of such inflammable material is incompatible with the well being of society and the safety of the colony.

I have arrived at the positive conviction that the submission of the convict population to the constituted authorities has been shaken by the licentious attacks of a radical paper edited by a time-expired convict and printed and published by an emancipated felon.[16]

The political opposition was led by prominent lawyers, merchants and landowners whose activities were focused in Hobart and Launceston while much of their effectiveness, as Arthur fully realised, came from the influence wielded by the opposition newspapers, the *Colonial Times* and *Bent's News* in the south and the *Launceston Advertiser* and *Cornwall Chronicle* in Launceston. While often violently opposed to the governor and his administration, the gentlemen radicals were not so much democrats as Whigs who wanted to gain the traditional British rights of trial by jury, freedom of the press and representative institutions based on a franchise limited to men such as themselves. There is little suggestion in their petitions, speeches and manifestoes that they were especially sympathetic to the large community of convicts and emancipists. Why transportation became an important issue was the growing realisation that while convicts continued to arrive authoritarian rule would continue, that it was an impassable road block to political reform. There was a strong anti-authoritarian element in opposition rhetoric due partly to temperament and partly to experience in Britain itself where executive government had long ceased to exercise powers available to the governors of Van Diemen's Land. Personal frustrations and disappointments could be subsumed in a crusade against irresponsible authority.

The first concerted political action of the opposition was a public meeting in Hobart in March 1827, which initiated a petition to the king that sought the introduction of trial by jury and a representative assembly. Addressing a large meeting the prominent colonist William Gellibrand declared that the occasion would be remembered with delight by 'all true hearted colonists' because it was one of the highest importance to the future happiness of their society. In arguing the case for reform he declared:

They were Englishmen – their birthrights were liberty and independence... They came from the Mother Country, where all the blessings of freedom are enjoyed in their fullest extent; and they approached His Majesty, therefore, for those privileges, without which independence was a mere mockery, and liberty an empty sound.[17]

Seconding the motion the prominent landowner and merchant Edward Lord commented:

In this new land which we have adopted, where we hope to plant a new race of Britons, enjoying the full privileges of British laws and British freedom. Could the rights – the freedom – and the independence of this newly adopted country be maintained – could we continue to our children that freedom to which we were born – and that happiness which we have known in the land of our nativity, without securing to them and ourselves, the grand bulwark of our national glory; namely, Trial by Jury and Free Representation.[18]

The meetings, the speeches and the petition achieved little. During the late 1820s attention was focused on the Black War and the Line, which had, as West observed, 'absorbed political animosities, and brought all parties together.'[19] But the momentum for reform built up again, culminating in another large public meeting in May 1831 that expressed a farrago of grievances. In the *Colonial Times* Henry Melville declared that a more numerous or more respectable concourse of persons had never before assembled together in the history of the colony. Those who opposed the government referred to the day of the meeting as the Glorious 23 May. The barrister Thomas Horne addressed the question of the application of political rights in the colony, observing that

Some would maintain that in emigrating to this Island we forfeit the privileges of Englishmen . . . No, no; I have forfeited no right, no privilege, which an Englishman considers his birth-right, by coming to this Island, and I will never consent to such a doctrine.[20]

The petition was forwarded to England in the hands of an agent but it had no demonstrable effect on British policy. Melville wondered if the document was ever presented or whether it was 'not thrown overboard during the passage' by friends of the governor.[21]

Arthur's departure heartened the opposition who welcomed the more liberal and certainly more personable Sir John Franklin, who took up the reins of government at the beginning of 1837. But the fundamental problem of local politics remained. Democratic reform was profoundly hampered by the continuation of transportation. And while Arthur's iron grip was replaced by more conciliatory policies the changing nature of the convict system pushed increasing numbers of colonists into the arms of the opposition camp. As will be seen below, almost all groups came to have legitimate grievances. The imperial government increased the inflow of convicts and charged the colony with larger amounts for the privilege. Assignment was replaced, which undermined influential landowners' support for the system, and convicts released from work gangs flooded the labour market, which forced down the wages of free labour. Franklin had more liberal views than his predecessor and was sympathetic to colonial grievances, but he was unable to influence the opinion of the British government or the Colonial Office. The problem he faced of finding sufficient funds to pay for the administration of the convict system and the ordinary demands of society was difficult enough in the prosperous years of the late 1830s but it became almost impossible in the depressed 1840s, as his successor Sir John Eardley-Wilmot found to the cost of his peace of mind and, ultimately, his career. Eardley-Wilmot's initial strategy of borrowing money was strongly opposed by the Colonial Office, leaving him with the only option of trying to raise the taxes paid by the colonists. This meant passing the necessary measures through his Legislative Council and against the vociferous opposition of the non-official members, culminating in the what became known as the affair of the Patriotic Six.

The governor called his Legislative Council together in July 1845 to pass a series of measures aimed at restoring the colony's battered finances. There were cuts to public sector salaries and increased taxes and charges. The Opposition used every possible measure to delay the proceedings of the council and addressed angry public meetings in Hobart. The issue came to a head at the end of October when the Appropriation Bill, having passed through its various stages on the casting vote of the governor, came up for its third reading. Finding that they could delay proceedings no longer the non-official members walked out of the council chamber, robbing the meeting of the required quorum. Their subsequent resignation caused a long delay in council business as the governor was forced to find reluctant replacements.

The walkout and resignations brought to a head problems that had been latent in colonial politics for years. Two broad currents had forcefully come together. The unofficial members of the council were frustrated by their limited powers. They were expected to advise not determine policy. They took their stand on the time-honoured principle of no taxation without effective representation, that is, without the ability to amend or reject the Appropriation Bill. More to the point was the fact that colonial revenue was expended on the police and gaols, which were seen as entirely a matter for the imperial government, which sent the convicts to Van Diemen's Land in the first place in the interests of Britain and in pursuit of policies over which the colonists had no say. As transportation became increasingly unpopular the financial burden borne by the colony became increasingly irksome. The colonists were paying for a system they increasingly reviled. In moving the motion to reject the budget – or, in the language of the time, to have it read in six months time – Richard Dry

called upon the members to pause before they voted away so much money for convict purposes, or plunged the colony further into debt on the same account. The people had borne the injustice in silence and with patience for a long time, and with an endurance that would not have been sustained by any other community; and although their grievance had at length engendered an anti-English feeling, yet the Colonists still retained feelings of loyalty towards their Sovereign.[22]

Though the governor's supporters stigmatised the Patriotic Six as members of a fractious minority they were a formidable and influential group. Kermode and Fenton were prominent landowners, and Fenton had a distinguished military background. Swanson was the leading financier and banker in the colony, and the *Colonial Times* observed that he conducted an 'immense monetary machine, in the working of which he has at his disposal the fortunes of three-fourths of the landed proprietors of the colony'. Gregson was the most experienced agitator in Van Diemen's Land and an inveterate opponent of arbitrary power, a man who was both a generous, open-handed host and a dangerous and vindictive enemy. He shot one of Arthur's coterie in a duel and horse-whipped another in the street. Thirty year old Richard Dry, by far the youngest of the group, had the advantage of appealing to the swelling ranks of the native born and, as the son of an Irish rebel convict, to many emancipists as well. And it was Dry who received the most extraordinary public affirmation for his stand when he returned to Launceston in December 1845.

As his carriage approached the town it was met by 150 horsemen lined up on both sides of the road. The procession grew as it approached the business district. Banners were unfurled and the local brass band could scarcely be heard above the loud and prolonged cheering. Dry's horses were unhitched and 'fifty willing men supplied their place' to pull the carriage through the streets to the Cornwall Hotel. The town's tradesmen marched four abreast behind a green silk banner with the colony's arms on one side and the words 'Unity and Concord' on the other. Behind the tradesmen a large number of 'the middle classes' walked carrying two banners bearing the words: 'The Patriotic Six' and' Dry For Ever'. Everyone wore blue ribbons and flags streamed from windows and rooftops with slogans such as 'The Independent Six', 'Dry and Independence', 'The Native Patriot'. Reporting on the occasion in a special edition the *Launceston Examiner* declared:

The universality of the feeling was shown by demonstrations, and the most respectable as well as the most humble spoke of 'Dry and Independence'.

It would baffle description to tell of the all pervading excitement; and the easiest and most accurate way of conveying any idea of the public feeling, is by stating, that, from the entrance into town to the arrival at the Cornwall Hotel, Mr. Dry was hailed by one loud, incessant and tumultuous cheer.[23]

But the affair of the Patriotic Six was merely a prelude to the intense politics of the following eight years, which focused almost entirely on the transportation question and subsided only with the formal end of the convict era in 1853. The problem dominated the terms of Governors Eardley-Wilmot (1843–6) and Sir William Denison (1847–54). Although economic conditions improved in the late 1840s and early 1850s feelings against transportation intensified and spread through many levels of society, although there were always people who, for a variety of reasons, wanted the system to be preserved or at least gradually wound down. It took a brave man to publically express support for the system or for the local and imperial governments. Those who tried to do so at public meetings were howled down and ridiculed and could barely be heard above the antagonistic clamour. The *Hobart Town Courier* reported that a supporter of transportation 'was not heard, the meeting having groaned him down, and hissed him down – voted him down'.[24]

The political temperature rose dramatically as a consequence of political decisions made by the Colonial Office, which initially signalled an end to transportation, and then three years later reversed the decision and intimated that the colony would become the main destination for convicts from all parts of the empire. As a precursor of that fate the remaining convicts from New South Wales and Norfolk Island were transferred to Port Arthur. The large imperial expenditure that had been so important in the colony's economic development seemed to increasing numbers of people to be accompanied by social and moral costs that were unsustainable. As more felons poured in, free migrants and enterprising emancipists sailed for Melbourne, which was a quick and relatively cheap voyage away. Many hopes and aspirations were woven in with the crusade against transportation. As had been the case for almost a generation the desire for free institutions was perpetually frustrated by the demographic dominance of convicts and emancipists. This was linked to the arbitrary power not just of the local governors but also of the distant and perpetually unresponsive Colonial Office. Economic engagement with and social commitment to the new society mingled with a bourgeoning indigenous patriotism. Parents worried about the world their children would inherit. The rapidly growing ranks of native born felt that they should decide the destiny of their homeland. The enthusiasm for Dry involved patriotism, local pride and a cry for independence. A sentiment that was heard with increasing frequency during the 1840s was that the physical beauty of the island made the continuation of transportation not merely anomalous but also sacrilegious.

Following the decision by the British government to suspend transportation for two years Governor Denison initiated a public discussion in 1847 about the future of the system. While he addressed himself to the magistrates the great question of the period was canvassed far and wide in the newspapers, public meetings, speeches, letters and poems, and certainly in innumerable if unrecorded conversations and arguments. All the evidence indicates that for years the colony became engaged in a period of intense, prolonged political activity. West observed that a massive volume 'would be insufficient to contain the petitions, letters, and dispatches produced in this controversy. Colonists well qualified to maintain the popular cause devoted to this cause the best years of their lives.'[25] It was, in West's admittedly partisan view, 'the most important colonial agitation in modern times'. He wrote that

In the progress of the struggle all classes ranged on the same side. Parents thought of their children – patriots of their country...The steps of the colonists have been cautious and deliberate, their perseverance and energy indomitable! Their success has been chequered by frequent disappointment but never was a battle more nobly fought – never was there a cause more worthy of triumph.[26]

In the middle of 1847 there were mass meetings in Hobart and Launceston at which the motion was put that transportation 'should for ever be abolished'. It was carried with overwhelming support. Opponents of the measure had trouble being heard let alone swaying the huge audiences, despite their often reasonable concern about the economic consequences of the abolition of transportation. It was also clear that the competing parties to the debate carefully stacked their meetings and sought to fill the chosen venues with their supporters. The moral arguments against the system drowned out reasoned counter arguments. Predictions of economic loss, of grass growing in the streets, were engulfed in the fervour of the crusade. In Hobart, solicitor Joseph Allport declared that consideration 'of pecuniary interests should be entirely banished from the feelings of the community' because the 'stigma should be wiped away from the Colony at any cost'.[27] In Launceston the sister meeting drew large crowds into the town. The streets were 'thronged and obstructed by knots of disputants'. The meeting began at noon and broke up just before 7 o'clock. Richard Dry told the receptive audience that

This country was never intended by God or nature to be a cesspool of filthiness, and everything that was abominable and horrible...they would seal their own degradation for ever, if they showed a disposition to tolerate, when the chance was offered to rid the country of pollution.

They should, he insisted, 'throw off the accursed thing...and stand fair with the world'.[28] Prominent magistrate and amateur botanist Robert Campbell Gunn sought to amend the motion, proposing a continuation of a modified form of transportation. There was some dispute as to whether 10 or 13 hands were raised in support. The motion for complete and total abolition passed with a vast, triumphant majority. The *Launceston Examiner* reported that 'As one man the meeting rose, and with raised hands and joyous shouts manifested the opinion of the mass of the community'.[29]

A local poet wrote in sympathy some 'Lines on Transportation', which ran in part:

> What! Shall we bear for filthy lucre's sake
> So vile a stigma? Shall we ne'er awake
> To our true interests, and, in union strong
> Fling from our shores a plague we've born too long?
> Why should we breathe pollution's blighting air
> When we may have a pure atmosphere?...
> Then arise my fellow colonists! Arise
> All you who would Tasmania's welfare prize!
> Unite; and in this cause combin'd appear
> Till Britain cease to send her convicts here.[30]

Launceston provided much of the drive behind the movement against transportation. The government, the military and the prison service had far less impact in the north than they did in the capital and far fewer jobs were at stake if transportation ceased. The moral intensity of the campaign was provided by earnest nonconformist clergymen such as Congregationalist John West, Baptist Robert Dowling and the editor of the *Examiner*, prominent Congregational layman James Aikenhead. Even on his own West was a force to be reckoned with. Editor of the *Sydney Morning Herald* during the 1850s and 1860s and author of a remarkably eloquent two volume history of Tasmania published in 1852, West was perhaps the most distinguished journalist in colonial Australia. The Anti-Transportation League was founded in Launceston in 1847. West provided the intellectual case for the movement in a pamphlet entitled 'Common Sense: An Inquiry into the Influence of Transportation on the Colony of Van Diemen's Land'. In it he argued that the question of transportation transcended every other political matter because it was a problem that 'came home'. It was, he asserted, 'domestic', affecting every man, his estate, his children, his posterity. While the convict system may have provided economic benefits in years past it had, in the 1840s, become an incubus of withering power. Though much of West's argument was about what he believed were the economic costs of the system, the peroration was an emotional appeal to 'the parents of Van Diemen's Land'. 'Can you hesitate?' he asked rhetorically.

Let the timid and sordid doubt, let them reckon the farthing they may lose; let the official men guard the system on which they live – they watch for their own interests; yours are immeasurably more valuable! Let your hearts dictate your answer . . . Let it be worthy Britons, Christians, and Parents. Shew that you prize your rights, and that you love your children.

It was only when the colony was free from the terrible stigma of the convict that the native-born children could 'go forth, the free among the free'. Otherwise the eyes of mankind would 'look upon you with abhorrence, and turn away with contempt'. The final sentence was a clarion call: 'Perform your duty, AND SAVE YOUR ADOPTED COUNTRY!'[31]

When West wrote his pamphlet there was a reasonable expectation that the British government would bring transportation to an end. But these hopes were dashed in 1850 when the colonists learnt that Secretary of State Earl Grey had changed his mind and intended to renew the process and concentrate the flow of felons to the island. There was an immediate sense of betrayal and anger about what appeared to be broken promises. What infuriated the islanders was that Grey questioned their moral right to resist the resumption of transportation and asserted without any sound evidence that opposition to the system had diminished on the island. Activists, angry and despairing, renewed the crusade. Agitated, earnest meetings gathered again in both major towns. The speeches and the motions were familiar but there was a critical innovation – the decision to call on the support of the other colonies. West observed that the phrase, 'The Australians are one' became the watchword of the abolitionists.[32] In August 1850 the Launceston Association for Promoting the Cessation of Transportation to Van Diemen's Land decided to send letters to politicians and other leading figures in Victoria, New South Wales and South Australia to seek support. In their appeal the committee members declared:

As a last resort we turn to our fellow-colonists who, united to us, by the strictest ties, are liable to the same wrongs; and who will not be indifferent spectators of sufferings which they may ultimately share.

Following a long passage detailing the dangers presented to the mainland colonies by convicts landed on the island and schooled there in further infamy, the committee repeated its appeal to fellow feeling and community of interest.

Communities allied by blood, language, and commerce, cannot long suffer alone. We conjure you, therefore, by the unity of Colonial interests – as well as by the obligations which bind all men to intercede with the strong and unjust on behalf of the feeble and oppressed – to exert your influence to the intent that transportation to Van Diemen's Land may forever cease.[33]

The intercolonial connection was cemented in January 1851 when two Tasmanian delegates, John West and prominent landowner William Weston, left Launceston for Melbourne. They had been accompanied through the town by a procession of supporters. At the wharf on the river bank a huge crowd gathered to see them off and gave three cheers for the Australian colonies as the paddle steamer cast off and headed down the river towards Bass Strait. In his farewell address West declared:

Van Diemen's Land must obtain a share in the general freedom or ever sink . . . Shall our children never know the pride and pleasure of patriotism? Shall we not ask all the colonies of the Australian empire to aid us in our struggle? Shall we not confide in the justice of Australasia?[34]

The Australasian League was formed at a influential meeting in Melbourne, where the League's flag, designed by West, was unfurled. He carried with him one made in Launceston and was presented in turn with another copy made in Melbourne. Later in the year West took his crusade to Sydney and Adelaide; by the end of the year the respective Legislative Councils had come out strongly against further transportation. Such a strong message could not be ignored in Britain, particularly as it embodied intimations of alienation from the empire. In December 1852 incoming Secretary of State for the Colonies Sir John Parkington wrote to Governor Denison explaining that growing public feeling against continued transportation in Van Diemen's Land and the mainland colonies had convinced the imperial government to 'comply with a wish so generally and forcibly expressed'. The alternative would be to force the colonists 'into a furious opposition . . . extinguishing all loyalty and affection for the mother-country'.[35] On 27 November 1852 the last convict ship sailed for Hobart, although it would be another 10 years before the last transport arrived, and that was in Western Australia.

Another unmistakable indication of local opinion that was difficult for the Colonial Office to overlook was the result of the first elections, which were held in October and November 1851. They were for the new 'Blended Legislative Council', which was to be composed of one-third nominees of the governor and two-thirds elected members. The British government had decided that the colony, the convict system notwithstanding, would receive the same sort of representative assembly as had operated in New South Wales since 1840 and that eventually all the Australian colonies would follow the Canadian path to full responsible government. The colonists took to electoral politics with relish. There were contests in many of the electorates. The two public occasions – nomination day and election day – brought large crowds out into the streets. Partisans gathered to march together behind bands to the point of nomination with banners, ribbons and flags in the chosen colour of the candidate. In Hobart one candidate chose rose pink, the second dark blue and the third light blue. Carriages decorated with the candidates' colours sped through the streets. In both towns the partisans came ready for trouble. They shouted and hooted and whistled in an attempt to drown out opposing speakers. They pelted their opponents with eggs, and skirmished and brawled with fists, sticks and clubs. When the result was declared, the successful candidates were 'chaired', that is, they were carried by their supporters on specially prepared chairs to the venue of victory celebrations. The successful candidate for Hobart, merchant T. D. Chapman, was enthroned upon a seat covered with rich pink silk velvet. It was attached to a carriage decorated with gay wreaths and bunches of flowers. His supporters dispensed with the horses: they themselves pulled the carriage through the town to nearby Battery Point, followed by a large crowd. As they passed the Glasgow Wine Vaults a large party of opponents attacked the triumphant crowd with bludgeons. But as the *Courier* reported, Chapman's party 'put them to rout, after a few heads had been broken'.[36]

For all the rivalry and roistering the elections were taken very seriously. The overwhelming issue was transportation and all successful candidates were opponents of the system and the governor. Many of them had fought for the cause for years. In a speech nominating Chapman, lawyer E. T. Macdowell declared:

On this day, and at this very hour, the death knell of Transportation is rung throughout the length and breadth of the land (cheers).

There is no difference of opinion on this point; that no man can lay the smallest title to success as a candidate except he pledges himself to the total abolition of Transportation (Hear, hear!).[37]

There was more to the election than a plebiscite on the convict system. It was as much about the future as the past and the first exercise in electoral politics inspired high ideals and matching lofty rhetoric. The returning officer for the rural seat of Cumberland, Mr Fenwick, told the small crowd in Bothwell that

The proceedings of this day will go forth to the world, and the neighbouring colonies, which have hitherto commiserated your condition, but will rejoice at this crisis of your political independence. The occasion of this great meeting will be inscribed in indelible letters in the historical annals of Tasmania, and long remembered, when we who have witnessed this scene shall have passed away – we who have seen the sun of political freedom rise in the horizon of a glorious and aspiring Colony; but future generations shall see it wending its way to its zenith of greatness... and the names of those noblemen who have arduously struggled for – aye, and obtained – the political independence of their country shall be engraven for ever in the hearts of a grateful and admiring posterity.[38]

Between 1830 and 1850 the political discourse changed significantly. The first political activists sought to restore what they saw as the traditional rights of Englishmen. They referred to the past and looked across the world to their homeland. By 1850 the rhetoric was much more about the future of the colony and the inheritance of native-born children. There was much talk of patriotism, independence and the impending role of the island in the world of nations. The election campaign of 1851 was significant because of the first organised political involvement of native-born Tasmanians who participated as a self-conscious group and who clearly must have had at least some rudimentary form of organisation and presumably customary meeting places and methods of communication. In Hobart and Launceston there were large public meetings of the native born. In Launceston 400 met at the Cornwall Hotel, and then marched in procession to the Temperance Hall where they were addressed by their hero Richard Dry, who observed that it was the first time he had 'addressed his own countrymen upon the political prospects of their native land'.[39] On Nomination Day the native youth formed a procession and marched through the town to the Cornwall Hotel to hear Dry deliver a speech from the balcony. At Longford and Westbury the native youth of the district, carrying banners, marched in support of anti-transportation candidate William Archer, eventually pulling his carriage through the town.[40]

But it was the large and well-reported meeting in Hobart that gives us a unique insight into the ideas of the young native-born men and women. The meeting was held under the flag of the Anti-Transportation League. Three hundred signed a petition that protested against 'the conversion of their country into a gaol', contrary to their feelings and wishes. There was a warning that if the policy was persisted with it would engender feelings in the breasts of the colonists hostile to the supremacy of Great Britain, and likely to engender attitudes 'inconsistent with the existence of any feelings of loyalty'. The meeting resolved 'that the native born ladies' should also sign along with their male companions and compatriots. The meeting concluded with three cheers for the Australasian League. The whole proceedings, the *Courier* concluded, did the young people much credit and 'would go far to remove the stigma under which they have laboured'.[41]

When they spoke the leaders of the native born displayed no sense of being troubled by a personal stigma. It was their country that they were worried about. Robert Garrett outlined the evil reputation that clung to Van Diemen's Land, and then added: 'But with pride be it spoken, the criminal records of our country disclose but few instances of native born turpitude'. It was a declaration that was met with loud cheers. He went on to emphasise that he did not seek to create distinctions between themselves and the convicts. They were opposed to the system not to individuals and in particular they were hostile to the threat of cheap prison labour. 'We are,' he observed,

bound by birth and interest to the soil, and never wish to leave it (hear, hear). They are not so. It is a principle in Human nature to cling to early associations; the bond long to leave a land remembered only as a scene of suffering . . . they can leave the colony, but we cannot. The land of our birth is endeared to us by many ties they cannot feel.[42]

The native born had been forced by the system to leave the island. It had already 'dissevered the dearest ties of country and kindred, and made us wanderers on the face of the earth'. In a call for action Garrett told his listeners:

We will combat against that system prudently and temperately; but if we find the warfare of words too weak, we will gladly embrace a stronger alternative, rather than remain quiescent in a land with the cloud of convictism hanging over it like a curse.[43]

Running like a powerful current through the speeches of the native born was an openly and proudly avowed patriotism and love of country. Like their contemporaries all over Europe they were lifted on the high tide of romantic nationalism. It had little to do with being British or of belonging to the empire and while the ideas may have arrived from outside, the source was thought to be the land itself and the natives' instinctive love of their homeland. Nor did the response to the land depend on status or wealth or education. A Mr Carmichael introduced a short speech with the declaration that for Tasmanians 'Love of country, a sacred and soul-ennobling feeling which could prevail in the human breast' had occasioned him and others 'to step forward this day'.[44] The presence of this feeling was 'suggestive of high thoughts and noble aspirations'. It moved and animated them in the accomplishment of wise and philanthropic ends and in the latest hour 'of lingering mortality only dispelled by death'. Another speaker, Frederick Wise, was an equally eloquent patriot who returned to an often repeated theme that linked the natural beauty of the island with political freedom. He asked his compatriots:

Who can ascend our noble and romantic hills without being imbued with a spirit of freedom? What reflecting mind can breathe the pure air of our mountain tops without feeling a desire to accomplish the freedom of his native land – without bemoaning the dreadful state of penal thraldom under which we labour – without entertaining a wish to place this our country on an equality with our neighbours.[45]

But the League and its native-born allies were opposed by a coalition of Denison's administration and the large and well-organised Tasmanian Union, established at an enthusiastic public meeting in Hobart in October 1850. Supported by two local newspapers, the *Guardian or Friend of Tasmania* and the *Irish Exile and Freedom's Advocate*, it drew its support principally from the emancipists, including many successful businessmen and tradesmen. Union members reacted strongly to the incessant and often highly coloured propaganda of the Anti-transportation League about the parlous moral condition of the colony. They were outraged at the obvious exaggeration and the very clear implication that they, as ex-convicts, were implicated in the putative degradation of their society. The earnest endeavour of so many individuals to achieve redemptive respectability was subverted by self-righteous, priggish 'false and slanderous statements against the colony and its inhabitants'.[46] There was also a strong current of resentment about the lack of recognition of the convicts' pioneering role and their contribution to the wealth of many of the prominent Leaguers. In a letter to the *Guardian* a correspondent using the evocative nom de plume of Spartacus cried:

Is it not unjust, cruel, and iniquitous to persecute further men who have already suffered for their offences? Is expatriation no punishment? Is exile from friends, home, and country not enough, but that they must be scouted and leagued against – like savages or beasts of prey? And who Mr. Editor are the persons composing this unholy alliance? Why! Many of these men, whose present affluence has been raised from the bones, the blood, and the sinews of the class who they are now so inveterate against.

The Tasmanians boast of the resources of their Island, yet, who but Prisoners opened up these resources – for how many lives were lost – how many lashes inflicted during the formation of the Launceston road alone, every mile of which was redolent of Triangles, and of blood.[47]

The Union, like the League, had its poets. In an 'Address to the Tasmanian Union' Mary Bailey declared:

> You who have so long in helplessness have borne
> Your vaunting fellow – man's unpitying scorn,
> Whose tears – whose blood have watered oft the soil
> Where deserts changed to gardens, own your toil
> Lift from the dust, once more, your sorrowing eyes
> The auspicious hour is come – arise, arise!
> Though ye have erred, and felt the penal woe
> Shall erring brothers aggravate the blow
> Are they quite pure, who cast the deadly stone.
> Since all have sinned – not only bond but free
> Let each express a mutual sympathy.[48]

Emancipist anger intensified at the end of 1852 when the Victorian government, urged on by the local branch of the Australasian League, passed what became known as the Convict Prevention Act, which was specifically designed to prevent the entry of most of Tasmania's emancipist population. It was seen as a profound collective insult, the responsibility for which was easily attributed to League propaganda. In Hobart, League members were driven first from the stage, and then from the hall at outraged public meetings 'under a shower of groans and protection of police'.[49] At the elections for the Hobart City Corporation a few weeks later the emancipists were triumphant. The *Guardian*, writing in ebullient mood, declared that 'Most nobly and most majestically have the People . . . consummated a victory, most glorious and most triumphant'.[50] In Launceston the League maintained its hold on the town and won control of the Corporation.

The political life of early Tasmania culminated on 10 August 1853 when the colonists gathered to celebrate the end of transportation and the 50th anniversary of the first settlement on the Derwent. It was an unofficial holiday, more widely celebrated in Launceston than in Hobart where the Town Corporation refused to sanction it and Governor Denison decreed that public servants were to remain at their desks. In a letter to the organisers of the festivities he observed that their celebration would enhance 'those feelings of antagonism of class against class' that operated so 'prejudicially to the comfort and happiness of the community'.

Despite the hostility of the governor celebrations began at dawn in the two large towns and the rural villages with the ringing of bells and the discharge of canon. Houses were decorated with banners and flags. There were special services in all the major Christian churches and in Hobart's Jewish synagogue. It was a great day of indulgence for the colony's children, who gathered and marched and were given cakes and sweets. All the children were given a ticket that entitled them to a medallion, which had been ordered in London, celebrating the end of transportation. In Hobart and Launceston the local pastry cooks produced the largest cakes ever seen in the colony. At the Hobart bakery part of the premises had to be taken down to get the cake out into the street. In almost every town evenings were lit with fireworks and blazing tar barrels. The ships in port flew their full complement of flags. Indigenous flowers and shrubs decorated tables and ceremonial arches. On the Derwent a 50 ton schooner, *Jubilee*, was launched. In Hobart there was a grand ball on the Tuesday evening. Couples danced till the early hours of the morning to the music of the band of the 99th Regiment, who concluded their performance with a rendition of the recently written jubilee anthem, 'Tasmania is Free', which the

company 'took up with a shout'.[51] Set to the tune of 'God Save the
Queen' the anthem ran:

> Sing! For the hour has come!
> Sing! For our happy home!
> Our land is free!
> Broken Tasmania's chain!
> Wash'd out the hated stain;
> Ended the strife and pain
> Blest Jubilee.
> Sons of Tasmania sing!
> Daughters sweet garlands bring:
> All joyful be
> Raise, raise your banner high
> Star of the southern sky
> Banner of victory!
> Cross of the free.
> God bless our Fatherland!
> God bless our patriot band!
> Staunch have they been
> Truth has confounded spite;
> Justice has conquered might
> Heaven has maintain'd the right;
> God save the Queen.

Launceston, which felt a sense of distinctive local achievement, celebrated the day with even more enthusiasm. The *Examiner* reported
that the holiday was observed by all classes with almost 'religious
exactness'. All the shops were closed and people poured in from
the surrounding districts, walking, riding or piled up into carts. The
crowds gathered in St John's Square in front of John West's church.
The native born, children and adults, marched through the town
holding League flags, followed by a cart carrying a printing press.
At the entrance to the square they walked under an arch of native
shrubs that had taken three days to prepare. In a speech at the
dinner for the native born, Richard Dry declared:

What a glorious picture was presented to them in contemplating the future.
(Cheers) No longer marked out to receive opprobrium, the beautiful climate
of their country would make it to be considered a place in which it was
desirable to dwell . . . the appeal of their fertile soil and sunny skies would
not be made in vain. (Cheers) Their country would hold a position second to

Image 6.1:   *Cessation of transportation celebrations,*
Launceston, 1853. (*Source:* Archives Office of Tasmania.)

none – it might become a rallying point of liberty and freedom to mankind.
(tremendous and prolonged cheering).[52]

Dry made another claim of great interest. He called for the 'emancipation of the prisoners now in bondage in the colony'. To the cheers
of his audience he declared 'that all who were fit for freedom should
have it'.[53]

In Hobart, the *Guardian* looked with portentous gloom on the
celebrations, particularly at the news that a medallion was to be
struck, and then given to the island's children. Why, it asked, have
medals to keep in remembrance that this was a penal colony? What
good would they do except to 'keep open wounds that ought at
once be closed forever'? The paper hoped they would be destroyed
when they eventually arrived from Britain.[54] A reader contributed
a poem in sympathy, which read in part:

> Tis not a gilded bauble that you offer as a prize
> Tis to rouse up saddened memories – to cause us tearful eyes
> For your gift will remind us how our parents came to join

The Badge of thraldom...
Why deck us with your 'Medal' unless 'twere to recall
A father's lapse from rectitude – a mother's shameless fall?[55]

The euphoria of the anti-transportationists did not last long. Their
opponents had a much better grasp of economic realities: soon after
1856, when the colony received responsible government, it was
mired in recession, which did not lift for almost 20 years.

7

The Convict System

Try as they might the Tasmanians found it hard to live down the legacy of the convict system. It had been there from the foundation of the colony in 1803–4 and had overshadowed every aspect of island life for the first 50 years of its existence. A free colony established at the same time would have had a very different history. The large number of impressive Georgian buildings, established to serve the system or constructed for private purposes, were built by convict artisans; the ambitious public works, initiated with gang labour and the expertise of military engineers, were ever-present reminders of the past and in more recent times have been promoted far beyond the island to illustrate the distinctive heritage awaiting the curious tourist. The convict experience, so richly and uniquely recorded by a small industrious army of clerks and other officials, has always been an irresistible attraction to novelists, poets and filmmakers. Every generation of historians have been drawn to the era of transportation in a way that is not true of more recent periods of Tasmanian history, which, in comparison, has appeared to be lacking in drama and colour. By the middle of the 20th century, the ancestral impulse to repress a shameful past had been overcome and families recovered and characteristically celebrated their convict forebears. In her recent book, *Tasmania's Convicts*, Allison Alexander observed how, from the 1970s, there was a new interest in convicts and there was 'little shame involved'. Tasmania, she declared, must be the only community in the entire world with such a large proportion of the population descended from criminals – and proud of it. Tasmania is known for its convict past, and this heritage is viewed not with contempt, or as a cause for shame, but with great interest. The convict past gives Tasmania a unique identity.[1]

While the community has developed a relaxed attitude to the convict past many people were surprised to read Alexander's estimate that 75 per cent of Tasmanians have at least one convict ancestor.

Convicts made up a high proportion of the colonial population throughout the early colonial period. They represented 54 per cent of the population in 1820 and 29 per cent 30 years later. Many of those who were free in 1853 were emancipists or were children who had at least one convict parent. The most obvious impact of the convict system was in the removal of people from Britain to Van Diemen's Land, few of whom would have otherwise made such a long, arduous journey. Between 1803 and 1853, 72 000 convicts arrived on the island. Men significantly outnumbered women who made up about 16 per cent of the total or 12 500 in all. Up until 1840 the overwhelming majority of convicts came from England with much smaller numbers arriving from Wales or Scotland. Irish convicts began to arrive in significant numbers after the end of transportation to New South Wales in 1840. In the years leading up to 1853 just over 10 000 Irish had arrived, although some of them had been convicted in various parts of mainland Britain. Large numbers of convicts left Tasmania – perhaps as many as half the total – upon regaining their freedom. The great majority crossed Bass Strait to the boom colony of Victoria. But despite the loss of population to the mainland, Tasmania depended almost completely on the regular arrival of the convict transports to augment its population. Between 1820 and 1851 convict arrivals outnumbered free immigrants by three to one. At the census of 1847 just over 50 per cent of the population were convicts or emancipists, 26 per cent were native born and a little under 20 per cent had arrived free.

The likely fate of the island without convicts can be seen by comparing it with the struggling Swan River colony. In the 20 years between 1832 and 1851, the Western Australian population grew from 1489 to a little fewer than 5000. In the comparable period the Tasmanian population increased from 24 000 to just under 70 000.[2]

Given the importance of the convict legacy, Tasmanians have followed with interest the long running debate about the nature of those who were transported. Answers to that question have varied widely over the 20th century. For a long time the view was that the convicts were more sinned against than sinning; they were victims of injustice, inequality and a brutal legal code that punished petty theft with banishment from homeland, friends and family. But in the 1950s and 1960s historians concluded that this picture was romanticised and unrealistic. The convicts came to be seen as members of a criminal underclass, many of whom had lived by theft in the slums of the large cities. The women, although usually convicted for theft, were frequently prostitutes who had 'been on the Town' long before they were transported. They were far from being the human material suited to founding new societies, pioneering the land and establishing stable home lives for first generations of native-born children.

The debate has swung again in recent years in the opposite direction: further detailed research suggests that the convicts were usually drawn from the urban and rural working classes of England and Ireland and were overwhelmingly convicted of petty theft in communities where thieving to get by was considered to be a normal way to behave. With an understanding of the most recent research on the subject, Alexander concluded that the convicts were ordinary members of the working class rather than serious criminals. The men were usually young, in their late teens and 20s, without dependents and therefore able to enter the workforce as soon as they arrived; the women were almost all of optimum child-bearing age. A considerable proportion could read and write and brought with them a wide range of skills of great benefit to the colony. They were in many respects valuable human cargo, who provided much of the labour that underpinned the island's rapid economic growth between 1820 and 1850.

While there was a good deal of uniformity in the convict diaspora there were always prisoners who stood out among the crowd of young working class Britons. There were foreigners who had been convicted in Britain, such as the Danish adventurer Jorgen

Jorgenson, seamen from many parts of the world picked up in English sea ports, freed slaves and their children left in poverty and transported bearing the sobriquet 'men and women of colour'. There were also the educated middle-class prisoners convicted of white collar crimes: the clerks who used their penmanship to forge documents, the printers and etchers who turned skilled hands to forgery and counterfeiting, ambitious bigamists and desperate seducers who procured illegal abortions. Many talented people arrived in the colony in this way – painters Thomas Bock, Knut Bull, W. B. Gould and Thomas Wainwright, writers and journalists Henry Savery, Robert Lathrop Murray and Andrew Bent. And then there were the political prisoners who ended up on the island throughout the convict era. There were the Irish rebels, such as Richard Dry senior, transported after the failed uprising of 1798, and those who followed after the also failed rebellion of 1848, men such as Smith O'Brien, John Mitchell and Thomas Meagher. In his study of political prisoners, *Protest and Punishment*, George Rude calculated that the island received 369 Irish rebels and several hundred more whose crimes such as arson or maiming of animals may have been politically motivated. One of the largest groups of exiles was made up of the 96 American and Canadian rebels who invaded Canada in 1837 and were dispatched by George Arthur to his old bailiwick of Van Diemen's Land. Then there were the rioters and rebels who reacted against the oppression and disruption of early industrial Britain, including machine breakers, rick burners and the so-called Tolpuddle Martyrs, transported for attempting to organise poverty stricken rural labourers. After the rural or 'Swing' riots of 1830 in southern England, 332 participants were sent to the island as were 91 Chartists who were transported there in the 1840s.[3] But as Rude pointed out his rebels, even when that term was generously interpreted, represented only about 2 per cent of all convicts sent to the Australian colonies between 1788 and 1868, when transportation ended in Western Australia.[4] The political exiles had little impact on island life, although a number of them wrote books about their experiences when they returned to Britain or the USA. Irish rebel Patrick O'Donaghoe edited a newspaper, the *Irish Exile and Freedom's Advocate*, in the early 1850s before escaping to Melbourne, and then to San Francisco. A number of them stayed in the colony, such as the Irish painter and early photographer William Dowling and the Welsh chartist Zephaniah Williams, who became a pioneer of the coal industry.

The human capital of brain, skill and brawn provided by transportation was only part of the story. Of equal importance to the rapid development of the fledgling colony was the large public investment that came from Britain with the convicts. In this way New South Wales and Van Diemen's Land were quite exceptional among white settler colonies. The most obvious element of the imperial contribution was the annual expenditure, which was reliable, predictable and did not depend, as did colonial exports, on seasons, trade conditions or fluctuating prices. Expenditure went up in depressed years when more convicts were dependent on the government, and down when returning prosperity increased the labour demands of the free settlers. During the 1830s government expenditure on the convict establishment averaged about £140 000 a year and increased to £240 000 in the next decade. In 1836 Governor Arthur estimated that each convict cost the imperial government over £18 to maintain, which was a little less than the £22 earned by the average labourer in a year. In some years imperial government expenditure ran at between 40 and 50 per cent of total value of island exports.[5] Much of this money went on maintaining those convicts not in private service – there were over 3000 of them in 1836 – and on purchases by the commissariat from the general community. The newspapers are full of notices seeking tenders for the supply of an extraordinary range of goods. Obviously, large amounts of grain, meat and vegetables were sought but so too were building materials, clothing and footwear, implements of all sorts, timber, sand and gravel and innumerable smaller articles such as pens and ink, paper, pencils, knives, forks, spoons, scissors, pins and needles. The commissariat paid fair market prices and did not default on its bills. It was good to do business with.

The government also used convict labour to carry out impressive infrastructure projects that would have been beyond the capacity of a small free colony. In 1836 just under 3000 convicts were working on public works, including 725 who laboured in irons. The sullen labour of the chain gangs may have been induced by fear and rigid discipline but it was ideal for large projects that could be carried out only with a mass of unskilled labourers supervised by army-trained engineers capable of effecting the surveying and construction of roads and bridges, and quarrying large quantities of stone for causeways and harbours. Convict labour built such important infrastructure as the main road from Hobart to Launceston, the New Wharf in Hobart and the causeway across the Derwent at Bridgewater, along with such key bridges as the ones over the Macquarie at Ross, the South Esk at Perth and the Coal at Richmond. Hobart's public buildings were on a scale that dwarfed anything that could be afforded in the early years in Adelaide or Perth.

Another distinctive feature of the two convict colonies was the unusually large bureaucracy they supported with many well-paid officials and army officers swelling the ranks of polite society and spending their reliable and regular incomes in the elegant shops and wine merchants, and in building or leasing substantial townhouses and maintaining an appropriate complement of servants in kitchens, gardens and stables. They could also afford to pay well for professional services from prospering lawyers and doctors and less well-paid tutors, portrait painters, dressmakers and tailors.

Private consumption notwithstanding the government was always omnipresent in the penal colonies. In the early years the governors exercised pervasive power, although they were answerable to distant imperial masters and subject to the rule of law. By the 1840s the governors had to deal with an often independent Legislative Council and were harassed by a free press but even so the reach of the state went very much father than that of the limited governments known in Britain at the time. Given that there had been no recognition of Indigenous land title the governors controlled all the landed property known as Crown land, could and did grant it up until 1831 to whomever they favoured, and exercised the capacity to determine individual prospects, to make or break private fortunes. The government also controlled the supply of convict labour, favouring large over small farmers, granting or withdrawing assigned servants according to personal judgement and sometimes private prejudice. The use of the large landowners as supervisors of their assigned servants allowed the government to interfere in the relations between masters and servants in a way that would have been unthinkable in contemporary Britain. The power of the government over the convict population was obviously vast and in many ways unrestrained. Although there were rules aplenty and customary ways that grew up over time, innumerable officials had enough discretionary power to make decisions and take actions that could determine the fate of the convicts in their power.

Given the distinctive character of the penal colony governors felt they had a responsibility to oversee the morals of the population, encourage marriage, build churches and schools, and subsidise their incumbents. The system also created a demand for publically funded charitable institutions, including hospitals, asylums for the insane and the large orphan schools for boys and girls at New Town. A key part of Arthur's administrative innovations was the establishment of a large, centralised professional police force controlled through the stipendiary magistrates in each of the colony's main districts. This was at a time when in Britain the justice system was still in the hands of local landowners in all places apart from London and a few of the new industrial cities.

The large expenditure that came with the convicts was a central issue when the future of transportation was being debated. The more practical minded colonists were concerned with what economic consequences would follow if the anti-transportation crusade was successful. They looked across Bass Strait at the greater attractions of Port Phillip, which lured large numbers of islanders even before news of the goldrushes burst upon the world. They wondered where the island would find sufficient labour and how it would fare when the abundant imperial purse snapped shut. Such income was, the *Guardian* declared, 'this politically life giving and life preserving fund', the source that replenished colonial coffers 'by the munificent issues of the inexhaustible British treasury'.[6] Moderate opponents of the League pressed for a gradual cessation over seven or eight years, which would allow the continuation of essential infrastructure projects. William Race Allison insisted that cessation must not be allowed to come upon the island 'like a thunderclap', destroying confidence and 'occasioning a commercial panic'.[7] But the zealots were deaf to such pragmatic concerns. Even though they were encouraged by the colony's recovery from depression in the late 1840s, the economy was not a central concern. It came a poor second to the drive for a promised moral regeneration. At a public meeting in Launceston in 1851 John West thundered:

Our stand must not be on commercial considerations, but upon Christian duty. Shall we stand, calculating as to what, from a pecuniary point of view, shall be the result of our decision? As men and Christians, we should declare in the presence of God that we are opposed to transportation – and that no bribe shall induce us to seek its continuance.[8]

West's moral crusade was greatly enhanced by the changes that had taken place in the system during the 1840s. Assignment was wound down and replaced by the probation system, which saw arriving convicts assigned to work gangs that were eventually scattered across the colony. The concentration of prisoners in so many areas aroused fears of breakouts and bushranging and an often obsessive concern about homosexuality. Referred to in hushed voices and multiple euphemisms, a moral panic was skilfully cultivated by the anti-transportation movement. There was no one to defend what was known as the abominable crime of buggery and no real evidence as to its actual extent. The very vagueness of the claims added to the anxiety and was accompanied by a fearful frisson.

Reflecting on his unwilling sojourn in Van Diemen's Land, Irish exile John Mitchell declared that the colony was 'a bastard, transported, misshapen England'.[9]

Visitors did commonly remark on the constant reminders of home, but Mitchell was right. The colony was both like and unlike Britain, with distinctive characteristics that arose as a result of the legacy of the convict system. The social structure had many aspects that were reminiscent of contemporaneous Britain, and this did not happen by chance. During the 1820s imperial policy was designed to create a structured, hierarchical society modelled on rural Britain, necessarily lacking an ancient aristocracy but with a wealthy, educated gentry who could exercise local authority, supervise their convict servants and maintain the minor decencies of everyday life.

Governor Arthur, ever alert to any levelling tendencies or lack of due deference, was pleased to report to the Colonial Office in 1836 that 'What is remarkable in this community, is the circumstances, that society has already proceeded far towards that division into various classes, which is usually found only in old communities'.[10]

By the time that Arthur was writing, the owners of large land holdings were comfortably established with large stone or brick houses and attendant farm buildings, orchards and gardens, drives lined with young trees and fields bordered with recently planted hawthorn or gorse hedges. There were sufficient families concentrated in relatively small areas to allow for the development of busy social lives characterised by constant visiting and meetings at church or for hunting and politicking. In the two large towns merchants, lawyers and surgeons mixed easily with senior public servants and army officers resident in the colony until further postings took the latter to other parts of the empire. Alongside the urban and rural elites were the owners of smaller land holdings, tenant farmers, skilled tradesmen and small business men who in their turn were able to distinguish themselves from the large mass of unskilled and semi-skilled workers.

So, as Arthur observed, Van Diemen's Land society was divided into various classes in a way that was familiar to anyone arriving from Europe. There was also a fundamental difference that was a consequence of the convict system. In parallel with the common class divisions was a system of status differentiation based on being either bond or free that often ran along the same lines as the class structure but at other times didn't. So there were well to do emancipists who had made their money as shopkeepers, publicans, builders, farmers and even as professionals, but while their income and lifestyle suggested a secure place in the hierarchy of class, their convict past kept them in social inferiority where many of the institutions of polite society were closed to them. They also had to harden themselves to the social condescension, and sometimes the outright contempt, of free immigrants and native born with less to their name and little else to distinguish them. The emancipists were more likely to find their friends among those similarly situated, regardless of where their formal class position placed them.

Hobart and Launceston had large working class communities made up of unskilled workers, day labourers and servants. While united by their income, place and type of residence and lifestyle they were divided into three quite distinct groups – the native born, the free immigrants and the ex-convicts, including those who had regained their freedom, held a ticket of leave or a conditional pardon. Very little is known about the interaction of these three groups – whether they mixed socially, drank at the same pubs, went out together or intermarried. There is some evidence to suggest that the native youth had a strong sense of identity and self-confidence and may have kept to themselves. One of the striking differences between these groups was their sexual composition. Among the native born there was almost an equal number of men and women, boys and girls. Among the emancipists there were four times more men than women. We have no way of knowing if this disparity led to sexual competition and whether the native born established informal taboos about forming relationships with the ex-convicts. For their part the emancipists, who were united, whether they liked the fact or not, by their unique collective experience, may have remained in touch with people they had been on the same ship with and anyone else who understood the pain and shame of exile. The island was much too small to allow emancipists to hide their convict past and that, as much as more inviting opportunities, may have been why so many left the colony to seek a longed for anonymity in Victoria's swelling crowds. The sensitivity of the emancipists about being publically reminded of their status was illustrated by the case of William Edwards, who was brought before the magistrate in Hobart in November 1836. The *Colonial Times* reported that

On being charged by a constable with being a prisoner, said he did not like to be exposed as a public character, and knocked down the constable. He was reminded of the nature of his situation by six months sentence in a chain gang.[11]

It was an incident that illustrated the fact that the holders of tickets of leave and conditional pardons were still subject to a far harsher set of laws than were the native born or free immigrants and they were no doubt constantly aware of their advantaged circumstances such as those of the young free woman who, having been released by the court without charge, declared in triumph: 'I am not a convict! I am my own property, and can do what I like with my own.'[12]

Most convicts were servants of one sort or another for at least some time of their servitude and a large number of the free immigrants above a certain level of prosperity were their masters and mistresses. It is quite likely that some of them acquired authority over servants for the first time when they arrived in Van Diemen's Land. Whatever their previous experience free settlers expected not only obedience from their servants but also deference, two quite distinct forms of behaviour. Obedience could ensure that tasks were completed with reasonable care and in an acceptable time. Deference was the way in which subordination was secured and the pleasure of command indulged. The free settlers had in their minds an ideal of paternal authority and respectful servants. If anything they wanted to be respected even more than they wished to be obeyed. Many of them obviously assumed that convict servants should be even more deeply deferential than free ones, that they should be humbly ashamed of themselves. There is no doubt that some settlers were able to inspire respect from their assignees, who often remained with the families they had served after their emancipation. But overall the convict experience of transportation, exile and frequent brutality had broken those traditional bonds of deference and it became a matter of pride to avoid ancestral forms of respect unless they were enforced by threat of lash and incarceration. Governor Arthur appreciated the problem and demanded that all convicts and holders of tickets of leave should remove their caps when passing a military or civil officer on pain of punishment. They had to be compelled to 'show due respect... towards their superiors'.[13] The free settler were equally concerned about the need to induce deference. In a letter to the *Hobart Town Gazette* in 1825 a correspondent observed that

In a country whose population is composed of discordant and combustible materials, the principle of 'subordination' is of paramount importance; for it is the basis on which is grounded the security of property and of person.[14]

The more obviously the master or mistress sought respectful deference, the keener the convicts were to deny them those pleasures that arose from elevated authority. Settler George Hobler believed that it was necessary to have one of his convicts flogged every now and then as an example to the whole establishment, although he obviously felt some compassion for Jim who had received 50 lashes, writing in his diary that

Jim is severely cut and unable to raise his arms yet, I saw his back and had it greased to soften the sores – he seems to feel the punishment and I hope all will benefit by the example.[15]

Hobler was quite clear as to what he wanted from his servants, observing that

I will feed them well and make them more comfortable than honest labourers at home, and in return I exact a fair proportion of labour, but above all things subordination and civility.[16]

The masters who had come from humble backgrounds with no experience of managing servants may have had the greatest trouble trying to extract deference and respect from the convicts. A good example was G. A. Robinson, a self-educated Cockney who, try as he might, could not hide his lowly social origins or his accent. His journals are full of his frequent failed attempts to be treated as an equal by the local gentry and as a legitimate authority figure by the convicts assigned to his Friendly Mission to the Aborigines and bristles with references to convicts who were 'impertinent', 'very impertinent', 'very rude', 'insubordinate', 'unruly and disrespectful'.[17]

There was a drawn out and repetitive clash of wills played out again and again in settler households across the colony. The most common offences that brought assigned servants before the magistrates alongside being absent without leave were those variously described as insolence, insubordination and drunkenness, often associated with what the more polite settlers thought was outrageous and insulting language. The more outspoken women were able to horrify their masters and mistresses with torrents of abuse the like of which they had never heard before. Hobler noted in his diary in 1829 that his servant Betsy had arrived back from Launceston drunk. She became 'quite outrageous in her language and deportment'. Hobler confessed that he had never heard a man, 'even in this land of blackguards use such beastly language as this young woman did'. In Hobart the young Mary Morton Allport kept a journal for six months in 1832 and 1833 that detailed her travails with four women servants, all of whom were sent back to the Female Factory for being drunk and absent without leave.[18]

But like many settlers Hobler found that judicious indulgence was more productive than flogging and less disruptive than giving up troublesome servants to prison or chain gang. During the harvest of 1827 he received two good reapers, Tate and Smith, from a nearby chain gang. But he found they were 'not disposed to work' without extra pay, which was quite illegal. He offered them 7 shillings an acre after which the harvest proceeded smoothly; when it was finished he provided his workers with 'a haunch of mutton and baked pudding washed down with abundance of strong whisky grog'. As he noted in his diary, 'all got jolly drunk and laid low'.[19] Boyes scornfully dismissed Governor Arthur's claim that assigned servants didn't receive any wages. With a sharp eye he depicted the realities of life in the colony, where a servant who was 'a nice calculator' could do quite well. The great majority of servants derived 'advantage from their situation over and above their food and clothing'. Many were paid in cash, others received tobacco, had their own gardens or were remunerated in one way or another by doing jobs for other neighbouring settlers.[20]

As well as artists, filmmakers, writers and academics, the way convicts experienced the system has interested many curious members of the general public over the years. The existence of such a massive archive of well-kept records has facilitated research and enlivened the task. But the experience of 70 000 individuals over half a century is hard to simplify. So many things changed over that time. The colony went from being the site of two struggling camps of tents and mud huts to a place with substantial towns and a prosperous rural hinterland. Convicts arriving in 1803 had a very different experience to those disembarking 50 years later. Britain itself underwent even greater change as a result of the dramatic impact of the industrial revolution and rapid urbanisation and the emergence of new ideas about society, about the citizen and the linked question of crime and punishment. But convicts did share the central experience of transportation, regardless of their crime, the location of their trial or the resulting sentence. And while historians have established that the convicts were unremarkable members of the British working class they sometimes miss the point that conviction and transportation to the far end of the earth was in itself an experience that changed men and women forever. While millions of Europeans who migrated to the New World during the 19th century shared the experience of long arduous sea voyages in small crowded sailing ships and separation from family, friends and neighbours, the convicts were under duress and had completely lost their freedom. What above all distinguished them from their free-born contemporaries was the utterly different impact of the state on their lives. In Britain the small, almost minimal, state had little direct impress on ordinary people. Many of them must have passed their lives without coming into contact with the military, the customs officers or the managers of the growing number of work houses. Contrast that with the offender: taken before the courts, sentenced, incarcerated for a long period in a prison or hulk, then shipped around the world to a penal colony where every aspect of their life would be recorded until they eventually received a full pardon and even then, often remained under police surveillance. For the convict the small British state had indeed become the leviathan. But the leviathan could and did act paternalistically. The average convict had a better diet than many poorer Britons and almost all of the European peasantry; they were also adequately clothed and had ready access to medical attention although that was often a dubious advantage. Summing up the results of recent research Alexander observed that analysis of the convict records showed that convicts had a considerably lower death rate than other comparable groups, such as soldiers living in barracks. It was, she wrote, 'actually healthier to be a convict than a soldier or indeed a working class British citizen'.[21]

Most convicts worked in the community either as servants assigned to private employees, or for government departments. When they were granted a ticket of leave or conditional pardon they could work independently of the government. Even the minority of convicts who served time in chain gangs or in penal settlements such as Macquarie Harbour or Port Arthur, had often worked in the community before their carceral sentence or after it was served. Many prisoners who were often in trouble went backwards and forwards between assignment and incarceration numerous times. This was particularly true of women convicts who were in and out of the so-called female factories in Hobart and Launceston many times over. The fact that there were convicts everywhere in the colony was one of the first features noted by visitors and featured in the books they wrote about their experiences at the antipodes. There was a certain frisson about being served by or waited on by convicted felons. It was also both the strength and the weakness of the system. Critics in Britain and the colonies pointed to the unpredictability of outcomes. Convicts with skills in demand in the colony were likely to fare better than the unskilled and the illiterate, regardless of the nature of their original offence. Luck also played a large part in the convict's experience. Masters and mistresses, who varied from the benign to the brutal, could make all the difference. For the convict a careless tongue, a hot temper or a rebellious nature could pave the way towards the harshest of experiences, to flogging, even to the gallows. Henry Tingley, serving his sentence on an east coast farm, explained the situation in a letter home to his family:

All a man has got to mind is to keep a still tongue in his head, and do his master's duty, and then he is looked upon as if he were at home; but he don't he may as well be hung at once, for they would take you to the magistrates and get 100 lashes, and then get sent to a place called Port Arthur to work in chains for two or three years, and then he is disliked by everyone.[22]

About 10 per cent of convicts committed serious offences in the colony and spent time in the penal settlements. At the other end of the scale 10 per cent had an unblemished record in the colony, while a further 25 per cent were admonished only once or twice. About half of the convicts were punished for a wide variety of offences, often minor ones such as being drunk, absconding, being caught in pubs or brothels, petty theft or using insulting or disrespectful language. The more serious offences were punished by short periods on the chain gangs, by flogging or by a session in the stocks or on the treadmill. Women were sentenced to solitary confinement on bread and water, to heavy labour at the washtubs in the female factories or they had their hair cut off.

The fact that the number of convicts who were heavily punished was matched by an equal cohort who escaped without any further convictions should not be allowed to disguise the fact that violence was central to the system and that its purpose was to instil a sense of communal terror. The minority of heavily punished convicts were not just unfortunate victims who fell by the wayside; they were necessary for the whole system, which needed backs to bloody, bodies to weigh down with chains and necks to snap on the gallows. The fact that flogging and hanging were public spectacles was clear evidence of the manifest need to infuse the whole penal population with hortatory horror. When the imperial government sent J. T. Bigge in 1819 to report on the colonies he was instructed to 'constantly bear in mind that transportation . . . is intended as a severe punishment applied to various crimes, and as such must be rendered an object of real terror to all classes of the community'.

The need to deter crime in Britain made it essential that transportation should be 'permanently formidable'.[23] Unless it was an object of fear in Britain itself, sufficient to deter crime, the great expenditure was wasted. The governors of Van Diemen's Land and New South Wales were frequently reminded in dispatches from London of the central purpose of transportation even while the economic importance of the colonies grew.

The ultimate power of the law was to execute prisoners, to illustrate in the most horrifying way that the state had command over life itself. In a letter to Arthur, his superior officer, Governor Darling of New South Wales, discussed the problem of bushranging and explained that he had on the day of writing collectively hung such a party. With implicit advice to Arthur he explained he had the troops out, 'assembled the convicts and have done everything to render the Ceremony this morning as awful and impressive as possible'.[24] Arthur scarcely needed guidance and used the gallows far more extensively than his counterparts in the larger colony. Through 1826 and 1827, during a prolonged festival of judicial killing, 103 prisoners were executed. In September 1826, 23 men died on the gallows in just five days. In his 12 years in the colony Arthur oversaw 260 executions. The peak in the mid 1820s was the ruthless response to the outbreak of bushranging and sheep stealing that confronted Arthur soon after his arrival at Government House in Hobart. Executions stood at the apex of the whole system of punishment and were an essential part of it. Throughout the convict era they were conducted in public and were watched by large crowds. No one in the colony could have been unaware of these demonstrations of the brutal power wielded by the state. But the public spectacles were complex events. Everyone present waited to see how the victims faced death and how they died. Characteristically, even the toughest prisoners accepted the promise of forgiveness and salvation in exchange for fervent prayer, public penitence and confession. Occasionally, there were prisoners who refused to respond to the importuning clergymen but the sight of the toughest convicts breaking down, overcome by paroxysms of weeping, was the dramatic climax sought by church and state.[25]

Flogging was an abiding feature of the system. The whips were unpacked during the first weeks of the colony's history. Knopwood, the Anglican clergyman, was appointed as one of the first magistrates. He recorded in his diary many of the floggings he ordered, sometimes as many as 200 and 300, along with accounts of his hunting and fishing expeditions and his many convivial dinners. Such floggings were extremely harsh punishments perpetrated with the infamous cat o' nine tails – a lash made up of nine long multi-knotted cords. Properly paced the torture could continue for an hour or more and was usually conducted as a public spectacle. The young settler George Russell recalled that when he was living near Bothwell he 'had a wish to see a man flogged', so he went to the local gaol one morning where a convict was to receive 25 lashes, and later explained how the victim

was tied up to a triangle, which consisted of three poles stuck into the ground and fastened at the top. The man's legs and arms were tied to two of the poles so that he could not move; his back was laid bare down to the waist; and the flagellator stood ready with his cat-o'-nine tails... The punishment seemed to be very severe. Each stroke changed the colour of the man's back, and when he had received the twenty five lashes his back was almost black, or like the colour of raw meat; but the skin was not broken.

He never moved a muscle, but kept chewing a piece of tobacco or something else which he had in his mouth.[26]

Every flogging was a dramatic exhibition of the fierce force of the law designed to humiliate and humble the victim. But as in the flogging Russell witnessed, the convicts often displayed their strength of will by not giving the authorities the pleasure of hearing the sounds of submission or pleas for mercy. The use of the lash diminished during the history of transportation. It was used less frequently and the number of strokes administered declined. All floggings were recorded by the meticulous convict administration. In 1836 there were over 14 000 male convicts in the colony outside the penal settlements. Of these, 9 per cent were flogged; the average number of lashes was 30. At Port Arthur there were over 900 prisoners, 13 per cent of whom were whipped; the average number of strokes was 42. At the Port Puer boys' prison there were 249 inmates. Over 40 per cent of them were flogged with the average punishment of 15 strokes.[27]

So the flogging continued although by the 1830s many experienced colonists were doubting its efficacy. One told the Quaker travellers G. Backhouse and W. Walker that while he had formerly thought flogging necessary he was now convinced that it was 'an ineffectual punishment, universally degrading in its consequences'.[28] Even the stern George Arthur believed that flogging should be 'resorted to as seldom as possible'.[29] He was aware that excessive violence provoked a dangerous spirit of rebellion. 'Coercive measure,' he wrote in a dispatch to the Colonial Office, 'must be bounded by humanity; if they are not, the criminals are driven into a state of mind bordering on desperation.'[30] In a private letter to T. F. Buxton, leader of the anti-slavery crusade in the House of Commons, Arthur explained his attitude to physical coercion, observing that

If we could supply men with an inward regulator, it would be ten times more effectual in every case in which it could be set up in the heart than all the fear and alarm than ever can be expected from without.[31]

What Arthur wanted to achieve was to provide the convicts with a clear set of options with the promise of upward advance by good behaviour to the receipt of a ticket of leave, a conditional and finally a full pardon. For those who rebelled or resisted, the way downward was equally well marked out, from flogging, to extension of sentence, to chain gang, and then to a penal settlement. He explained that there was

maintained throughout the colony a continual circulation of convicts, a distribution of each in his proper place; in short a natural and unceasing process of classification, the mainspring or moving power is not the authority of the Government, but the silent yet most efficient principle of self interest.[32]

What Arthur wanted was a system that was predictable in its outcome. With good policing, constant surveillance and meticulous record keeping the convicts were encouraged to feel that the system was all-seeing and invincible. He explained that he did not wish to impose the punishment of transportation by means of 'harshness and severity, but by vigilance in the prevention of crime, by certainty of detection when it is committed and by the regular exaction of labour'.[33] What Arthur wanted above all else was that the convicts repent, have a change of heart and realise the error of their ways. He wanted abnegation. There is no doubt that some did as he wished but more often the prisoners wanted to conform sufficiently to the demands of the system to escape its penetrating, censorious eye as soon as they could. Backhouse and Walker spent a lot of time investigating the system and they concluded that 'The generality of prisoners look upon themselves as the aggrieved parties which is much to be regretted! When they take an opposite view it is to be taken as a token of reformation.'[34]

Arthur had an implicit political agenda. He wanted the convicts to become obedient and above all deferential servants on the large estates. Writing of the life of the assigned servant he explained that 'idleness or insolence of expression or even of looks, anything betraying the insurgent spirit' subjected him to the 'chain gang or the triangle or to hard labour on the roads'.[35] The state was to underwrite a degree of industrial discipline beyond the reach of employers in contemporary Britain. Convicts were to be kept 'in undeviating respect to the authorities'.[36] He wanted to secure permanently the hierarchical nature of island society, which was still a very recent and in that sense an insecure creation. His strong objection to any upward social mobility among the prisoners, of the kind that had been encouraged by Governor Macquarie in New South Wales, was clearly due to his political beliefs as much as to what he considered were the requirements of penal discipline. Beyond the concern with the shape and structure of island society was the anxiety about the democratic forces unleashed by the French and American revolutions that were troubling contemporary Britain. Arthur clearly hoped that insurgent beliefs could be left behind in Europe or lost in the process of exile and punishment.

But the insurgent spirit lived on. Many men and women learnt how to hide their feelings, hold their tongues and play the roles expected of them. An outburst of anger or, more commonly, a brief drinking binge often undid the pretence, leading to a release of pent up frustration, boredom or impacted impatience with the endless condescension of self-righteous masters and mistresses. The authorities had great difficulty controlling the rebellious women who were collected together in the female factories and who often intimidated prison officials and other inmates. There were comparable groups of men who retreated into remote parts of the island in an endeavour to live beyond the reach of the magistrates. While leading one of the roving parties pursuing the Aborigines, prominent settler Gilbert Robertson came across a number of men living in a remote stockman's hut. They characterised themselves as 'staunch men' who would have nothing to do with the government and showed complete contempt for the convict constables in Robertson's party.[37] Such men undoubtedly provided support and information for the bushrangers who most clearly manifested the 'insurgent spirit' and who for that reason were admired by many prisoners and correspondingly feared by the authorities.

Bushranging began in the earliest days of both pioneer settlements as prisoners were encouraged to venture out into the hinterland to hunt the kangaroo and emu needed to keep the struggling settlements from starvation. As knowledge of the bush grew it became easier to bolt into the interior. The more serious problem of bushranging gangs developed during the governorships of Thomas Davey (1810–17), William Sorell (1817–23) and George Arthur (1824–36). The prominent historian of the convict system, H. Maxwell-Stuart, estimated that 328 individuals spent time illegally at large in the bush between 1807 and 1846. Many of them are unknown but a few, men such as Mike Howe, Matthew Brady and Martin Cash, were infamous at the time and are also recalled in the written history and oral tradition of Tasmania. Bushranging was easy and difficult in Van Diemen's Land. It was often easy to escape into surrounding hills and be out of sight in a matter of minutes. The country provided ready concealment and innumerable high vantage points afforded easy surveillance over the settlements in the nearby valleys. In more rugged country soldiers and police had to abandon their horses and pursue their quarry on foot. Bushrangers and the often sympathetic frontier shepherds, stockmen and splitters knew the country better than most members of pursuing parties. The country itself provided kangaroo and emu and, increasingly, stray sheep and cattle, as well as a ready supply of water. But the island was small and very difficult to escape from and the more remote areas were the least hospitable to the Europeans. So the gangs needed to stay within striking distance of the settled farm land to access fresh supplies of gunpowder, shot, flour, sugar, tea, tobacco and replacement clothing, especially footwear. Many of those who bolted stayed out for a short time before being recaptured or surrendering to the authorities but the larger gangs were often at large for a number of years committing many robberies and raids on settlers' households. Most were caught in the end. Maxwell-Stuart estimated that of his 328 bushrangers, 120 were executed, 21 were shot down in the bush and 117 were returned to the penal colonies. A few were pardoned for betraying their comrades and 35 either managed to escape from the island or possibly died out in the bush.[38] Most of the bushrangers were on the run from the penal settlements or the chain gangs, where they had been subjected to the most brutal regimes of endless toil. There was little motivation for them to return to the settlements to seek clemency let alone sympathy for their circumstances because absconding itself was a capital offence.

Many bushrangers had more in mind than plunder. They, too, had a political agenda. They were often motivated by a strong sense of injustice, particularly about their treatment in gangs and on settlements, and the impossibility of receiving a fair hearing about justifiable grievances. When they raided the homes of the gentry they performed carefully thought out rituals of insurrection, called on assigned servants to judge their masters, and forced the masters to don servant's clothes and serve the bushrangers at the table and in every possible way to humiliate the often cringing master and mistress. It was a direct challenge to the overriding emphasis in the colony of deference and subordination. Many masters were shocked by their own servants who generally avoided the two extremes of siding overtly with the bushrangers or taking up arms to defend the property. A poem written in blood found in one captured bushranger's pocket expressed what were no doubt common sentiments:

> We are the boys that fears no dangers,
> And what you term us is bush-rangers
> If it is our lives you do demand,
> True to our guns then we must stand.
> We are all young and in our prime,
> To meet our hardships we incline
> And if our blood you mean to shed,
> Life for life before we yield.
> Tis in the bush we are forced to go –
> You settlers prove our overthrow:
> To rob and plunder is against our will,
> But we must have a living still.
> Now to this country we are come,
> Banished from our native home,
> And if we can't go back no more,
> We will rob the rich and feed the poor.[39]

The young man 'in his prime' was executed a few days after this poem was published.

When bushranging was at its height it presented a serious threat to colonial progress. Ever-present was the rarely expressed fear of a general convict uprising or a union of the larger gangs, with prisoners scattered across the country in chain gangs and penal settlements. It was impossible for members of the government or the prominent settlers not to be aware of how much sympathy there was for the bushrangers. Even where there was no overt support there was a keen understanding that convicts who sided with the gaolers or the masters were unpopular and often in danger of ostracism, or worse. The general fear and insecurity presented the possibility that settlers would abandon their farms at a time when the colony had come to depend almost totally on its own successful harvests. Governor Arthur discussed the problem in his correspondence with Governor Darling. In September 1825 Arthur reported that the 'boldness of these determined offenders' was so great that settlers were abandoning their farms and resorting to the town. He was sending more soldiers into the interior 'to dissipate the panic'.[40] In the first days of 1826 he declared that bushranging 'must be put down, or colonisation cannot proceed'. Darling shared Arthur's concern, writing that 'every exertion' should be made to prevent settlers from abandoning their farms. If they did, 'the country will be ruined'.[41] After venturing into the interior himself he wrote to Lord Bathurst in London outlining his difficulties:

It is impossible to convey to your Lordship a just idea of this most discouraging warfare. In addition to the natural facilities of a mountainous Country to an armed Banditti, there is such a combination and communication kept up between the bushrangers and the Stock-keepers throughout the Colony, that, whilst the miscreants acquire the most accurate information of all the measures that are resorted to for their apprehension, their pursuers are misled and imposed upon by every device that can be practised.[42]

But the networks of supporters, informants and fences that were so important to the bushrangers and so frustrating to the governor were ultimately the undoing of the gangs. The offer of free pardons, return to Britain and absolute confidentiality tempted enough informers to provide the crucial information that enabled the military and police to track down the bushrangers and shoot them there, in the bush, or to bring them in heavily chained to be pinioned until they, too, faced death on the gallows in Hobart or Launceston.

While many old hands may have admired the bushrangers they did not join them. Everyone eventually passed through the system and regained their freedom, although just over 4500 men and women died while they were still under sentence, mainly from disease or accidents. There were hundreds of often elderly emancipists who, while legally free, remained and died in institutions for paupers, invalids and the insane.[43] They were the most obvious victims of the system, the ones who never escaped it and in many cases probably didn't want to leave the threadbare, grudging security of the institutions to try to make their way in a world that had very little time for them.

Many of the tens of thousands of emancipists suffered physically while under sentence. Those who had been flogged were often scarred for life and deeply embarrassed by their disfigurement, although there were many stories that were once told in Hobart

Image 7.1:   Invalide Depot, Launceston.
(*Source:* Archives Office of Tasmania.)

of old lags who would show their scars for a sixpence. But what of all those others who had rarely been in trouble? Were there hidden injuries, which went largely unnoticed, because they were psychological rather than physical and as a result were never recorded in the great registers that provide historians with so much of their evidence?

It has been established beyond reasonable doubt that the convicts came from the ranks of the poor working class in England, Wales and Ireland, but too much can be made of their normality. From the moment of their sentence to transportation until the moment they received their absolute pardon their life became radically atypical, creating a vast gulf that separated them from their erstwhile peers. They were uprooted from their familiar surroundings, separated from family and friends, in most cases forever, kept closely confined with an ever-pressing crowd of utter strangers for months in hulks and then in the stinking, pitching prison of the transports. One can only guess at the mental and emotional impact of these no doubt unforgettable experiences. The 19th century historian James Bonwick recorded the comments of an old hand who declared that when the judge passed sentence of transportation 'he opens up an ulcer in the heart that neither time nor penitence can wholly heal'. Although the assignment system gave the appearance of providing a reasonably normal environment in which to serve one's sentence, it is hard to overestimate the tension that must have been created by the ever-present fear of the lash and the chain gang, the constant anxiety about keeping out of trouble. These tensions may have been more oppressive among those who did manage to escape serious punishment. The timid may have been more traumatised in this way than the bold and rebellious. William Ashton, a chartist from Yorkshire, was rarely in trouble and became a police constable, but he recalled that

Oft have I wept in the darkness of the night, and deplored the inauspicious moment that my poor mother gave me existence... Months and months passed away, and I was the same miserable object, liable for the smallest offence to have my back lacerated by the dreadful lash.[44]

Getting drunk and abusing the master or mistress, even a flogging, may have acted as a cathartic experience not shared by those who behaved well. The constant drunkenness of many servants, despite the certainty of consequent punishment, must have had some relationship to a desperate need to relieve pent-up anxiety. It is important to remember that the system was designed to produce a sense of terror and to cower convicts into subordination. Its administrators were quite open about that. One can only wonder about the psychological damage this perpetrated on a massive and collective scale among those who had no physical scars to remind them of their time as convicted felons or the inhumanity of the system.

Did the system leave behind a legacy of behaviour and belief in Tasmania and New South Wales that helped shape the Australian identity? It is an intriguing question that has interested many people over the years. The sheer magnitude of the system would suggest that shadows must have been cast onward into the post-convict era and while it is true that the way individuals experienced the system varied widely there was an inescapable commonality of experience.

In Tasmania at least it was hard to ever escape the fate of being an old hand. Evidence strongly suggests that the collective and utterly distinctive experience of transportation did shape views about society and politics. The deference that was almost instinctive in English society and which men such as George Arthur sought to impress on the new one, was an early casualty of the system. It was clearly dependent on traditions that did not ship well and on mutual respect and mild paternalism. In Van Diemen's Land deference was enforced with the lash and chain – or fear of them – but what was achieved was grudging obedience or deliberate, self-conscious performance of the necessary rituals, often with barely disguised mockery. Once out of the system there could be no return to manners imposed by force. To dispense with deference was a kind of freedom, a declaration of personal independence. Irreverence became a popular pastime, one embraced early by Tasmanian children. Governor Denison lamented the fact that the children of the small settlers were 'self-willed, presumptuous, and unwilling to submit to any control'.[45] The emancipists also reacted to the hierarchy of status that was central to the system and manifestly more rigid in Van Diemen's Land than in New South Wales. No matter what one did the only ways to escape the status of ex-convict was by flight or dissimulation. Consequently, status itself was called into question while leaving the class structure based on wealth and income in place because anyone, emancipists included, could aspire to accumulation. So wealth was admired while status was eschewed as was any associated assumption of superiority. This was yet another way in which the convict colonies diverged from British society. The same was true of attitudes to the state. To an extraordinary degree the convicts had suffered from its brutal power, and while they were only too well aware of its might they rarely admired its majesty. There is no doubt that many convicts emerged from the system with a deep hatred of authority, but because they had firsthand experience of the power of the state very few imagined it could be overthrown, although it could be avoided whenever possible and treated with disdain. An official 1860 report into the reasons for the poor attendance at government schools declared that emancipist parents had 'an antipathy to the schools because the government supported them. This almost instinctive aversion is very powerful with the considerable section of the population who have been prisoners.'[46] Paradoxically though, many emancipists believed that governments that had handled them with such overwhelming authority had a life-long duty of care to provide for them when they were old or impoverished or sick.

8

Post-penal Depression, 1856–70

In the colony's short history 2 December 1856 was a big day. It was the moment when the recently arrived Governor Henry Fox-Young opened the new parliament. The 30 recently elected members of the House of Assembly and the 15 legislative councillors took their seats in the council chamber watched by what the *Launceston Examiner* called 'between 60 and 70 of our most influential colonists' as well as a 'large number of ladies...The scene,' the paper declared, 'was brilliant and worthy of the occasion.'[1] Despite its distinctive history as a penal colony the island had travelled in the wake of the mainland colonies – New South Wales, Victoria and South Australia – and accepted responsibility from the imperial government for its own internal affairs. It was a decisive constitutional change, and one of global significance. From the first day of 1856 the tainted words 'Van Diemen's Land' were officially replaced by the new name, Tasmania, a change sanctioned by the queen in an Order in Council issued on 21 July 1855. The governor, as the queen's representative, with words appropriate for the first day of the Tasmanian parliament, declared:

At the first meeting of an entirely elected Parliament I perform a very gratifying duty. I congratulate you, and through you the Colonists at large that Tasmanian freedom has passed from a name into a reality, since it is now guaranteed, not by positive laws merely, but by the enduring bulwark of free popular institutions.[2]

Tasmanian politicians had faced the same challenges as their mainland counterparts in adapting British parliamentary institutions to the quite different conditions of the New World. All the colonies decided to establish bicameral – two chamber – parliaments without a hereditary aristocracy, members of which occupied the crowded benches of the House of Lords. The conventional view at the time was that the lower house would represent the people at large and be elected on a wide franchise while the upper houses would speak for wealth and property or what were called the fixed interests of the community. While the popular house would seek change and reform, the upper house would council caution and stability. The report of the Tasmanian committee tasked with drawing up the Constitution assumed that the instincts of the lower house would be 'movement–progress–innovation; generally it is hoped of a useful character'. The instincts of the more conservative body would be 'caution–deliberation–resistance to change if not fairly and fully proved to be beneficial'.[3]

Yet for all the rhetoric about balancing change and stability the large landowners and their urban allies created a more conservative political system than was being established in the mainland colonies. A property qualification for voters in the House of Assembly enfranchised less than half the adult male population and embraced the more successful skilled workers and small business men. Few members of the rural workforce had the vote. The franchise was not significantly widened until the 1880s and full manhood suffrage was delayed until the end of the century. Many wealthy property owners had multiple votes. Hobart and Launceston were seriously under-represented to the advantage of the rural districts. But it was the Legislative Council that represented the most powerful bulwark against reform. Elected on a restrictive property franchise it was created to have a kind of permanent existence. Whereas the Assembly was dissolved at each election the Council was protected from changing political moods by never facing a general election. Rather, there was to be a series of by-elections at which one-third of the members were up for election, leaving two-thirds of the chamber always in place. There was no provision for a double dissolution even when the two houses were in dispute. Whereas any adult male could seek election to the lower house, councillors had to be 30 years of age.

There is no doubt that the leading politicians were afraid of democracy and anxious about the potential power of the largely emancipist working class, especially in Hobart where the emergence of the Protection Association had illustrated a capacity for effective political mobilisation. John West's disdain for the politically active emancipists was probably representative of respectable opinion. They were, he declaimed, a 'caste embittered by ignorance and revenge'.[4] The rise of an emancipist party presented a dilemma to the demagogic leaders of the Anti-Transportation Movement who prided themselves on their capacity to whip up popular opposition to the governors and the imperial officials. T. G. Gregson was the most aggressive and vociferous opponent of all the governors over a 20 year period, but in 1851 he confided in Boyes, telling him that if sworn to an opinion upon the subject he would assert his belief that the colony was not now in a state to receive free institutions. 'The convict population,' he declared, 'have now too great an influence.'[5] The man who had mastered the art of haranguing large crowds told his colleagues in the Legislative Council that he hoped and trusted 'never to hear of any meeting being called in Hobart Town, where you can hire a ruffian for half a crown or five shillings to insult any man'.[6] The leading conservative politicians also looked fearfully across Bass Strait at the other colonies, where manhood suffrage had been adopted, and where what they considered vulgar, plebeian democracy appeared ascendant. The electors of rural Morven believed that it was only a limited franchise that would save the colony from the fate of the mainland colonies where

Democracy in all its unblushing audacity is riding roughshod over the best, nay vital interests of those communities, as too sadly indicated by its inevitable results, the systematic exclusion from their legislatures of men of education, intelligence and established character . . . [and] the admission thereto of illiterate needy and unprincipled adventurers.[7]

Agreeing with his anxious constituents the local member and leading conservative politician F. M. Innes said he hoped that Tasmania would remain a land of 'settled government, of law and order, in which the natural subordinations of society are maintained'.[8]

The ambivalence that Tasmania's leading politicians felt towards the new parliamentary institutions can be well illustrated in the case of the introduction of the secret ballot. In company with the other colonies Tasmania adopted the measure prior to the first elections in September 1856. It has always been regarded as a major democratic reform pioneered in Australia and, as a result, known widely as the Australian ballot. It achieved two major objectives. Bribery had been widespread during the elections of 1851 and many candidates spent considerable sums on treating potential voters. The secrecy of the new polling booths greatly reduced opportunities for outright bribery and prevented powerful men from intimidating voters, particularly in the small rural electorates. The use of printed voting slips was not introduced to prevent the illiterate from voting as they were permitted to be accompanied by a literate companion. There were other advantages that arose from the fact that voting extended over a whole day and that each electorate went to the polls on a different day. This, combined with the contemporaneous abolition of public nominations, greatly reduced the likelihood of crowds gathering to express their passion and partisanship. Even though this took much of the fun and festivity out of elections, the political leaders were always anxious to avoid situations that allowed large roistering, boisterous crowds to congregate. The nomination process had not been 'adapted to good order'; it led, so the attorney-general believed, to 'a disturbance of the peace and all kinds of scurrility'.[9] A writer in the *Mercury* pointed out that in the colony,

so far from manifesting any democratic tendencies, we have by one act taken a vast stride in the opposite direction – we have abolished public nominations. By this the Colony has deprived all non-electors of their long enjoyed privilege of expressing their approbation or disapprobation of candidates for legislative honours, thus excluding them from all participation in elections.[10]

If the conservative politicians wanted to restrain the political passions of the electorate they appear to have been successful. In the four elections for the House of Assembly between 1856 and 1866 the average turnout of registered voters was around 40 per cent. Numerous seats were uncontested, particularly in the countryside. Eight members were returned unopposed to the House in 1856 and

1861. Fifteen members, or half the House, were unchallenged in 1862 as they were 14 four years later. As did their counterparts in the other colonies the Tasmanians had difficulty learning how to manage the political system, which was based on the assumption that two rival parties would compete for office and be able to provide reasonably effective governments and oppositions. Without them stable government became dependent on the capacity of leading figures to hold together skittish coalitions long enough to legislate and do so with a mixture of charm, coercion and the promise of the many rewards of office. Tasmania began its history of responsible government with a period of instability. There were four governments in the first seven months. This unsettled period was followed by an era of greater stability but there were 11 different administrations in office between 1856 and 1875. The central problem for this whole period was the difficulty of managing the budgets with revenues falling and costs rising. Yet it was never just a fiscal matter. Where the tax burden should fall was a question of wide political significance. The largest source of revenue was the duties levied on imports, especially on items of everyday use such as tea and sugar. While easy to collect and predictable in return they weighed most heavily on the poor. Like many indirect taxes they took a much higher proportion of income from the indigent than from the rich. To raise them was to face the public anger of the working class in both cities, as well as accompanying protest meetings, marches and petitions. But to levee taxes on land or income or luxury goods required acts of self-denial from the politicians themselves that were not forthcoming.

The leading politicians who fought the governors in the 1830s and 1840s and who shaped the new Constitution in the early 1850s were successful in retaining power in their own hands. As the visiting British politician and traveller Sir Charles Dilke observed in 1869, Tasmania was 'cast in more aristocratic shape' than the other Australian colonies.[11] But their victory was pyrrhic. It eventually brought little joy or sense of achievement, which must have been particularly sobering for the leading members of the anti-transportation crusade who had insisted that moral regeneration must trump commercial considerations. Having ostentatiously celebrated the end of transportation they found that the portentous warnings of their enemies, such as Governor Denison and his allies among the settlers, were prophetic.

The economic consequences of the sudden cessation were just as they had predicted. Neither the colony's new name nor the fledgling parliament added anything to the ailing economy. The rapid withdrawal of imperial funds and the diversion of the flow of convict labour to Western Australia could not have come at a worse time. Tasmania experienced 20 years of chronic depression at a time when the other colonies were booming. During these years the island fell out of the cavalcade of colonial progress. In the lifetime of the political leaders of the 1860s Tasmania had been the second colony in seniority, population and economic performance. In the years when they were young pioneers there was serious speculation about the prospect of the island eventually rivalling New South Wales. Even the measured George Arthur marvelled at the speed of development in the 1830s and like almost everyone else assumed it would continue. But Victoria, in many respects Tasmania's own colony, had more people by 1851, South Australia by 1855 and Queensland by 1868. Tasmanians made up about 16 per cent of Australia's population in 1851; 50 years later they were a mere 5 per cent. The sense of being bypassed and left behind took root in these years and has remained as a residue in island attitudes ever since.

Visitors who came to Tasmania in the depressed 1860s and early 1870s were sharply aware of the colony's economic plight. Perhaps the observation that hurt most was delivered by the celebrated English novelist Anthony Trollope, whose visit was greeted with great enthusiasm. He liked the place and declared that if he were to emigrate he would pitch his staff in Tasmania. But he referred to poor little Tasmania and found that the fixed opinion of the politicians he met was that the island was 'going gradually to the mischief'. His private thoughts were that he had never found himself among a people 'so prone to condemn themselves as these Tasmanians'. In the opening lines of his four chapters about the island he declared that it was hard to say of a new colony not yet 70 years old that it had seen 'the best of its days, and that it is falling into decay, that its short period of importance in the world is already gone', and that for the future it must exist on the 'relics which the past has left behind'.[12] English journalist John Martineau who was

in Tasmania a few years before Trollope left a graphic picture of
the Hobart during the depression:

The streets are almost empty. Nobody looks busy. Nobody is in a hurry.
Converse with anyone about the state of the Colony, and the word depression is one of the first you hear and it will come over again and again until
you are weary of it. Different people mean different things by it, and feel the
tendency from prosperity to adversity in different ways, but none dispute
the fact. Elderly ladies lament the old days when there was more society,
and a more abundant supply of soldier and sailor ball partners; merchants
and tradesmen the time when Hobart Town promised to be the emporium
if not the metropolis of Australia. It is seldom indeed that anyone can be
heard to speak cheerily of the present or hopefully of the future.[13]

There was indeed little to be cheerful about as the statistics dramatically illustrated. Tasmania's greatest problem was the loss of
people. The outflow began with the movement of settlers to Victoria in the late 1840s. The momentum increased dramatically with
the discovery of gold. The number of adult males fell from 21 000
in March 1851 to 13 000 at the end of 1853. Many disappointed
diggers returned but there was an overall loss to the colony that
could no longer be disguised by the large intakes of convicts. We
have no means of knowing exactly who left and who returned
but it is possible that the island lost many of its more enterprising and adventurous residents. The sluggish economy and resulting low wages meant that the colony was unable to compete with
the mainland colonies for a supply of free immigrants. From the
middle of the 19th century the tradition developed that saw the
community losing more people than it gained by immigration and
natural increase. Between 1856 and 1875 the growth rate was only
1.5 per cent; emigration exceeded immigration by 4500. By the
1870s women outnumbered men in all cohorts from 20 to 50. Tasmania's folk traditions are, therefore, more about departing than
arriving. For its size it has had a much more significant diaspora
than any other part of Australia.

The depressed colony saw a steep decline in living standards.
Wages fell significantly, far more dramatically than prices. Government expenditure dropped from £400 000 in 1856 to £225 000 ten
years later. Imperial expenditure on the prison population declined

from £280 000 in 1854 to £70 000 in 1864. Trade, too, fell dramatically away. Between 1856 and 1870 imports were almost halved from £1400 000 to £800 000. Exports declined in sympathy and fewer ships called at the once busy island ports. The old settled districts had reached a peak of productivity and the sheep population levelled out after 1850. The small settlers pioneering the forest lands were only beginning to have an impact on the economy in the last decades of the century. Whaling was in steep decline and the once flourishing ship building industry was long past its prime. From the early 1850s Tasmanians longed for a mining boom and there were many optimistic assessments about the prospects, but it was not until the late 1870s that the colony began to uncover the great wealth in its remote mountains and valleys. Given the depth of the depression it might be considered surprising that more people didn't take the easy option of flight across Bass Strait, but by the 1870s many families had been in the island for several generations and were no longer sojourners willing to walk away from what had become their homeland. For better or worse they had become Tasmanians and many of those who did go away dreamt of an eventual return. One Tasmanian farmer, writing to his nephew in South Australia, explained his predicament:

The Island cannot compete with the Mainland. Its soil is expensive to cultivate, & its natural grass inferior & kept back by a colder winter & backward spring. Without doubt the people on the soil are discouraged.

He reported the comments of a neighbour, who said: 'We have no chance against the people in the other colonies. Its all hard work here. I don't know why we stop here at all, unless it is because we love the old Island.'[14]

The end of transportation in 1853 and the royal approval of the new name did not mean that Tasmania was finished with the system. The successful propaganda of the opponents of convictism in Australia and Britain had convinced many people that the island was both site and source of moral contagion, a society deeply stained with vice and crime. It was a reputation that was very hard to live down and added a sense of shame to the contemporaneous feeling of economic disappointment. Once again it was much as the opponents of the anti-transportation crusade had predicted.

Governor Denison observed that the colonist 'had given to themselves a name ... which will stick to them for some time, though I
believe undeservedly'.[15]

The bitterness arising from the battle over transportation lived
on for years. Heated rhetoric once cast could not be withdrawn;
nor was it forgotten. J. D. Balfe, the powerful spokesman for the
emancipists, asked

How can any reflecting, impartial, or humane person join in that inhuman
outcry against unfortunate fellow creatures and which must act on the
sensibilities of a most important section of the community like an alarm bell,
ever and torturingly awakening in their souls the unpleasant reminiscences
of by-gone misfortune.[16]

We don't know if John West had second thoughts as he watched
Tasmania's travails from the far off comfort of the editorial chair at
the *Sydney Morning Herald*. Many of the emancipists left Tasmania
and we have no certain way of determining the numbers remaining
after the census of 1857, which found that 50 per cent of adults
and 60 per cent of adult males were convicts or ex-convicts. Later
censuses kept well away from the contentious question of social
origins but the rapid rise of the native born from 37 per cent of
the population to 73 per cent between 1857 and 1881 was clearly
an indication of the passing of the ex-convicts, and incidentally,
of the small numbers of free immigrants enticed to settle in the
faltering colony.

The system cast long shadows. The *Launceston Examiner*
observed in October 1857 that while transportation had ceased
there was 'a residuum of crime, disease and poverty'.[17] Bushranging
persisted until the end of the 1850s. Men known as Rocky Whe-
lan, Hellfire Jack, Long Mickey and Black Peter Haley kept anxiety
levels high in the rural areas. Sheep stealing continued on the large
unfenced summer pastures of the Central Plateau where emancipist
shepherds 'whistled nigger melodies in the balmy air' and caroused
with other old lags on grog distilled from ration sugar. Remoteness
provided its own protection. The sight of a policeman riding up
from the settled valleys resulted in smoke 'curling to the sky from
the first hut he reached, and in ten minutes the same warning signal
passed from north to south and east to west'.[18]

The penal settlement at Port Arthur continued to operate until 1877 and the presence of the large albeit declining population of mainly long term prisoners was a constant source of anxiety. There were frequent calls for the parliament to vote funds to send them all back to Britain. It was a proposal that met with little favour in the Colonial Office. The British decision to withdraw troops from the island in 1870 exposed fears about the surviving convict population. Prominent settlers warned the governor that 'some serious disturbance or perhaps catastrophe, might follow the announcement'.[19] Governor Du Cane seconded local concerns when he argued that the troops were 'an essential element for securing, in the case of an outbreak, the complete isolation of the settlement on Tasman's peninsula from the mainland'.[20] The regular release into the community of prisoners with tickets of leave was a constant source of alarm. A parliamentary committee of 1861 reported that

From Port Arthur, therefore, through the criminals it is constantly sending forth into society, arises . . . the whole of the Crime in the Colony with all its dangers and moral evils together with the enormous cost of restraining and punishing that crime.[21]

The committee thought that the presence of the prison just a few hours away from Hobart 'afforded to the Colony but a sad and distant prospect' of escaping from the 'frightful evils resulting from this continuous circulation of criminals through the community'. An examination of the records of the 161 men discharged during the preceding nine months revealed a 'long catalogue of desperate and revolting crime'.[22]

All the available statistics point to the massive involvement of the emancipists in the colony's crime. In 1866 and 1867 convicts and emancipists committed 70 per cent of the serious crime. Even in 1875, long after the end of transportation, the emancipists committed 44 per cent of major crimes, although by then the population was much diminished and many ex-convicts were elderly and frail. While large numbers of emancipists sought respectability and tried to live down their past by conforming to the exacting standards of behaviour demanded by the more self-righteous free settlers, there were others who continued to live in the way they pleased. Hobart and Launceston had many rowdy, notorious, pot houses where the ex-convicts could escape the censorious gaze of the respectable and find companionship in raucous drinking, cock fighting, gambling and more or less casual sex. They scorned the worthy middle class reformers who wanted to save them and no doubt had fun shocking their genteel sensibilities. A visiting clergyman found that the language of the streets was 'often fearful', providing 'much matter for painful thought'.[23] Earnest young Quaker J. B. Walker recoiled from the frequent sight of 'poor wretches' carousing in the streets with 'drunkenness, oaths and shame'.[24] Polite, often timorous, visitors who ventured into the rowdy parts of town were particularly taken aback by the loud, lewd women they encountered. A visitor who wandered into a disreputable pub in Launceston was disgusted by what he termed the drunken harridans who sat 'drinking gin from broken tea cups and smoking villainous tobacco from short, black pipes'.[25] There was a depth and passion about this common rejection of polite society that was related to the enduring outrage that many emancipists felt about the way they had been dealt with by the system. Theirs was a personal and social rather than a political rebellion.

A distinctive feature of Tasmanian society during the second half of the 19th century was the large number of institutions, a legacy of transportation, that housed prisoners, invalids, paupers, lunatics and orphan or abandoned children. The island had a far larger population of people dependent on the state than any other of the Australian colonies and what was, in effect, a version of the welfare state long before that term was invented. In 1856 there were 820 prisoners under sentence, 223 paupers, 370 invalids, 343 lunatics and 511 orphan children. Convicts and emancipists made up the bulk of this large institutional population, accounting for 94 per cent of the invalids, 89 per cent of prisoners, 85 per cent of paupers and 84 per cent of the lunatics as well as over 60 per cent of all patients treated at the Hobart Hospital.[26] There were still over 800 invalids and paupers in island institutions in 1890, an overwhelming proportion of whom had been transported to the colony.[27] Tasmania spent more on prisons and charitable institutions than any of the other colonies. They were a burden on the depressed economy. In 1866 this social expenditure took up 17 per cent of the budget. At much the same time New South Wales spent 6 per cent of its budget on comparable institutions and Victoria only 4 per cent. At the time investment in charities amounted to £305 per 1000 people in Tasmania and only £138 in the other colonies. This trend was apparent even later in the century. At the end of the 1880s the island spent 40 per cent more per capita on hospitals and charitable institutions than the rest of Australia.[28]

The statistics could be so precise because emancipists could never escape their past. Government records were voluminous and ready at hand and people's memories were almost as comprehensive as the large official ledgers bequeathed to the colonial government by the convict administration. As Trollope appreciated, the records were 'recent, fresh and ever present'.[29] The police continued to subject ticket of leave holders to 'an unremitting supervision', visiting their homes by day and night. While they had no such authority over the emancipists who had received their pardons they continued to exercise 'a certain surveillance over them'.[30] The social barriers to upward social mobility remained in place after 1853. Trollope observed that it was still felt necessary to adhere to the rule that 'no convict, no matter whatever may be his success, shall be received into society'.[31] The prisoners released from Port Arthur were frequently shunned, which rendered their 'search for employment often tedious and difficult'. A parliamentary committee reported that there was a 'growing dread of the frightful practices to which it is known many of them are addicted'.[32] E. N. C. Braddon, the retired Indian public servant who settled on the northwest coast in the 1870s, was surprised to discover the prejudices against the emancipists that persisted even in regions settled after the end of transportation. 'They were convicts once,' he explained to his Indian readers,

and must remain under suspicion until the end of their days... Young Tasmania cannot forgive those of a former generation who bear the convict brand, cannot believe any sort of good of them... keeps the 'old hands' under police surveillance and delights always to think and speak ill of them.[33]

The relations between masters and servants were a source of constant contention in the era after the end of transportation. Many of the larger employers had become used to wielding power and authority over their convict servants, which came with the assignment system. The desire to maintain rigid hierarchies, to enforce subordination and maintain the deference they felt they were entitled to, persisted after transportation ended. They sought to maintain the old controls over the new workforce, which was made up of emancipists, free immigrants and increasingly of native born. They brought to their aid legislation that granted masters control over their servants, legislation unlike any other in the other Australian colonies. For their part the free workforce was well aware that island employers wished to maintain the ways of doing things that belonged in the era of the chain gang and the triangles.

The Masters and Servants Act, passed by the old Legislative Council in the last days of its existence, bestowed great powers of coercion on the employers. A servant who broke his contract, refused to work diligently and carefully, or was guilty of 'any other misconduct' could be arrested without a warrant, taken into custody, held for a week before a hearing and was not permitted to speak in his own defence. If found guilty he was liable to a £10 fine, the equivalent of several months income, the loss of wages owing to him or both penalties. A servant convicted of drunkenness or of using obscene language was liable to a £20 fine or to three months in gaol. Any member of the master's family could place a servant in custody. When the new parliament met, Attorney-General Francis attempted to amend the legislation, seeking, as he said, to adapt the laws to the 'new state of things now growing up, and they must remember they had not now a population requiring to be controlled by the apparatus of gaols'.[34] After a storm of protest burst forth from the leading rural families the Act lapsed in committee. Attempts at reform in the following two years were equally unsuccessful; the sought after amelioration was not achieved until the 1880s.

The petitions that came in from the rural districts were awash with anxiety. Petitioners from Morven insisted that the proposed changes afforded 'no protection to the master' and was 'subversive of all discipline'. Those from Glamorgan believed the provisions of the new legislation 'did not secure to the Master that protection which the circumstances of the Colony demand'. Alarm was even greater in Fingal where it was believed that the effect of the new legislation would be to 'disorganise society . . . and to depopulate the island, so far as its most worthy and valuable inhabitants are concerned'. Landowners in Brighton expressed concern for the 'labouring classes' who, relieved from 'wholesome restraint', would become 'dissatisfied, insubordinate and utterly careless of their own or their master's interests'. At a meeting in Longford pastoral patriarch William Archer declared that the proposed legislation was 'altogether inapplicable to the circumstances of the colony', and would give 'all servants perfect immunity in misconduct however gross'.[35]

The harsher aspects of the legislation fell into disuse in the towns but were still applied in the rural areas where they were the means of acts 'little short of cruelty'.[36] Working class opposition was pronounced. Reform of the legislation became a key objective of liberal reformers. It was, they argued, a relic of 'convict barbarism'; it was 'with slight alteration the same as in the black old days of convictism'.[37] A correspondent writing in the radical *Southern Star* argued that harsh laws drove working men away from the island. 'How is it,' he asked, 'that Tasmania cannot keep her people at home?' The fault, he declared, was that the government had always

stuck to the old conservative book, the remnants of white slavery. The Masters and Servants Act has been a curse to Tasmania and should be swept away. When 500 miles in the interior of South Australia, I have heard it denounced by men who came out at Tasmania's expense. Those men did not know what freedom was until they reached Australia's shores. During the last twenty years I have been thrown among some hundreds of migrants and I can safely say that not one in a hundred of them knows this island by the name Tasmania; but it is well known as Van Diemen's Land; the land of white slavery.[38]

The ability of the large landowners to resist reform of the masters and servants legislation for a generation indicated one of the most striking features of Tasmania in the middle years of the 19th century – the power and influence of the gentry. It needs some explaining because it arose as a result of distinctive features of the history and the geography of the colony.

The first substantial wave of settlement occurred during the 1820s at a time when British policy was designed to 'create and uphold an opulent gentry'.[39] Land grants were in proportion to income and possessions, and were almost all concentrated in the so-called Midlands – that area of open lightly wooded grassland in the valleys of the Derwent, the Macquarie, the Meander, the South Esk and their tributaries. But land was limited and by the time that free grants were replaced by land sales in 1831 most of it had been taken up. This was in strong contrast to the mainland where vast grasslands beckoned the squatters ever-outward away from the coast. The families who received their land in the 1820s were sitting pretty. They normally had frontages along permanent water courses, fertile soil and assigned convict servants. They were wealthy and influential enough to keep small freeholders out of their districts, thereby forcing the land hungry into the dense forests where many years of back-breaking labour was required to establish a viable enterprise. Sheep farmers were untouched by the depression of the 1860s. Wool prices remained high while the price of labour fell. It continued to be the principal export, earning 48 per cent of total export income at the end of the 1860s. The Hobart *Mercury* remarked that 'every industry but the pastoral industry is in a depressed and ruinous condition'.[40]

The power of the gentry was based on their dominance of land over several generations. In 1875 ninety-two of the largest 100 rural estates were owned by families who had acquired their land before 1832. Only one estate seems to have been acquired after 1850. The 12 largest landowners held about 440 000 acres or just over 10 per cent of the colony's stock of freehold land; the Van Diemen's Land Company owned a further 350 000 acres in the far northwest. The 100 largest properties took up over 40 per cent of all freehold land. When the numerous family aggregations were considered the concentration of land holding was even more pronounced. Seventeen families held 46 of the largest 100 estates. Extensive intermarriage among the gentry families threw a web of kinship over the interlinked pattern of land ownership. The colony's sheep flock was concentrated on the estates of the gentry. Ten family groups ran 20 per cent of the total flock, while the 25 most substantial flock masters owned just over one-quarter of all the sheep; many of them had developed flocks of superfine Saxon merinos and exported their rams all over Australia. The economic dominance by the gentry families was accentuated by the lack of any competing interests.

While some landowners were willing to encourage tenants, they were hostile to independent small farmers and the rural towns of the Midlands were dependent on the big properties whether they liked the fact or not. In 1870, of breadwinners in the Midlands 71 per cent were labourers or servants and only 12 per cent were owners or lessees of land.

The social position of the gentry was enhanced by the fact that so many of their employees were or had been convicts, which added to their assumption of preeminence and to the barriers obstructing the path of anyone aspiring to social mobility. Only a handful of the 100 largest landowners had been convicts and almost all of them had arrived in the colony in the very earliest years before the social structure had solidified. Otherwise the prominent settlers who had come to the colony in the 1820s were people with modest capital and above average education – military officers on small pensions, aspiring solicitors, merchants and surgeons and ambitious yeoman farmers. All had immigrated with the intention of maintaining or improving their social position and if possible emulating in the New World the life of the more prosperous British landowners. The social uniformity and the smallness of the island fostered a collective way of life that allowed for constant visiting and mutual attendance at local churches, and gathering for hunting and cricket matches. A visitor in the 1850s thought the landowners of the northern Midlands 'more given, perhaps, to the country house hospitality of the old country than in any other of our Australian dependencies'.[41] Many of the gentry's children attended a few chosen schools and subsequently intermarried. Visits to Hobart and Launceston were easy to undertake and professional and personal links were maintained with the urban elite of merchants, solicitors, accountants, doctors and senior public servants. Strong class identification and solidarity developed early and persisted for generations, as did the sense of exclusiveness acquired in the time of transportation and, once assumed, lived on even when all the old hands had died.

There is no doubt that the prominent landowners sought and savoured the subordination of their workforce. They wanted deference as much as they needed labour. But some of them were strongly paternalistic and thought the restraint they exercised

Image 8.1:   Distance view of Mona Vale, with Blackman
River in the foreground. (*Source:* Archives Office of
Tasmania.)

was necessary and wholesome. The book *On Improvements in
Cottage Husbandry*, published in Launceston in 1849, sang the
virtues of 'well-ordered neighbourhood' and the 'interchange of
friendly offices' between master and servant 'where the domestic
services of the young female are repaid by kindly counsel and sympathy for her family'.[42]

Because many of the large Midland properties were mixed farms
with dairies, orchards, gardens and fields given over to grain, it made
economic sense to provide valued permanent employees with cottages and garden plots although casual labour probably came from
the small rural towns. The larger estates had almost as many people
as the towns, and they were often long term residents. There were
many contemporary stories of old hands who had been assigned
servants, and then stayed on after they had gained their freedom.
The Hobart *Mercury* referred to the faithful retainers who had been
so long in service that they were as 'much part of the estate as the
most valued trees and as little likely to leave'.[43]

The paternalism was often real enough. Ebenezer Shoobridge of 'Bushy Park' in the Derwent valley established a school and a library with 600 books and 15 papers and periodicals for his 'own people' and presided over their Mutual Improvement and Garden Societies. With 85 cottages on his estate he was 'one of the largest employers in the Colony'.[44] The Kermodes of 'Mona Vale' were also interested in the education of the children on the estate.

Mrs Kermode spent two hours with them every day and the chief inspector of schools thought her husband 'a proprietor who looks at the school as his own interest'.[45] On 18 June 1859, the *Launceston Examiner* lauded Kermode's benevolence. One reporter wrote that

On his large landed estates he has, above all others, cared for the welfare of the numerous hands he employs and their families. They are provided with superior accommodation, have important advantages; and at his own exclusive cost, he maintains a school master for the children growing up on his wide domains.

On New Year's Day the Reibeys of 'Entally' feasted all the children of the district and many other landowners provided food and beer or homegrown cider to enliven traditional harvest festivals. At a hop festival at 'Lisdillon' on the east coast, 120 tenants and workers on the estate and their families sat down to 'a most substantial repast consisting of roast and boiled joints, puddings, pastry, etc. etc.'. The children 'adjourned to a neighbourhood paddock, where they indulged for the rest of the day in various games, such as cricket, horsey, kiss in the ring etc'.[46] Local historian K. R. von Stieglitz described a similar hop feast at 'Mayfield', where 70 had lunch in the open air, and then spent the afternoon playing cricket and rounders before dancing in the oast house.[47] William Gellibrand of the Ouse kept bank accounts for his workers, while others involved themselves with the religious life of their estates, many of which had their own small churches.[48] Francis Groom of 'Harefield' insisted that his servants attend church every Sunday and read prayers to the assembled household morning and evening.[49] John Leake of 'Rosedale' lived some distance 'from a place of worship' but always assembled his servants and family 'to hear the Church service and sermon read'.[50]

Clearly, the leading rural families believed that they had a responsibility to represent their districts in parliament and they had the substance and the leisure to do so. The short distances on the island and the convict-built roads facilitated their self-appointed mission. During the first generation of responsible government the Midlands returned eight of the 30 members of the House of Assembly and four of the 15 legislative councillors. Elections were often uncontested, a situation that may have been informally arranged among the gentry. Even when an election took place the candidates came from the same small group of families. In 1875, of the 100 largest landowners 31 had sat in parliament at some stage over the preceding 20 years. Six Archers had been in parliament as had three Gibsons, three Scotts and three Gellibrands, as well as two members of the Bisdee, Meredith, von Stieglitz and Sharland families. Despite their engagement in the government of the colony many of the large landowners were strongly opposed to bureaucratic intervention in their lives. An Inspector of Sheep reported in 1872 that he had great difficulty with men of an ultraconservative class. Their faith was that they knew best what was in their interests. The idol they worshipped 'with intense devotion is the boasted liberty of an Englishman who they persist in asserting...can do what he likes with his own'. They were 'men of substance and deservedly good repute', but nothing would induce them to conform to a law that they disliked except compulsion, which they called tyranny and denounced as unconstitutional'.[51]

With these attitudes it is not surprising that the large landowners were determined to take control of the local councils that were formed throughout the Midlands within 10 years of the passage of the *Rural Municipalities Act 1858*. While this legislation delegated authority to the regions it also handed local power to the gentry. The £15 household franchise was higher than the voting qualification for the House of Assembly and it seems likely that only about 30 per cent of adult males could vote in local elections, and even then there was never much choice. Council membership was restricted to owners or occupiers of property worth £50 per annum at a time when most houses in the small towns were valued at between £10 and £15. Of the 100 largest landowners in 1875, 37 of them had served on one or other of the 11 midland councils. Their tenure was very secure because multiple voting existed on a scale unique in Australia, ranging from two votes for property worth between £50 and £100 and up to 10 votes for land worth £450 and over. It was apparent that somewhere between 15 and 20 per cent of electors held a majority of votes and that a few families were able to dominate the councils, which, among other things, assessed the value of properties, decided on local roadworks and, above all else, controlled the police.

The police had been one of the most contentious aspects of the system established by Governor Arthur. Instead of a force controlled by the local magistrates, as was the case in rural Britain, Arthur centralised it through the appointment of salaried officers directly responsible to the administration in Hobart. What was even more galling to many of the large landowners was that almost all the police were convicts under sentence or emancipists over whom they had no control. One of the reasons for the rapid development of local government – and it was unusual in Australia – was to take control of the police force. In each municipality a small coterie of like-minded landowners had the means to use the police in their own interests and to favour the owners of the big estates over townsmen and small holders and masters over servants. It was a form of local power that the gentry fought to preserve, the result of which was that the small, highly inefficient forces were not centralised until 1898. The concentration of local power became a constant focus for agitation. A petition presented to parliament in 1872 outlined the dissatisfaction of many rural dwellers. The petitioners explained that when the rural municipalities were set up,

Many of them feared that the measure would prove unequal and unjust, inasmuch as the powers conferred on the different classes of ratepayers might enable the wealthier sections when combined to dominate over the poorer and more numerous.

Your petitioners regret to state that those fears have proved to be well founded; for it is well known that in every municipality it is only necessary for some ten or twelve of the greater ratepayers to unite, when their own votes of ten each, together with the influence naturally attendant on their social position, enable them to rule at will their respective municipalities, to the absolute exclusion from all share of power . . . of the general body of their fellow citizens.

Your petitioners have long felt the evils consequent on the law as it stands. They feel themselves powerless to oppose in their own interests a combination only too certain to prevail.[52]

While writing in 1852 about the settlement of Tasmania John West observed that

The dignity and independence based on landed wealth are ever the chief allurement of the emigrant. Whatever his rank, he dreams of the day when he shall dwell in a mansion planned by himself; survey a wide and verdant landscape called after his name; and sit beneath the vineyard his own hands planted.[53]

The middle class settlers who received land grants in the 1820s went far towards fulfilling these dreams. In the early days they had feared attacks from Aborigines and bushrangers and had to find ways of managing convict servants. Many of them took up the cause of political reform and eventually turned against transportation. They successfully engineered the transfer of power from Downing Street to the Tasmanian parliament while facing down demands for greater democratisation and ran their own municipalities from their elegant drawing rooms. Most of them had children who survived infancy and were eager to inherit what had become grand estates, which were at their best in the 1870s when death was thinning the founding generation. The flocks of superfine Saxon merinos won awards and fetched a premium at annual wool sales. The drives and parks lined with exotic trees, the fields hedged with hawthorn, briar and gorse, planted half a century before by the abundant convict labour, were widely admired. The estates presented a picture of 'nature subdued and trained by art'.[54] The visitor found 'no broken fences, no gates without latches' and the cleared land was 'quite unblemished by stumps'.[55] Willows clustered 'emerald bright' along the streams while gardens, abundant with English flowers, 'looked and smelt like home'.[56] Deer grazed in the parks of Panshanger, Clarendon and Quamby; larks, linnets, pheasants and sparrows flittered through the trees and salmon swam in the cool island streams.

But as the sons inherited the midland properties the age of the gentry was coming to an end. Their economic importance declined as wool ceased to dominate the resurgent economy. Its share of total export income fell steadily from over 40 per cent in 1875–80 to a mere 14 per cent 20 years later. The tide of migration turned in the colony's favour and after stagnating for a generation the cities recovered. Legislation of the 1880s whittled at the base of gentry power.

Image 8.2: *'Panshanger', the seat of Joseph Archer, Esquire.*
(*Source:* National Library of Australia, an6016322-v.)

The Master and Servants Act was stripped of its severity while both parliamentary and municipal franchises were significantly widened. The colonial government asserted its authority over public works in the 1880s and over police in the 1890s. Unionism emerged as a factor in island life and organisers began to stir the millpond of rural life. The young native-born workers, who had no desire to stay in the Midlands, sought greater freedom and higher wages in the new farming areas or at the mines. The pioneers who lived deep into old age lived just long enough to 'see the servants become the masters'.[57]

But not the convict servants who had built the grand houses, planted and maintained gardens and hedgerows, tended the domestic animals and prepared abundant meals and cleared them away again. It is likely that only a few of them were ever able to vote in parliamentary or municipal elections and many of them were dieing away at much the same time as the leading landowners. The gentry were eulogised at large funerals and handsome headstones were raised to dominate country graveyards in death as they had bestrode their neighbourhoods in life. The convicts passed quietly away, their graves marked in most cases with no more than a simple wooden cross. Launceston expressed its continuing hostility to the old hands by burying them on an unused hillside out beyond the boundary of the town. Tasmanians could not conceal their satisfaction as the ranks of the old hands thinned and the official statistics recorded a progressive decline in crime, consumption of alcohol and the numbers resident in the institutions inherited from the convict era. The *Tasmanian Official Record* of 1891 noted 'how remarkably fast the old foreign element in our Gaols and Pauper Establishments is dying out'.[58] By then Tasmania had a lower crime rate than the rest of Australia and drank less alcohol. 'The advance in material progress,' the Colony's statistician observed, 'is not half so cheering as this indication of her power to eliminate from her social system the noxious poisons of pauperism and crime.' They were 'simply noxious foreign plants' that found 'no congenial soil in Tasmania for their propagation'.[59] When the last day of 1897 bushfires ravaged the decaying penal settlement at Port Arthur a Hobart paper observed that many people would 'make no concealment of their satisfaction at the destruction of the penitentiary'.[60]

As the convicts and the free settlers who had built their fortunes with assigned convict labour died a new Tasmania was emerging. The island merged with the other colonies that, for a generation, had left it behind although the past would continue to influence those many families whose roots were already deep in the local soil.

9

Reform and Recovery

The death of Trugannini in May 1876 was one of the best known events in island history. For most Tasmanians it represented the end of an era and the disappearance of a race. In the wider world scientists and ethnographers saw it as compelling evidence of the iron laws of evolution, which elevated the progressive races and drove more primitive people to destruction. The fate of the island's Aborigines was a portent of further extinction. By the time of her death Trugannini was a celebrity in Hobart and her funeral was a significant event attended by the premier, cabinet ministers and religious leaders. Extraordinary precautions were taken to prevent a repeat of the notorious desecration of William Lanney's cadaver seven years previously. Her body was guarded by the police while it was in the Hobart hospital, and then moved secretly to the old convict Female Factory at the Cascades. Many people gathered in the streets to pay their last respects, only to find the body had already left the town. The service was carried out at a small Protestant chapel and the coffin was buried outside the door where it would be beyond the reach of any potential grave robbers. As it was lowered into the ground a bouquet of native shrubs was placed on the lid. A plan to erect a monument at the site never came to fruition. Her skeleton was removed from the grave a few years later and was taken by the Royal Society, which put it on display until 1951 at the Tasmanian Museum and Art Gallery.

The death of Trugannini was not the only reason for contemporary scientific interest in the Tasmanian Aborigines. While many scholars wrote about dying races, others found equal significance in the mixed descent community on the islands in the Furneaux group. Books written in Europe and the USA noted the passing of the Aborigines, while others were equally impressed by the fact that there was a flourishing population of people who combined the heritage of Europeans and Aborigines. Their interest was stimulated by the fact that at the time the orthodox scientific view was that people of mixed descent were biologically impaired and could not produce healthy children. So the evidence of leading British seaman Captain J. L. Stokes, in a book published in London in 1846, was taken up by those scholars who rejected the idea of mixed-descent inferiority. During a surveying voyage Stokes, who had been in Hobart on the *Beagle* in 1836, visited the Bass Strait islands and reported that he found a flourishing community that included many intelligent, healthy children. Such was their skill in the way they handled their boats that he regretted that he could not take some of them away to become apprentice seamen.[1] The community had only occasional contact with mainland Tasmania where they sold their smoked and salted mutton birds, along with their feathers and purchased essential supplies. Few other Tasmanians knew of their unique way of life and even when they did it did not shake the conviction that Trugannini's passing had signalled the death of the race.

Beyond the opening of the new parliament and the difficulties of dealing with the aftermath of the convict system much changed for settler Tasmanians and their children after 1856. New areas of the colony were opened up for settlement, the population moved decisively away from the gentry-dominated Midlands, great mineral fields were discovered and a new generation of reform-minded politicians brought Tasmania into line with the larger mainland colonies as they edged slowly towards federation. Of the many changes the most significant related to the abiding question of land ownership.

In the early years of settlement the government had granted small plots of land to emancipists and their children. Many lost or sold their grants but there were always small farms and commercial gardens close to Hobart and Launceston. From the 1820s policy moved decisively in favour of free immigrants with capital who were granted most of the island's readily available land in just over

10 years. The other arm of policy saw the introduction of measures that made it very difficult for the poor, whether emancipist, immigrant or native born, to acquire either land or livestock. The large landowners implemented their own unofficial policy aimed at preventing small, independent farmers from establishing themselves in the Midlands. Such widely variable access to land was a major instrument in securing the desired social hierarchy and impelling subordination. The majority of the population was condemned in a completely conscious way to remain landless and therefore dependent and available to provide their labour for wages. It was in a way a heroic attempt to counter the observed tendency for settler societies to flatten out hierarchy, dissolve deference and to distribute land more widely than was common in the Old World.

The widespread desire for land was facilitated by legislation passed during the second half of the century, beginning with the *Waste Land Act 1858*, which introduced two important innovations: first, it allowed individuals to select blocks of land under 320 acres, and second to secure them with a deposit, and then pay off the remainder over a number of years. As with all such legislation land was frequently taken up by speculators who had no intention of farming. But gradually, amending legislation tipped the balance in favour of the genuine selector and put landownership within the reach of working men and women with small savings. It did not pit selector against squatter in the way common on the mainland because Tasmania's large landowners were safe behind their original freehold titles. What it did achieve was a radical change in determining which Tasmanians could became landowners, where they took up their selections, how they farmed and the sort of society that emerged in what became known as the 'new country'.

Selectors moved into pockets of Crown land all over the island and many small, raw farming communities sprang up during the late 19th and early 20th centuries. The most sustained development took place along the northwest coast between Port Sorell and Circular Head, in the northeast between Launceston and the east coast and in the Huon Valley south of Hobart. During the second half of the 19th century there was a constant stream of people moving out from the old districts into the new, particularly along the northwest coast. Between 1861 and 1891 the population west of Deloraine increased by over 400 per cent, from 5400 to 22 500 or from 6 per cent to 15 per cent of the total population. The new towns of Devonport, Latrobe and Ulverstone grew rapidly, easily outpacing their older rivals in the Midlands. By the turn of the century the northwest had become the most productive region of the colony and the products grown on the small farms – potatoes, fruit, cheese and butter – were more valuable than the wool clip. The Huon was becoming renowned as an orcharding centre and for the production of apples, pears and berry fruits. The achievement of the small farmers was a success story that would have seemed improbable to the first generation of settlers whose hopes had soured among economic stagnation and demographic decline.

The new country had remained unoccupied during the convict era because of the dense forests thrown up by rich, deep soil and abundant rainfall. The Aborigines had cleared patches here and there in the forest and opened up their pathways but otherwise, the country was dominated by large overarching trees and dense undergrowth. The cost of clearing the land was so prohibitive that settlement had stalled for a generation on the outer fringes of the open grasslands. Many stories were told of the extraordinary density of vegetation, of travellers getting lost only a few steps away from their destination, of the sunless gloom of the forest floor and the perpetual dankness of the vegetation, of the necessity to laboriously hack a way with an axe and hook through the entangling undergrowth. It needed many years of relentless labour with the simplest tools to carve a viable farm from the forest, a venture particularly suited to men and women without capital but with physical endurance and an unflinching determination to win their independence, even if it took a lifetime to achieve it. Many of the pioneers were native-born men and women who had grown up in the old districts and watched as their emancipist parents performed those rituals of deference demanded on the big Midland estates. It was this experience that helped shape the vastly different social environment that emerged in the new country.

There was little previous experience in the colonies or in Britain that could provide guidance to solve the unique difficulties of settling in the great forests. The initial problem was to find and mark out the chosen selection. The first task was to cut down the undergrowth, pile it up and wait until it was dry enough to burn. This job was usually carried out while sheltering in a tent on the selection but living elsewhere. When the conflagration was complete, grass seed and potatoes were thrown into the ashes and the selection left to look after itself till there was enough grass to feed a horse. The next and most decisive task was to ringbark all the large trees, and then wait until they eventually fell down, which might take years to occur. So farming proceeded and houses and fences were built among the dying trees and the stumps left behind by those already burnt or cut up. It often took a lifetime to reach the desired condition of cleared pasture free of stumps. When it was finally achieved the visitor might gain no impression of the years of labour that had been required to turn forest into farmland.

The selectors were, according to parliamentary committees, labourers, tradesmen, poor immigrants and tenant farmers' sons. The new country was 'emphatically the land of the cockatoo or peasant farmer'. It was a land 'where muscle and skill are all in all'. There was 'no opening for educated intelligence or capital'.[2] The few educated middle class settlers faced the problem of having to spend their capital on local labour, which was expensive, or roll up their sleeves, do the hard physical labour themselves and be willing to accept the advice of their more humble neighbours and learn to cope with the blistered hands, broken nails and strained backs. There were few men with soft hands in the new country. The pioneers took pride in their skill with axe and crosscut saw, a new sport that emerged to be enjoyed at local shows and carnivals. On returning from a visit to the Huon a middle class visitor observed that it was 'a most objectionable settlement for the best class of colonist'.[3] Small holdings predominated in the forest lands. In 1891 the average size of properties was only 143 acres compared with 1174 in the Midlands. Few selectors had any money or any equipment beyond axes, hoes, spades and sickles. Their bark and timber houses were rudimentary and for years they lived without much profit from their farming, often depending for long periods on credit grudgingly extended by local shopkeepers. A frequent visitor to the Huon observed that he

often wondered how the people ... manage to live. Many of them are so attached to their little farms that they will subsist on turnips carrots etc. rather than eat their potatoes which they save up for seed.[4]

Even when the farms began to produce a surplus and potatoes were the most favoured early crop, there was no local market and it was often impossible to transport them even to nearby ports due to a lack of passable roads or serviceable bridges. Beyond a certain distance, transport costs took away any profit margin. Many selectors cut their own trees into palings and shingles, and then carried them on their backs to where they could be sold. What saved many selectors was their ability to find wage labour in the timber mills, at the mines or on public works projects while wives and children remained behind to look after the selection and feed the chooks, the pig and maybe a horse and a cow, perhaps to water the geraniums.

The social structure of the small farming districts was very different from what could be found in other parts of the colony. Many more people owned or leased land, which meant they were able to vote in local and colonial elections. There were few large employers of labour. Labourers often owned small selections, farmers worked willingly for wages. The collector of agricultural statistics on the northwest coast observed in 1872 that there were 'no regular employers of the capitalist class . . . the master of the day is often the servant of the tomorrow'.[5] Educated middle class settlers who arrived on the northwest coast were struck by the egalitarianism they experienced. Arriving from India Edward Braddon found that

Forth society is yet a mystery to us, so great is the difficulty of deciding where the line is drawn and who is, or is not, of it. Its society is mixed very considerably and storekeeping seems to be regarded almost as one of the professions to which a gentleman may commit himself without loss of position.[6]

Louisa Meredith came to the region from her gentry-dominated world of the east coast when her husband Charles was appointed police magistrate. As did Braddon she found it difficult to work out where the social boundaries were or, indeed, if there were any at all. She wrote:

As to the tender question of esquirearchy, I am convinced that the only prudent principle now is to bestow the envied title on everyone alike – on the friend you invite to partake your dinner, and the butcher from whom you brought it.[7]

The selectors had far greater problems to surmount than the amused condescension of patrician observers. Their overwhelming difficulties were transport and travel. One of the great advantages with the Midlands had been the ease of movement across the land. As so many visitors noted, it was possible to drive carts and even carriages over dry firm ground among widely dispersed trees. It was so different in the forests. The rainfall was higher, the soil was deeper, it turned to mud for much of the year and became worse every time it was travelled over. Being bogged on the rudimentary tracks became one of the pioneers' most commonly shared experiences. Everyone had a story about horses and bullocks sinking into mud up to their bellies. Travel was difficult enough but the movement of goods was almost impossible for long periods every year. There were also numerous rivers and creeks to cross. It was difficult to get supplies in and harder to take produce out, particularly heavy items such as potatoes and split timber. Not surprisingly, the settlers in the forests were at the forefront of the demand for large expenditure on roads, bridges and jetties, which came to dominate colonial politics during the 1860s and 1870s. There was clearly a problem of funding such works but there was powerful political resistance as well from the conservative gentry politicians, particularly in the Legislative Council, who time and again rejected Bills for public works schemes. They took the view that each district should fund and manage its own roads and bridges and that it was an imposition to charge such works to the general revenue, which was an attractive option for them because their districts still benefited from the work of the convicts. But as well there was almost certainly a latent hostility towards the outlying parts of the colony where servants were becoming landowners. Legislative councillors may well have personally known poor families who had left their districts and even their own estates to select land in the forests.

The colonists began to talk of railways in the 1850s but it took another 18 years before the first tracks were laid. Visitors from Britain were charmed to see the coaches like the ones they had known as children still passing up and down the highway between Hobart and Launceston. English journalist John Martineau remarked that most Tasmanians had never left the island since their arrival or were native born. It was, therefore, 'quite a new sensation to live among people, comparatively few of whom, rich or poor, young or old, who have ever seen a railway'.[8] The story of the first railway from Launceston to Deloraine 50 kilometres away, through some of the most productive land in the colony, was long and tortuous, pitting the enthusiasm of the northern community against the resistance of the government. A Railway League was formed in Launceston and eventually a poll of landowners along the line indicated a willingness to give financial support to the project, which led to the formation of a private company. The line was surveyed and rails and rolling stock ordered from Britain. Cheered on by a large festive crowd the visiting Duke of Edinburgh turned the first sod at the site of the terminus in Launceston in January 1868, although work did not begin till six months later and was disastrously set back by unprecedented floods that washed away track and collapsed cuttings. Eventually, on 10 February 1871, Tasmania joined the age of steam. Two trains, with streamers flying and freighted with the colony's elite, set off for Deloraine at more than 20 miles an hour, past cheering crowds and returned in triumph six hours later. The *Launceston Examiner* expressed the pride of the northern community in doing so much to bring to fruition 'the greatest work ever achieved in Tasmania'.[9] But the euphoria of attained modernity did not last long. The company struggled to make a profit and when storms and resulting landslips brought the trains to a standstill the company was forced to suspend operations; it was taken over by the government in August 1872. A campaign by the authorities to recover money owing by the landowners led to passive resistance by the well to do and riots by angry crowds in Launceston.

The line from Hobart to Launceston had an even more laboured birth. During the 1850s there was much talk about the project, a royal commission and an associated parliamentary debate. An English company forced the issue by offering to build the line with the support of government guarantees and the contract was signed in March 1872. Intense controversy over the projected route arose, but not enough to halt work, which proceeded in early 1873 with a large imported labour force; the first journey was completed in November 1876. But the partnership between unstable ephemeral governments and an assertive company was a troubled one. Dispute followed dispute, inquiry was piled on inquiry, mediation failed and both parties turned to the courts. The contention was not resolved until late 1890 when the government took over the company. By then public ownership of the rail networks had become commonplace in the Australian colonies. It was a step that Tasmania had already taken in 1883 when, with money borrowed in London, the government decided to build important branch lines up the Derwent and Fingal Valleys, from Launceston to Scottsdale and from Deloraine to Devonport. Tasmania's ability to borrow money in London at an acceptable rate of interest was due not to the virtue of the legislators but to the dramatic improvement in the economic outlook brought about by the growing understanding of the richness of Tasmania's mineral provinces. Debate on the required legislation for the rail network saw the final showdown with the old men in the Legislative Council who had been opposing public work construction for many years. When the Bill was thrown out by 8 votes to 7 there was an immediate communal revolt. The *Mercury* reported on 'an outburst of popular indignation which has rarely been equalled', and in Launceston the returning northern legislative councillors faced a hostile, vociferous crowd, hooting, groaning and hissing, when they stepped off the train from Hobart. William Grubb was pelted with eggs, gravel and stones and was hustled by harassed police officers back into the train, which retreated, puffing down the line.[10] There were worried comments about mob rule but the public anger convinced the council that resistance could not be sustained; in a special sitting of parliament the contested legislation passed and the central developmental role of government was finally accepted.

As did so many people in the Australian colonies and beyond, the islanders had witnessed the transforming impact of mineral discoveries, initially the prosperity bestowed on struggling South Australia by the copper boom of the 1840s, followed by the spectacular goldrushes in California, and then much closer to home in New South Wales and Victoria in the early 1850s. Thousands of Tasmanians crossed Bass Strait to find their fortune or just to experience the sheer, unprecedented excitement of goldrush Victoria. Some of those returning arrived with stuffed purses but everyone, enriched or not, had colourful stories to tell their friends and relatives who had stayed at home. The same question arose simultaneously in the minds of the sedentary and the itinerant: If such riches could be unearthed in Victoria, why not in Tasmania? That tantalising prospect lured hundreds of men into almost every corner of the island over the next 50 years, remote places that no one had ever visited since the Aborigines were driven from their land. There were enough indications everywhere to maintain the hope of a bonanza. Traces of gold were found all over the island along with encouraging intimations of silver, copper, tin and iron. The newspapers of the 1850s and 1860s were crowded with stories of promising finds until repeated disappointment dulled the appetite for over-optimistic forecasts. The *Mercury* reported in June 1859: 'That we possess rich and inexhaustible Gold Fields there can be no doubt.' The evidence was 'too reliable and too exciting'.[11] There are many sites of abandoned mining camps, even of semi-permanent villages, all over Tasmania that are reminders of this age of incessant prospecting but there were many other sites now completely forgotten where hopeful miners pitched their tents for a month or two before they moved on to try elsewhere. The surprising thing is not that significant mines were eventually discovered but that it took so long to find them.

James 'Philosopher' Smith discovered the first truly significant mine in the western wilderness in 1871.[12] Amid the tangled undergrowth at the base of Mount Bischoff he found one of the richest tin mines that had ever been discovered. Smith's life had many aspects that made him the quintessential native-born hero. The abandoned child of convict parents he was austere, abstemious and dedicated to self-improvement, educating himself in geology among many other subjects. He was typical of his generation in selecting and developing a bush block at Forth on the northwest coast but making many journeys out into the rugged inhospitable country to the southwest, becoming an exemplary bushman in the process. He had been prospecting throughout the 1860s and discovered gold close to home on the Forth and silver on the sea coast at Penguin, but it was the great tin deposit that made his name and began the island's process of recovery from depression. Smith sold his shares before the mine reached its full potential but it greatly enriched the Launceston investors who provided the initial capital. The problems of developing a mine in such a remote area were gradually overcome. The town of Waratah mushroomed, a tramway was built to the mine from Burnie by the Van Diemen's Land Company and a smelter was established at Launceston on the banks of the Tamar in 1878; the profits cascaded into the town. By 1884, 75 dividends had been declared and £462 000 had been paid to shareholders. It was an unprecedented stream of wealth in Tasmania and the mining investors were suddenly and dramatically far wealthier than even the most securely established of the Midland pastoral families, who would never again re-establish their financial preeminence.

Prospecting parties ventured out into the bush with renewed enthusiasm, speculators floated new companies with fanciful names. During 1878 there were reports of finds of silver, bismuth, antimony, coal and copper. The *Mercury* declared:

With our rich hoards of minerals ever opening out we have resource of wealth which only need treatment on a broad basis of enlightenment and spirit, to make Tasmania what only what she now deservedly is, the Island sanatorium of the Southern Hemisphere, but a respected and quoted unit in the Colonial commercial world.[13]

By 1881 even the sanguine *Mercury* was taken aback by the 'mining mania' and the 'blind, reckless, extravagant speculation' that was underway.[14] But there were discoveries that led to enduring developments. Renison Bell, an associate of Philosopher Smith, found alluvial tin over a wide area in the northeast and many miners soon began working as contractors packing their ore over rough, muddy tracks to the north and the east coasts for shipment to the smelter in Launceston or the one that opened in Hobart. The nature of the tin deposits in the northeast, which could be exploited by groups of men with little capital working cooperatively, attracted Chinese miners into Tasmania for the first time. The *Official Mining Report 1887* noted the presence of 700 or 800 Chinese miners; while there was uneasiness about their presence among the Europeans on the tinfields, local officials reported that they were 'peaceable, law abiding men', who conformed 'with creditable strictness to mining laws and regulations'.[15]

Among the many goldfields discovered and developed during the 1870s the Tasmania Mine at Beaconsfield was the most enduring. Unlike many of the other mines of the period it was conveniently situated in settled farmland on the left bank of the Tamar River, close to water and only 50 kilometres north of Launceston. The rich reef gold was discovered in 1878 and development was rapid. Within three years the district had a population of 1500. Six hundred men worked at 16 mines and the town supported four hotels, three churches and five schools. By 1881 the Tasmania Mine had produced gold worth £460 000 and paid £279 000 in dividends, mainly to Launceston investors. The northern city was without question the centre for the mining industry. In the early 1880s, 157 mining companies were registered in the town compared with only 33 in Hobart. Population grew quickly, property values spiralled and merchants, banks and insurance companies began a decade-long building boom that transformed the streetscape that created the legacy of Victorian architecture that survives to the present day.

The whole colony prospered in the 1880s. It remains one of Tasmania's most sunny decades when the movement of population tipped in the island's favour. For the first time since the 1840s more people arrived than departed. Migrants came in and the young native born stayed at home as wages rose and opportunities expanded. The mines offered well-paid work to unskilled and semi-skilled workers and provided an expanding domestic market for food, timber and services. Export income from minerals – mainly tin and gold – exceeded the value of wool for the first time in 1879 and continued to grow until they made up 60 per cent of earnings at the time of federation. But the growth of the industry in the 1870s was dwarfed by the even more spectacular developments on the west coast, particularly the silver mines in and around Zeehan and the even greater gold and copper mines at Queenstown. Despite their isolation, rain-drenched and rugged terrain they were rich enough to attract what for the time was massive interstate and overseas investment and to decisively change the distribution of population and, ultimately, of political power. The large companies were bigger undertakings by far than any previous ventures in Tasmania. The Mt Lyell Company, with the great mine, smelter and railway, overshadowed every other island company. It employed 2600 workers in 1899 and its revenues matched those of the government. One million tons of copper had been exported by 1901.

Image 9.1: Mt Lyell Mine, Queenstown, 1900.
(*Source:* Archives Office of Tasmania.)

The west coast was largely unknown and uninhabited once the local Aborigines had been exiled and the penal settlement at Macquarie abandoned. The prospectors who tramped through the region in the late 1870s and 1880s were entering an utterly strange environment. The climate was quite different to what they knew in the settled districts. Here, the untamed westerly gales drove wild surf onto a rugged coastline and brought rain more intense and more frequent than what was experienced on the far side of the knotted mountain ramparts that separated the west coast from the Midlands. The vegetation was exotic as well, with distinctive plant communities as different as button-grass plains and horizontal scrub. Access was an abiding problem. Mountains and deep, steep valleys stood between the coast and the Derwent and Huon Valleys, which cut into the highlands on their eastern side. The wild stormy coastline lacked safe havens apart from Macquarie Harbour, with its notoriously narrow and difficult entrance. But the great mines attracted immigrants and Tasmanians. By 1900 the coast supported

25 000 people or one-seventh of the total population, and Zeehan
and Queenstown had become the third and fourth largest towns in
the island, easily outstripping the old towns of the Midlands and
even their new rivals on the northwest coast. With a population of
8000 people Zeehan was one-third the size of Hobart.

The west coast was as exotic socially as it was physically, and very
different from the Midlands and the small farming areas. There had
been some opportunities for small prospectors or contract miners in
areas of shallow alluvial deposits but the main mining fields needed
large capital investment for extraction, processing and transportation. Big companies dominated the fields, employing large armies
of wage labourers who were far more likely to rent than own their
houses. The communities were strongly masculine. Miners were
either single or had left wives behind in towns or on selections. In
1901 men outnumbered women by two to one in Queenstown. At
the time, one-third of dwellings were single roomed. The lack of
family life and primitive living conditions produced a vibrant social
life. There was a continuous succession of sporting carnivals, band
recitals and concerts. The hotels were centres for crowded con-
viviality. The small middle class of managers, office workers and
professional men remained aloof from the swelling crowds of miners, tradesmen, navvies and smelter hands. Hobart's radical paper,
the *Clipper*, printed a piece from their Queenstown correspondent
who declared:

> For a mining town this is the greatest place for snobs I have ever
> struck ... There are no less than eight lawyers on the field ... all manfully
> striving to maintain the class distinctions upon which their cult has been
> suckled. Several doctors and some twopenny ha'penny employees in the big
> company's office make up the snobocracy, and ... never hold communica-
> tion with the ordinary Tom and Bill, except for business purposes.[16]

The outright predominance of working class wage earners produced
a very different political environment on the west coast than was
common anywhere else in Tasmania. There were also many more
workers there who had come from the mainland colonies. But political life was slow to develop and it took some time for the coast to
achieve its fair share of electoral power. The potential was clearly
there, as the visiting British trade union leader Ben Tillet recognised.

His audiences reminded him of 'Yorkshire Socialist meetings – so hearty, so responsive'.[17] The full political impact of the west coast did not become apparent until the early years of the new century when Tasmania joined the federation and found the introduction of full adult suffrage irresistible. Hobart remained the main centre of nascent working class politics before the turn of the century.

Skilled workers had formed benefit societies during the 1840s, often to protect themselves from cheap convict labour. Many of them faltered with the great exodus of men to goldrush Victoria and the succeeding depression. But the economic growth of the 1870s encouraged further organisation, and the rapid spread of unionism in the larger colonies provided examples of what might be achieved locally. At a November 1883 meeting of tradesmen, where letters of advice from the Melbourne and Sydney Trade Councils were considered, the Hobart Trades and Labour Council was formed. During the next few years most of the trades affiliated with the council, which came to represent over 700 workers. Attempts to expand the reach of the organisation to other parts of the island were unsuccessful, but links with the intercolonial movement were strengthened, culminating in the decision to hold the sixth Inter-colonial Trade Union Congress in Hobart in February 1889. It was a great occasion for Tasmanian unionists. The social and political acceptability of the movement was accentuated when Governor Sir R. G. Hamilton addressed the congress and prominent merchant politician Premier P. O. Fysh and his ministers attended the official banquet. Fysh also entertained delegates at a picnic at his New Norfolk country retreat. The mainland unionists helped organise further groups of workers and by the end of 1889 most skilled and semi-skilled workers were affiliated with the council. In August the Northern Trades and Labour Council was established in Launceston, the newly elected secretary declaring:

Trades Unionism was something new to him: in fact, six months ago, he might say he had not given the matter a thought, and it was not until after the success of the Trades and Labour Congress that the working classes seemed to realise their power.[18]

The two councils extended their engagement beyond industrial matters and quickly emerged to be among the most powerful lobby groups in the colony, developing close connections with the Liberal government led by Fysh. An executive committee was formed and given the task of 'defending the political rights of the working classes'.[19] Influential Council Secretary Hugh Kirk declared that the workers were 'the chief power in the world' and he looked forward to the time when Tasmania would 'keep pace with the other colonies and the rest of the world' and so hasten the time 'when the whole of mankind shall be as one whole brotherhood'.[20] But the main work of the council was much more mundane. The major issues of the day were debated at council meetings. Press statements outlined union views and, where necessary, public meetings were called and petitions organised. At colonial and municipal elections the council enrolled voters, interviewed candidates and listed their preferred ones. Ministers were lobbied on a range of industrial and political reforms; evidence also suggests that the council had a major influence on the government. The cooperation was symbolised in January 1890, when, to the disgust of conservative Tasmanians, Premier Fysh was seen walking arm in arm with Hugh Kirk 'the agitator' down Macquarie Street.[21]

Indeed, that year opened auspiciously for the unions. The first Eight Hour Day march was held on 25 January. Premier Fysh accepted the position as patron of the event and declared a public holiday, while sympathetic employers provided transport for the procession, which, led by local bands, marched from the Working Man's Club to the cricket ground for a sporting carnival. New unions were established for mill hands, carters and labourers. Discussions were held with the government about legislation to attend to factory inspection, employer liability and mining regulations. But before the end of the year the movement was under siege as it experienced the backwash of the great maritime strike. The council had received an intimation of trouble to come at the August meeting when a letter from the Amalgamated Shearers Union appealing for help in the expected conflict with the wool growers was tabled. In August and September wharf labourers in Hobart and Launceston refused to unload or provide coal for ships arriving from the mainland. But non-union labour was readily available and the police protected them while they worked. By the end of October the unionists had returned to work. Many public figures spoke out against the strike and Tasmanians feared for the consequences of any disruption to essential shipping services. Letters that were unanimous in their condemnation of the strikers and hostile to the unions flooded the papers. The Anglican Church called for the stamping out of socialism; the mayor of Launceston declared that the strikers were madmen. Employers in Hobart and Launceston established powerful organisations to defend what they called freedom of contract. It is clear that many Tasmanian unionists were shocked by the turmoil of the time, and the southern and northern councils deplored the illegal action that they believed had been taken by mainland unionists.

Worse was to come as depression struck, manifested most dramatically in Tasmania by the failure of the Van Diemen's Land Bank in August 1891. The long boom that had reached Tasmania only in the 1880s had come to a dramatic end. Markets shrank, trade dwindled, wages fell and employment evaporated. The government slashed expenditure and curtailed public works. Hundreds were thrown out of work and carefully accumulated savings necessarily dissipated. Conditions were worse in the winter of 1894 when hundreds were out of work. Beggars appeared on the streets for the first time in a generation. In 1895 the Launceston Benevolent Society gave help to 1300 people in one week. Government relief was tardy and grudging. Distress produced intellectual turmoil. Unequal land distribution was debated and schemes for settlement and taxation were canvassed at meetings and from the pulpit. In an address to the Anglican Synod in 1894 Bishop Montgomery asked why the rich attended church while the poor stayed away. He urged his clergy to study sociology and get in touch with the masses.[22] Catholic Bishop Delaney declared that the strikes were wild, rough, untutored protests against 'greed which denies justice . . . and privileged strength which refuses concession and conciliation'.[23] Tasmania's first labour newspaper, the weekly *Tasmanian Democrat*, appeared on the streets of Launceston soon after the crash of the Van Diemen's Land Bank. 'The great citadel of capitalism,' announced its first editorial, 'must be razed to the ground, and upon the ruins thereof will arise a nobler and grander structure.'[24] It called for the complete nationalisation of land and capital and the obliteration of all class distinctions. Lectures by English Fabians were reprinted along with quotations from the American land reformer Henry George and Karl Marx. Hobart's comparable radical paper the *Clipper*, was first published in April 1893. Modelled on the Sydney *Bulletin* it was red-covered, irreverent and republican.

The labour movement was crippled. By the end of 1892 six of Hobart's unions had collapsed or had abandoned the council. Two years later only four remained. In Launceston only one union, the Typographical Society, survived. Eight Hour Day marches were staged until 1895 but the number of marchers grew smaller each year. The *Mercury* thought the final march an 'eloquent epitaph'.[25] The council finally closed its doors in 1897. The union movement did not recover from the impact of strikes and depression for another decade. During that time attention turned to politics and to the task of winning political power. The fruitful alliance of the 1880s between union leaders and liberal middle class politicians did not survive the turmoil of the 1890s.

There was a changing of the guard in parliament during the late 1870s and early 1880s. Most of the politicians who had fought the governors and debated the merits of transportation had died or retired. Links with the convict era were lost along with the personal antagonisms and family alliances that had their origins in that troubled era. Only four members of the lower house of 1882 had been elected before 1870. A period of great instability in the 1870s came to an end in October 1879 with the formation of a coalition government led by the able, native-born and locally educated lawyer W. R. Giblin. It held on to power until 1887. In 1882 the government reformed the contentious Master and Servants Act and two years later Giblin introduced the first significant extension of the franchise in 30 years, increasing the number of eligible voters for the Assembly by 10 000 or 60 per cent. It was not manhood suffrage. The percentage of adult men who could vote increased from 52 per cent to 76 per cent. As it was conservatives feared the outcome, and even the reformers worried about enfranchising anyone else. After a conversation on the matter with Giblin, his friend and confidant, J. B. Walker noted in his diary:

Safeguards in the bill – six months contin. employment.
   Manhood suff. Pecul. Dangerous here – a few good mines bring over some thousands of miners – nomads.[26]

During the debate on the Bill the Liberal member for Central Hobart called for a division on manhood suffrage. It was defeated by 26 votes to one, but what was significant was that Giblin and Walker, the two well-educated middle class Tasmanians, were worried about a flood of men from the mainland, not the surviving community of ageing emancipists. For the island this was a significant change.

A number of motives fired the desire for extension of the franchise. Like their contemporaries in many parts of the world, island liberals felt they were living at a time of great change. They were aware of what they considered to be Tasmania's political backwardness. The liberal *Tasmanian News* published a long list of franchise qualifications in 26 other countries and the mainland colonies, the editor observing how 'terribly behind' Tasmania was, 'even with respect to some of the old countries in Europe'.[27] The colony, he thundered, needed a revolution 'and at that a radical one, and assuredly we have need of a Danton in every village of the island'.[28]

For all the references to political developments overseas Tasmanian reformers were more engaged with their own distinctive history. The 'honoured name' of Thomas George Gregson was 'still often on the lips of men in Hobart'.[29] The limited franchise was directly related to the legacy of the convict system. In a letter to the *Tasmanian News*, a correspondent who signed himself simply as 'Native' declared that the native born were 'the unfortunate hand and feet fettered white slaves of their native land'.[30] At public meetings orators called for the 'badge of inferiority' to be removed from the working class. To the surprise of many erstwhile supporters Fysh took up the cause of franchise reform. In a letter to the *Tasmanian News* he explained why he was 'in advance of his former self'. He had, he declared, been 'liberal to the backbone' before he left England, 'but coming to a country with peculiar institutions' he did not advocate his opinions. In a veiled reference to the passing of the old hands he declared that 'the population has aged, the youth become men, the industries which attend upon railways and mining with accompanying activities have developed, and a new age in our political history has been turned'.[31]

Between 1887 and 1900 Tasmanian politics merged with the Australian mainstream. The reforming ministries led by Fysh (1887–92) and by Braddon (1894–99) were similar to those that held power in many parts of Australia in the late 19th century. Like them they were made up of middle class liberals who were interested in political reform and who were comfortable with expanding the power of the state in the provision of services and the building of infrastructure and in intervening in the economy to create a balance between the interests of labour and capital. Tasmanian liberals were aware that the island had been left behind for a generation and that the desired agenda of necessary reforms had already been carried through in one or other of the mainland colonies or in New Zealand. They frequently consulted earlier legislation passed elsewhere. They sought to introduce what, at the time, were well-known innovations such as triennial parliaments, payment of members, abolition of plural voting, legalisation of trade unions, proportional representation and votes for women. There was also a group of reforms aimed at the workplace – legislation for shorter working hours, abolition of child labour, inspection of factories, mines and machinery. It was this generation of politicians who carried Tasmania into the federation. The two Liberal governments drew their electoral strength from the two cities and the small farming districts and, by the late 1890s, from the mining electorates on the west coast. They had the support of the *Tasmanian News* and more qualified approval of the labour papers that emerged in the 1890s. They also drew great strength from their close alliance with the trade union movement as it expanded and grew in confidence in the 1880s. Very few of them had the prescience to see that it was the labour movement that would supersede them early in the new century.

The leading figure in Hobart's reform movement of the early 1880s was the young Andrew Inglis Clark who was native born (in 1848) and locally educated.

The son of Scottish migrants who established a flourishing engineering business, Clark trained as both an engineer and a lawyer. By the time he was in his mid 30s he had already emerged as a major intellectual figure in Hobart and the leading light of a group of like-minded radicals who founded the short-lived but intellectually impressive monthly journal the *Quadrilateral* in 1874. Along with their concern for reform at home to dispel the lingering convict legacy and undermine the continuing power of the landed families and their urban allies, the young intellectuals had

Image 9.2: Andrew Inglis Clark. (*Source:* Archives Office of Tasmania.)

ecumenical interests and cosmopolitan sympathies. While proud islanders they were anything but insular in the sweep of their imaginations. Clark read widely, consuming books on literature, history, political economy and jurisprudence. Familiar with contemporary British thought, above all with the writing of John Stuart Mill, Clark also developed a life-long interest and expertise in the history, jurisprudence and politics of the USA. He also venerated the heroes of Italy's struggle for national unity and independence. On his first visit to Europe he made a pilgrimage to the tomb of the great nationalist Mazzini in Genoa and was moved to write a long poem celebrating the heroes of the Risorgimento. A portrait of Mazzini hung in his richly stocked library, which the visiting English politician and man of letters C. W. Dilke declared to be the best private library in the colony and 'one of the best in the southern hemisphere'.[32]

Clark was to play a major role in the campaign for federation but his most important contribution to Tasmanian politics was as a great reforming attorney-general in the Fysh and Braddon governments. Clark's industry and legal expertise were such that he was without doubt one of the most creative liberal politicians in the Australian colonies in the closing years of the 19th century. He sought to carry through reforms that would expunge the last remnants of what he called the colony's 'peculiar history', the memory of which legislators had 'striven rather to perpetuate than to outgrow'.[33] He endeavoured to centralise the police force and to reset the balance of taxation to favour the poor and the small settlers as against the large land owners. As did many earlier Tasmanian reformers Clark saw many of his Bills rejected or amended in the Legislative Council. He also spent innumerable hours reforming and consolidating the Tasmanian statutes. During his time in office he drafted and introduced to the parliament a total of 228 Bills on a wide range of subjects, although he had only a small staff to assist him. Tasmanian legal historian S. Petrow argued that

In the number and range of Bills he saw passed into law, he can lay claim to being the most capable and productive nineteenth century Attorney General, not just in Tasmania, which he certainly was, but also Australia.[34]

Clark's most enduring reform was the introduction of proportional representation for the 1896 elections in Hobart and Launceston. Known ever since as the Hare-Clark system, it was eventually adopted for the whole of Tasmania in 1909 and has remained in place for the past century. It was a bold, innovative move on Clark's part. Proportional representation had been frequently discussed in liberal circles in Europe and the USA during the late 19th century, but he was the first person to carry out a practical application of the method in the English-speaking world. Given the universal spread of various forms of proportional representation during the 20th century it can quite legitimately be seen as a development of global importance.

Like other intellectuals in politics Clark was mocked for being too earnest: he lacked easy demotic humour, talked at listeners rather than to them and spent too much time attempting to explain abstract ideas to disinterested audiences. But when it came to electoral reform he was able to successfully employ Liberal ideology to deal with abiding local problems. From the first years of the local parliament there had been contention about the best way to elect the five members returned in Hobart and the three in Launceston. The division of both cities into single member electorates became a continuing subject of Liberal agitation because it allowed many wealthy property owners to cast multiple votes and tip the balance in tight contests. This was of immediate concern to Clark who was a member for Hobart for 11 years and a close confidant of the members of the Trades and Labour Council who pressed for electoral reform. He had been an advocate of proportional representation for a long time. As a young man he read Thomas Hare's 1859 book, *The Election of Representatives*, and advocated the cause of proportional representation in an 1874 article in the *Quadrilateral*. It had a double appeal to Clark. He declared that 'it was the only system that gave real and perfect representative government', in that it gave every voter the same electoral power while allowing minorities to retain a voice in the mass electorate.[35] Clark must have been aware of the symbolic importance of introducing an electoral system that sought to give every voter a mathematically equal share of political power in a society that had been founded on convict labour and for a generation after the end of the system strove with anxious endeavour to deny the vote to all but a minority of the emancipists.

Clark's other great political role was as an early and consistent supporter of Australian federation. He had advocated the cause as a young man in the *Quadrilateral* as the most certain way to assert Australian nationalism and throw off the burden of British institutions, or, as he termed it, 'for disencumbering ourselves of the institutions and customs derived from feudal Europe and which have proved themselves unsuited to Australian democracy'.[36] His most important role was played while representing Tasmania in two major intercolonial meetings – the conference of 1890 and the convention of 1891, which drafted the first federal Constitution. With C. C. Kingston from South Australia and S. Griffiths from Queensland Clark worked on the draft later submitted to the full convention. Clark had prepared his own model Constitution in advance of the meeting of the convention and his wide understanding of federalism in general and the US Constitution in particular enabled him to exert a significant influence on the eventual federal constitution, especially in relation to the structure of the Senate and the important role of the High Court. He did not attend the Federal Conventions of 1897 and 1898 but played his final role in the creation of federation by shepherding the necessary legislation through the Tasmanian parliament in July and August 1897, just prior to his resignation from the Braddon ministry on a matter of principle, which was the letting of contracts without his knowledge. He was appointed soon after to the Tasmanian Supreme Court, which removed him from active political life. By then many other Tasmanians had taken up the federal cause and the colony voted strongly in favour of joining federal Australia in the referenda of 1898 and 1899.

Tasmania surrendered much of its independence to the new federal government, as did the other colonies. Even so, the 20th century continued to provide problems that were distinctive to the island and which related to its history and geography.

10

Federation and War

The 20th century opened auspiciously for the island. Nature seemed to bestow her blessing. In Hobart 1 January 1901 was 'a perfect, fragrant, exhilarating Tasmanian day'.[1] After 53 years of rule by governors and Colonial Office officials, and a further 44 years as a self-governing colony, Tasmania entered the new Australian federation having voted in favour of the amalgamation by very large majorities in the two referenda of 1898 and 1899. The issue was stoutly contested but the outcome was never in doubt. Being the smallest and poorest of the Australian colonies Tasmania had nowhere else to go and could not seriously consider independence and isolation. Tasmanian politicians had shown interest in some form of federation when the issue was discussed in the 1850s and John West had written a series of distinguished essays promoting the cause. Throughout the second half of the century island leaders sought, with little success, to promote free trade among the colonies and were deeply frustrated by the protectionist trade policies of Victoria, which was the natural market for Tasmanian produce. Union with Victoria was often promoted, particularly among the Launceston business community, which characteristically looked north across Bass Strait rather than south to Hobart. As in the rest of Australia the momentum given to the cause by the Federal Convention of 1891 faltered; legislation endorsing the draft Constitution passed the House of Assembly but was shelved in the Legislative Council. A Tasmanian delegation attended the Federal Convention of 1897–8 in Adelaide, Sydney and Melbourne and island politics sprang into life with the approach of the federal referendum in June 1898.

The Federal League launched the most creative and sustained political campaign seen in Tasmania since the Anti-Transportation Movement of the 1840s and 1850s. It was led by young business and professional men, who carried the cause into every district in the island. Some small communities had never had political meetings before the federalists raised their standard in small local halls. To fortify the message 20 000 copies of the League journal, the *Federalist*, burdened the bags of postmen all over the colony. A federal medal was struck: it bore the words 'Australian Commonwealth: 3/6/98' and was topped with red, white and blue ribbons. The league banner carried the message 'Tasmania Expects Every Man To Do His Duty'. Sympathetic poems were written, songs composed and sung. The poet W. H. Dawson composed a song, 'The Sons of Australia', which was sung with great enthusiasm at Federal League meetings:

> From the north to the south, from the East to the West,
> The cry has gone forth, from our strife let us rest!
> One in race, one in speech from the shore to the shore,
> The barriers that part us shall part us no more!
> With faith for our guide,
> We shall not be denied,
> And the sons of Australia stand fast, side by side.
> We will tarry no more – we have tarried too long;
> We have dared to be weak – let us dare to be strong!
> Be the cost what it may, we will break from the past,
> One in race, one in fortune – a Nation at last!
> With faith for our guide,
> We will not be denied.
> And the sons of Australia stand fast side by side.

As referendum day approached large rallies were held and local bands led marchers through the main streets in Hobart and Launceston. Speakers appealed to high ideals and to national destiny but mixed their message with the material enticements promised to many sections of the community by the opening of mainland markets. In his history of the federal campaign, leading advocate Herbert Nichols caught the nature of the crusade in a much quoted reference to the federal campaigner who addressed his audience with the assorted exhortation:

Gentlemen, if you vote for the Bill you will found a great and glorious nation under the bright Southern Cross, and meat will be cheaper; and you will live to see the Australian race dominate the southern seas, and you will have a market for both potatoes and apples; and your sons shall reap the grand heritage of nationhood.[2]

Such compelling rhetoric notwithstanding, the federalists faced articulate opposition. There were many farmers, manufacturers and merchants who feared free trade and the consequent mainland competition. Conservatives looked askance at the more radical politics of the bigger colonies and the certainty of manhood suffrage in federal elections and female suffrage foreshadowed in South Australia. There was genuine concern about Tasmania's fate in a federal union. The highly influential statistician R. M. Johnston predicted that the projected financial arrangements would ruin the colony because it was far more dependent on customs duties, which were to become a Commonwealth preserve, than the other colonies, which had been far more successful than island governments in imposing direct taxation. Johnston's case was a powerful one and foreshadowed Tasmania's continuing struggle in the federation to achieve a better financial deal. It shook the confidence of influential politicians, including the father of federation in Tasmania, A. I. Clark, who withdrew from the campaign and refused to recommend the draft Constitution. Clark's friend and city librarian A. J. Taylor produced a poster urging working men to vote no because the proposed Bill placed the colony 'in a position that every man having a love for his country and a regard for his fellows must shrink from accepting'. Taylor explained that he was a federationist at heart and a proud native-born Tasmanian and that he had no object in view but the 'welfare and the good of the land of my birth'.[3] Leading Hobart businessmen set up the Federation With Safety and Advantage Association, which advocated a vote against federation. The *Tasmanian News* declared in sympathy:

Federation under the present Bill will cost the people of Tasmania a heavy income tax, a heavy land tax, a surrender of our customs duties thus giving away the security of the State and preventing the carrying out of public works to develop our latent industries, for no federated state can borrow on the same favourable terms after she has surrendered a great portion of her security.[4]

But the newspapers in Launceston, Burnie, Devonport, Zeehan and Queenstown campaigned strongly for federation. In the *Church News*, Anglican bishop H. H. Montgomery declared that he longed 'to step on to that loftier plateau, and see those nobler visions'. He hoped his fellow Christians would see their way to accompany him.[5] The editor of the paper wrote that amid the prevailing uncertainty the Christian position was to 'trust to the final working of the great principles of good embodied in the Bill'.[6] The problem was that were Tasmania to stay outside the federation it would never again receive such advantages, including equal representation in the Senate with the much larger states and a guarantee of five House of Representative seats regardless of the movement of population. On the night before the referendum J. B. Walker noted in his diary:

After getting over the first shock of Johnston's figures and realising that Federation was in many respects a leap in the dark, thoughtful men looked at the other alternative – what would be Tasmania's position if she was left alone outside the federation with United Australia bonded against her. Slowly many of us came to the conclusion that this was a worse alternative than the possible financial risk of joining.[7]

The uncertainty about public opinion was swept away as the results came in the following evening. Tasmania had come out overwhelmingly for union. Just over 80 per cent voted yes although less than half the eligible electors had bothered to visit the polling stations. It was a low turnout, although similar to that in the mainland colonies. But the large majority that was chalked up for the colony as a whole cloaked the striking regional variation that enables us to understand Tasmania's diversity, despite its small size, and also the factors that helped determine the reasons why people voted one way or the other. The yes vote varied widely across the 29 electoral districts from as high as 98 per cent to a low of 39 per cent. Of the farming communities of the northwest coast, 97 per cent voted yes. Free trade with the mainland was a powerful incentive to the small farmers. The two local newspapers, the *Emu Bay Times* and the *North-West Post*, urged the cause of union; local Federal League branches were also active. The mining towns of the west coast were equally in favour of union. The economic motive was strong but sprang from quite different circumstances. Every item of food and clothing was imported at great expense and free trade promised lower living costs. The *Zeehan and Dundas Herald* remarked that miners whose children were 'going without fresh meat and butter, and eggs and bacon owing to prohibitive prices', needed little added incentive to opt for federation.[8] The mining towns had strong ties with the mainland. Many miners had followed their luck across Bass Strait and in travelling time Melbourne was as close as Hobart, which was only accessible by sea. The promised democratic franchise was attractive to men who were still without the vote in local elections. The certainty of a white Australia appealed on the minefields where anti-Chinese sentiment was strong. A leading union official came out in favour of federation in order 'to prevent the undesirable shipment of these most objectionable people in our midst'.[9] Launceston and its hinterland were strongly pro-federal, with only 6 per cent of electors voting no. Launceston had significant historic ties with Melbourne and the three local papers, the *Launceston Examiner*, *Daily Telegraph* and the *Tasmanian Democrat*, all came out strongly in favour of federation. There were vigorous Federal League branches throughout the region. Launceston had given support to intercolonial cooperation from the days of the anti-transportation meeting and the movement for annexation to Victoria had been centred in the town; there was also the long standing, almost ancestral, rivalry with Hobart, the importance of which would diminish inside the federation.

Opinion in and around Hobart was evenly divided and the most striking fact about the vote was the difference between the north and the south. In the 17 electorates in the north only 6 per cent voted no; in the 12 southern districts the figure was 37 per cent. Of electors in and Hobart and its suburbs 40 per cent voted no. The three local papers were united in their opposition to the draft Constitution if on precious little else. The conservative *Mercury* insisted that it contained 'gross, open, palpable absurdities' and objected to the democratic franchise.[10] The *Tasmanian News* foresaw impending insolvency, while the radical *Clipper* believed the Constitution was not democratic enough. Free trade threatened numerous local manufacturing enterprises that made furniture, soap, candles, biscuits, shoes and clothing. Meat and grain producers in the old settled districts also feared mainland competition and followed the lead of the capital. The threatening prophesies of the Federation With Safety and Advantage Association had an impact, as did Clark's equivocal attitude, which Walker thought would lose the cause 1000 votes.[11] But the reluctance of many people in the south to embrace federation could not stop the momentum in favour of union.

The result of the second referendum in 1899 was a foregone conclusion. The critics moderated their message or retreated into resigned silence. The no vote dropped dramatically. Minds had changed or opponents of the cause stayed home on polling day. The Federal Leagues maintained their momentum. In Launceston 3000 supporters crowded into the Albert Hall on the eve of the referendum. Even the *Mercury* changed its tune and declared in an editorial:

> The discussions which have taken place since the last poll was declared have not lessened but increased the ardour for union . . . for in the end there can be no loss – the need for union makes all else seem mean and trivial in the extreme.[12]

Like all the local papers the *Mercury* greeted the nascent nation and the new century on 1 January with banner headlines: 'New Era', 'One People', 'One Destiny'. The celebrations merged events to mark the coming of federation with the traditional ringing in of the new year. Patriotic decoration abounded and the Parliament House in Hobart was lit with what was considered a spectacular display of gas lights. Federal iconography, including the names of the states and the slogans 'One people: one flag' and 'United Australia', sat beside such religious and royal statements as 'praise God, honor the Queen, long may she reign'. Jubilant members of the Federal Leagues partied for the last time before formally dissolving their branches. In Hobart and Launceston local volunteers were able to fire their artillery pieces, a rare experience for them, and in both cities fireworks splashed colour across the clear sky. There was general agreement that Hobart's best fireworks had come from a visiting German gunboat. The more pious went to church to seek the blessing of the Almighty for their families and for the new nation; the church bells pealed out across the night. Yet the nation's very newness caused some indecision about how the event should be commemorated. The claims of empire, nation and state each exerted their attraction. The Union Jack was flown everywhere, yet while there must have been many of them readily to hand in the community, there was nothing new about it; nor was it distinctively Australian. The *Clipper* lamented that the Tasmanians were not 'proclaiming nationality' because they continued 'under the British Flag'.[13] But other islanders saw the achievement of federation as a building block in the evolving structure of empire, the *Launceston Examiner* urging its readers, with a remarkable passage of imperial rhetoric, to support the cause:

We cannot all be a Clive, a Rhodes, or a Hastings, but we can be Empire builders in a humble way, and each elector will have an opportunity of doing his share in consolidating the foundations of the British Empire.[14]

But as everyone was aware the ceremonies to mark the inauguration of the Commonwealth were mild and half-hearted when compared with the ecstatic celebrations that had greeted the raising of the sieges of Ladysmith and Mafeking in South Africa just a few months before and were therefore fresh in everyone's mind. The *Mercury* observed that many people, though enthusiastic at heart, did not know how to decorate suitably. The occasion, the writer argued, was not 'patriotic in the recent sense and it did not seem that the Union Jack could be aptly used again as the keynote of effect. Nor could the patriotic mottoes be set out again appropriately.'[15] A number of questions present themselves. In retrospect the two events, federation and the war in South Africa, were not equal in importance. The war has largely been forgotten, federation remains and the roots of the movement for union go deep into Tasmania's colonial past. The first problem to confront then is why the small, poor colony at the bottom of the world was involved in South Africa at all. Such an engagement would have seemed highly unlikely to contemporaries at any time in the years leading up to the outbreak of war in 1899.

The military had been an obvious presence in the colony during the early colonial period and the last British soldiers were not removed until 1870 causing lingering concern about convict insurrection. Old colonists regretted the loss of a tangible link with Britain and referred darkly to the departure of the Roman legions from ancient Britain. Defence was a low priority in the depressed colony and the part-time citizen soldiers, the 'volunteers', were not effectively organised until the 1880s when there were about 1000 officers and men in units based in Hobart, Launceston and on the northwest coast. But volunteering was little more than a hobby and there was never enough money for large scale manoeuvres; even ammunition was often scarce. It was a popular amusement to mock the pretentions of the colony's tinpot soldiers. Not that Tasmanians were unaware of the great events in their world – the Indian Mutiny, the Crimean War, the American Civil War and the Franco-Prussian War – but until the telegraphic cable was permanently established in 1869 news was always weeks, even months, out of date. Like other Australian colonists the Tasmanians were ambivalent about their isolation from the wider world. While some people felt distance kept them safe others fretted about their lack of security. Every now and then war scares rippled through the community. Anxiety about a Russian squadron sailing into the Derwent in 1885 created a momentary panic and the more anxious families packed cases and made plans to retreat into the interior.

More portentously, Tasmania was drawn into the debate of the 1880s about the future of the empire and the contending forces of separatism and integration. Branches of the Imperial Federation League were set up in Hobart and Launceston in 1888. Meetings and debates were held and membership reached 300 by March 1889. It was a very respectable organisation that gained the allegiance of the Anglican bishop, several judges, leading politicians, professional men and business leaders. Yet for every person attracted to the idea of closer ties with the empire there were others who were hostile to the idea. The working class organisations showed no interest in the project. Tasmanian patriots were openly hostile, as was publically illustrated at a league meeting in Hobart in June 1889 during which opponents of the cause only narrowly failed to pass an amendment rejecting the imperial dream. The overwhelming objection of speakers on that evening was that imperial federation would be the means for Britain to continually embroil Australia in her quarrels. Edward Ivey, a friend of Clark, argued that if Australia was permanently united to Britain 'it would be the means of the Mother country continually embroiling her in her quarrels'. Ivey insisted that Australia should be allowed to work out its destiny 'untrammelled by Imperial complication'. Trade union leader Hugh Kirk asked rhetorically: 'Was there any necessity for the Colony to be implicated in European wars? Why should Australia be made to pay for the wars of England?' Another dissenter 'strongly objected as a colonist to being mixed up with the wars of England'.[16] In a debate in the following year Taylor provided a more detailed objection to the imperial project because closer connection with the Mother Country 'would certainly tend to involve the Colonies in wars not of their own making'.[17] The opponents' fears of closer union with Britain were realistic and prophetic. Within 10 years young men from all the Australian colonies had marched off to fight in Britain's war of conquest in South Africa. The reason why is a tangled tale.

The Boer War was very much the project of Secretary of State for the Colonies Joseph Chamberlain, a fact that increased the likelihood of colonial involvement. The conflict was controversial and faced strong opposition within Britain and in the wider world to such an extent that during the war Britain became unpopular and isolated. Chamberlain decided that he needed the support of the settler colonies – Canada, New Zealand and Australia – but to have its full political value the offer of assistance had to appear to be spontaneous and the initiative of the colonists themselves. To arrange the matter Chamberlain had at his disposal the governors of the colonies and the commanders of the colonial armed forces, normally, serving British officers. What was needed was an offer of troops from one colony that would be sufficient to spark the spirit of intercolonial competition and emulation. And so it turned out. The Queensland premier, without parliamentary approval, offered a small force and slowly over the following weeks the other colonies felt obliged to fall into martial file, often with some reluctance. Initially, there was no strong public support for the involvement. The Boer republics, small and landlocked, were a long way away. They could never in the wildest flight of imagination be seen to be a threat to Australia. Still, there was some sympathy with the Boers who, language apart, had strong similarities with Australia's rural pioneers. Attitudes to race were virtually interchangeable. Very few people knew anything about South Africa although in mining communities there were often links with men who had gone to work in the goldmines on the Rand. The treatment of the foreign miners – *Uitlanders* – by the Transvaal government was a major purported reason for intervention; hostility was whipped up by a ruthless propaganda machine controlled by the fabulously rich mining magnate Cecil Rhodes and his associates. In Australia there was a degree of hypocrisy in the rising concern for the Uitlanders, who fared far better in the Transvaal than did British subjects from India, Singapore and Hong Kong in the Australian colonies.

Braddon's Tasmanian government found itself obliged to join the larger colonies in offering a small contingent. One incentive to send troops was provided by the fact that Tasmania alone among colonies had not sent a military contingent to Queen Victoria's diamond jubilee celebrations in 1897, a disgrace that royalists had not forgotten. When the matter of troops was discussed in parliament there was some pointed criticism of the venture although the debate was poorly reported, as Tasmania lacked a *Hansard* or any other official record of parliamentary speeches. There was some sympathy with the Boers, serious doubt about the need for a Tasmanian contribution, suggestions that food would be a more appropriate export than inexperienced soldiers and arguments that the money being sought by the government would be better spent on local defences. Much of the comment was sensible and sceptical. When it came to the division, the government had its way by a vote of 18 to 11, though that was scarcely a ringing endorsement for such an unprecedented venture. Once the contingent of 80 was chosen, trained and kitted out, the doubt and scepticism were flushed away in a flood of sentimental imperial rhetoric. At the official inspection of the force before they boarded the train for Launceston, Acting Governor J. S. Dodds observed that the event was 'certainly a unique one in the history of the Colony'. Britain had accepted Tasmania's services 'not because she needs them, but much as a loving parent accepts with proud feelings a service of affection and devotion from an offspring'. The volunteers had done more than this, however; they had 'given an object lesson to the whole world of the homogeneousness of the great Empire to which you belong'.

Dodds brought his speech to a crescendo when he read a telegram, said to be from the old queen herself, thanking the people of Tasmania for the 'striking manifestation of loyalty and patriotism in their voluntary offer' to send troops to cooperate with the imperial forces. It was acts such as these, Minister for Defence G. T. Collins declared, that 'bound us to the British nation'.[18] Local poet W. H. Dawson produced on cue a patriotic poem titled 'Tasmania's Gift' to mark the occasion:

> To prove our love complete
> Once again the ancient spirit stirs
> Go then, our own! And remember well
> What trust in your hands is laid;
> Let dauntless, courage tell;
> What men in our isle are made!
> Prove to the world we have kept the strain
> Of the old true blood.[19]

The excited enthusiasm of the milling crowds who watched the small band of soldiers march off to war was far outreached by the spontaneous public reaction to the dramatic events in 1900 when the tide of war began to turn against the initial brilliant successes of the Boer farmer army, which caused a loss of British prestige and morale. The two dramatic occasions were very similar. Ladysmith and Mafeking had been surrounded by the Boer army but held out against the siege until they were eventually relieved by the imperial forces. Their relief aroused enormous excitement throughout Britain and the white settler colonies. Tasmania joined with gusto in the general exultation on 3 March when news of the relief of Ladysmith was telegraphed through and on 21 May when similar messages about Mafeking arrived. On both occasions the events were announced by the firing of guns from the batteries on the harbour. The guns crashed through the sleep of the whole town at 4 o'clock on the morning of 3 March but boomed out across the Derwent more conveniently at noon on Saturday, 21 May. On both occasions people poured out into the streets. They milled around in ever-changing groups talking, shouting and singing patriotic British songs. Impromptu groups held small spontaneous marches back and forth around the streets. Every union jack in the town was unfurled and those without one brought out ribbons, towels and sheets in red, white and blue. The excited hubbub continued for hours, well into the succeeding night. Alcohol, often drunk in multiple toasts, kept the enthusiasm alive, mollified hoarse throats and justified excess. A *Mercury* journalist wandered through the crowds who were marching up and down 'carolling joyously all the way'. Each countenance 'bore the imprint of fine exultant thankfulness'. Grave men of business, elders of repute in various seemly circles lost their accustomed 'dignity of demeanour and deported them selves like street boys'. Moody and reserved men became 'as brisk as bees and open as sunlight'. One reveller excitedly shouted for all to hear: 'Man, this is the glory of war.'[20]

Public enthusiasm for the war never again reached the heights of the first months of 1900. Local newspapers carried extensive war news provided almost entirely by British news services, none of which could be considered to be objective. Soldiers' letters home were also often published. While Hobart's *Clipper* made a brave attempt to provide a different view of the war, doubt was continually elbowed away by the many other occasions that brought out crowds and drew forth pro-imperial rhetoric. The contingent that marched away in 1899 was only the beginning. Two hundred men followed them in three batches in February, March and May 1900, another 250 in April 1901 and 300 between March and May 1902. Over 850 Tasmanians fought in South Africa, a commitment that would have seemed totally improbable to the politicians who voted to send away the first small party in October 1899. Each contingent that left Tasmania was officially farewelled and every returning group was feted when it arrived home. The declaration of peace in June 1902 followed the established pattern of public celebration. The volley of canon shot from the local battery announced the cessation of hostilities. Milling crowds carrying flags and ribbons flocked into the streets and listened to triumphal rhetoric. School children were given a half holiday and many businesses closed for the day. Twenty-four soldiers did not come home to receive their hero's welcome, but twice that number arrived back with imperial medals of one sort or another, including two of the only five VCs awarded to Australians troops. Monuments were erected in many towns or, more humbly, photos of local men mounted in elegant frames were hung in small town halls. In Hobart the base of the most important memorial was opened on the public domain by the Duke of York in July 1901, watched by local dignitaries considered important enough to be within earshot of the royal visitors and their entourage. The duke declared that such memorials were not only a tribute to the dead but also to that 'living spirit of pride of race'. Is not this sentiment, he asked his eager listeners,

which has given, yes, and will give again, your brave contingents and has made even death easy to their gallant comrades whose names will be engraven, not only on the monument you raise, but in the hearts of their loving fellow countrymen, of pride of a common heritage, and of a fixed resolve to join in maintaining that heritage, which sentiment, irresistible in its power has imposed and united the people of this vast Empire.[21]

At the turn of the century it was still possible to relish the excitement and the glamour of conflict and Tasmanians fell in love with war in 1900, a dangerous liaison in the long run. Tasmanians like their fellow Australians came to believe that their young men had a special talent for soldiering. They were all dash and daring-do. But during those years of the Boer War Tasmanians also showed an intolerance of dissent that had not been obvious before. Critics of the war, called pro-Boers, were routinely condemned. The few meetings called to criticise the conflict ended in uproar and violence. In January the editor of the *Clipper* James Paton was campaigning for the forthcoming state elections. He called a meeting to hear an address by the young New South Wales Labor politician W. A. Holman, a known opponent of the war. After 20 minutes the stage was stormed by a hostile crowd, including sailors from a visiting British ship. Holman was knocked down, beaten, and then punched again as police escorted him from the hall, actions applauded as manifestations of laudable patriotism by the conservative press. Paton's subsequent meetings were similarly broken up and he had difficulty finding anyone willing to act as chairman or even to move motions for fear of being branded a Boer sympathiser.[22] As in the other parts of Australia there was remarkably little dissent given the fact that in Britain itself the war, though initially popular, was opposed by many of the leading liberal politicians, intellectuals and artists. There was little colonial disquiet about the causes, morality or legality of the war. There was also none of the outrage that emerged in Britain about the tactics in the final phase of conflict with the burning of farms, destruction of livestock and the incarceration of Boer women and children in concentration camps where over 20 000 of them died. Had he not been sitting on the Supreme Court bench Clark may have provided the kind of moral leadership given on the mainland by people such as the academic G. A. Wood or the liberal politician H. B. Higgin. Clark made his attitude to the war clear in an unpublished essay, 'The Future of the Australian Commonwealth: A Province or a Nation?', written, it seems, soon after the end of the conflict.[23]

Clark clearly felt that the war had borne out his fear that the tie with the empire would stunt Australia's development and condemn it to provincial rather than national life. At the very moment that the federal union was consummated the Australian colonies or states became more deeply involved with the empire than at any time since the achievement of self-government in 1856. The contrast between the imperial celebrations in March and May 1900 and those for federation in the following January was apparent to everyone. Australia's enthusiasm for the war evoked pleasant surprise in Britain. Tasmania's Agent-General in London, P. O. Fysh, observed that

Reports of the loyal rejoicing in Tasmania – second to none in the world on the various successes as to British Arms – have been greeted here with the greatest pleasure, and in some restricted circles by a surprise that Tasmania had any common cause with Imperial interests.[24]

The single most important lesson learnt in Britain was that Australia had shown a surprisingly uncritical support for the empire and that it had chosen to express its loyalty with military, not purely diplomatic, support, and asked little in return beyond the ritual gratitude of royalty, praise from the top brass and a brace of British medals. It was, as Fysh realised, a welcome display for a Britain that had a chronic problem of military manpower given the strong domestic resistance to conscription. Support in future wars was now expected. The Duke of York had said as much in Hobart when he looked forward to the time when Tasmanians would once again deliver up their 'brave contingents' to die in Britain's wars.

For all the imperial fervour it was federation that brought the most significant changes to the island. There was a flurry of activity to rearrange and reassign government departments and their staffs between the state and the new federal bureaucracy. Construction began on the first federal building, an imposing Customs House, on the waterfront. Herbert Nichols, the leader of the federal cause, reflected on the impact of union in 1913, writing that

The realization of their oneness with their brethren all over the Continent across Bass Strait has given Tasmanians an outlook so broad and tolerant as to frequently cause astonishment amongst new arrivals. The phrase 'othersiders' has disappeared.

The past is no longer lamented; the man in the street of Hobart (once called Sleepy Hollow) now talks of the future, and points proudly to the hundreds of new houses which are being erected in every direction.[25]

Federation also brought full manhood suffrage to Tasmania, an end to plural voting and, after 1902, the even more contentious innovation of votes for women. It was a reform that had been advocated in a limited form by Giblin in the 1880s and by Clark in the 1890s. It had been forcefully promoted by the Women's Christian Temperance Union, which, with branches in the two cities, 14 country districts and over 300 active members in 1896, became the largest and best organised women's organisation in the colony. During that year female suffrage was accepted by the House of Assembly by a significant majority but as was so often the case with progressive reform, was rejected in the Legislative Council, one member declaring that the measure would 'destroy that chivalrous feeling of men towards women', and that they would lower themselves by 'dabbling in the dirt of politics'. It would be the 'worst thing that could happen to woman, pure woman'.[26] Commenting on the measure the president of the WCTU, Mrs Blair observed:

Much ignorance and prejudice still remains against the measure, especially amongst women who are content to live for their own interest, satisfied to go down to their graves without having made a single creature better or happier outside the narrow circle they call 'home', but which is really self... These are women who do not want to vote; they take no interest in the burning questions of the day... The persistence with which certain men oppose women's advancement forces one to the conviction that they are desperately afraid that if we have our way we shall make the world too good for them to live in.[27]

The adoption of female franchise for the federal parliament in 1902 forced the issue in Tasmania. The same reform was adopted for state elections, reluctantly so in the Legislative Council, where one member declared that the relevant federal legislation was 'absurd and ridiculous'.[28] And so, in the federal election of 1903, Tasmanian women voted for the first time, making them global pioneers in this regard. Fewer qualified women voted – just over 34 per cent – less than men at 54 per cent. At one mining town on the west coast a 70 year old woman walked 5 miles along a rough road in the rain to cast her ballot.[29]

Involvement in federal politics hastened change in Tasmania: the first 10 years of the new century saw a complete recasting of the way the game was played. There was a move towards more permanent political organisation among the three main forces – conservative, liberal and labour – culminating in a genuine three-way contest in the 1909 state elections, which resulted, as it did in federal politics, in the destruction of the Liberal Party, which was caught and destroyed in the conflict between the Labor Party and the conservatives. The rise of labour was undoubtedly the most remarkable development in a decade of dramatic change and while it had been prefigured by events on the mainland after 1890 it still unfolded in Tasmania in its own distinctive way.

The first federal election saw two decisive developments. For the first time the vote of the west coast mining communities, greatly enhanced by manhood suffrage, impacted on the overall result. Two members were returned almost solely on the miners' vote. Union leader Dave O'Keefe won a seat in the Senate and the extraordinary US showman King O'Malley won second place in the race for the House of Representatives just behind the former Premier Edward Braddon. O'Malley had decided to launch his political career on the west coast and stood unsuccessfully there in the Tasmanian elections in 1900. Totally irrepressible, he campaigned hard, enrolled voters in mine and bush camps and on street corners and won over an initially sceptical community with his cheek and gusto, a combination of the flowing rhetoric of a revivalist church meeting and the overblown advocacy of a frontier salesman. Tasmanian had never seen anything like him. But behind the calculated clowning was an astute mind and a strong commitment to innovative policies.

O'Malley joined the Labor caucus when he took his seat in the first parliament, was a cabinet minister in the Fisher government between 1910 and 1913, and again under Hughes in 1915 and 1916. His election and that of O'Keefe was a moment of jubilation for Tasmania's enfeebled labour movement. In his *Clipper* editorial James Paton exulted. The election, he declared, was a moment of 'gorgeous ecstacy and solemn joy'. Democracy, he cried,

has at last triumphed in Tasmania, triumphed as it never triumphed previously . . . The people have made a great leap forward and commenced to come into their own. We are living in the purple of the dawn, and somewhere ahead is the glory of the full day.[30]

Paton's full day did arrive. After a number of false starts the Labor Party established a permanent statewide organisation, the Tasmanian Workers Political League, in 1903 and at each election the vote bounded upwards. At the state election of 1903 the first three working men were elected. Jubilant miners forsook their homes 'and school children in the small town of Linda were given a half holiday'.[31] The Labor vote in federal elections rose from 16 per cent in 1903 to 33 per cent in 1906 to 54 per cent in 1910. The state election of 1909 was the most significant contest because it saw the electoral destruction of the Liberal Democratic Party, which had inherited Clark's traditions and was led by a protégée, Herbert Nichols, who had served his articles in Clark's office, and L. F. Giblin, the son of the 1880s premier and later leading economist. Despite having the support of the new liberal paper, the *Daily Post*, the party won less than 10 per cent of the vote and returned only one member. Giblin observed that the electorate had showed a preference for parties with extreme views and would drive men of liberal opinions either to the Right or the Left. There was no longer any political space in the centre of the electorate. Giblin joined the Labor party soon after, was elected in 1913 in the Hobart seat of Denison and became the economic adviser to the government of John Earle, which came to power after gaining the support of an independent in April 1914, just four months before the outbreak of war. It was a challenging time for the new government. No one had experience of government, the party did not command a majority in the House of Assembly and was opposed by a hostile Legislative Council.

War arrived suddenly and unexpectedly. If Tasmanians were interested in the wider world they were more concerned with the crisis in Ireland than events in central Europe. News of Britain's declaration of war reached Australia on 5 August; given the country's lack of external sovereignty it, too, was at war. Precautions had already been taken in Tasmania. Naval authorities took control of the port and the forts overlooking the harbour were manned. A German ship loading timber at Port Huon was commandeered and the crew taken into custody. Public servants met to express their loyalty and municipal councils passed votes of support at special meetings. But even at this heady moment there were dissidents. A local Labor Party branch passed a motion declaring its belief that all modern wars were 'waged for profit and not for patriotism' and urged workers of all countries to use their combined power 'to prevent the return to barbarism at present contemplated in Europe'.[32] But such dissent was uncommon during that first wave of enthusiasm for what many people believed would be a short and heroic war. Tasmania was set a target of 1070 recruits to be part of the first expeditionary force. Twice that many came forward, many from the west coast where unemployment was rising as a direct result of the war and the cessation of trade with Germany. Large numbers of willing recruits were rejected after their medical examination, many of them because of tooth decay, which was a Tasmanian characteristic. Many of the chosen were veterans of the Boer War; they marched away singing the heroic songs of that conflict. In her study of the period Marilyn Lake observed how

Railway stations in country towns became increasingly the scene of sad farewells. Accompanied by the district Brass Band, the men marched from the local drill hall to the station, there to bid their families what was often a last goodbye.[33]

The contingent marched through Hobart streets and sailed away on 20 October. The crowds sang 'Rule Britania' and a specially composed song called 'Goodbye Tassie'. As was the case in the rest of Australia, Tasmania was placing more than 1000 of its young men in the hands of the imperial authorities with little say on when, how and who they would fight. It was the ultimate act of faith. By the end of the war over 15 000 Tasmanians had enlisted and just under 13 000 embarked for active service, that is, 38 per cent of Tasmanian men aged 18 to 44 enlisted. Just under 2500 of them were killed.

The war was a long way away and until the beginning of the Gallipoli campaign there was little to report. What Tasmanians were able to read was heavily censored and designed to maintain morale. The community raised money for the war effort at concerts and fairs. School children joined in while their mothers became members of newly founded Red Cross branches or more informal groups of women who knitted and sewed, baked biscuits and wrote cheerful letters. In the Brighton municipality alone seven Red Cross branches raised money, made garments such as socks and shirts, collected old clothes for bandages and sent a huge variety of gifts to the soldiers. The branch in the Bagdad district had 43 workers who between them made 2612 garments and held 60 fundraising events in four years.[34] In Hobart Henry Jones' large jam factory took on extra workers to fill enormous orders for tinned fruit and jam. Throughout summer the smell of stewing raspberries wafted over the waterfront. But for many people the war added to the burdens of life. The mining industry was heavily hit. Mines closed and unemployment spiralled. The shortage of shipping had a serious effect on the island economy: it limited imports and frustrated producers who exported to the mainland and beyond. Unemployment rose into double figures and the cost of basic commodities rose rapidly. Patriotism could not ameliorate penury.

The incessant need for new recruits intensified tensions already emerging as the question arose as to who was bearing the heaviest burden imposed by the war. In the absence of conscription young men had to be persuaded to enlist. The Commonwealth government waged a constant campaign to encourage and to shame those who held back and who soon came to be derided as 'shirkers'. Patriotic busybodies took it upon themselves to confront young men and challenge them as to their intentions. They expressed outrage when they saw young civilians playing or watching sport or drinking, smoking and obviously enjoying life. As in other parts of the country loyal young women collected white feathers to send to men they believed were shirkers. To such zealots cowardice seemed the only possible reason for not enlisting. Patriotic employers tried to persuade their workers to enlist or face dismissal. In country districts the police called on the homes of young men and asked them about recruiting. In Brighton the local recruiting committee was given a quota to fill during 1916: 17 at once, and then six a month. A returned soldier was sent around the district to call on possible shirkers even though 140 local men had already enlisted and 60 more did so by 1918. Alexander estimated that only 24 fit, single men were able to withstand the inner urging of patriotism or the outward pressure of the local community. An old man in the nearby Richmond district related how a local landowner tried to make him and his brother enlist and sacked them when they rejected his overtures. He recalled:

We had been thinking about it Mr. Swan, but now you've done this, I wouldn't go and fight for you or your bloody property! You can take your bloody job and your bloody rifle and stick it as far up your bloody arse as it'll go!! I wouldn't fire a shot for you and if I did I'd shoot meself first![35]

The terrible impact of the war was more apparent in such small communities than in teeming, anonymous cities. In Richmond the large extended families farewelled sons, brothers, nephews and cousins, including five Kearneys, four Cooleys, four Smiths and three Barwicks, Bowdens, McKenzies, Tillacks and Wrights. One family lost three sons. The war memorial outside the old Richmond Council Chambers lists 42 young men who died in the war. It was a catastrophic loss of life for a small rural community to sustain. But of all the historical sites in the town it is the one that today is totally ignored by the milling tourists who walk along the main street to learn about Tasmania's heritage.

The tension and the anxiety in the community was displayed in many ways. The temperance movement stepped up its campaign to clamp down on the liquor trade and persuaded the government to hold a referendum to coincide with the 1916 state election. A substantial majority voted to enforce 6 o'clock closing on hotels and taverns the better it would seem to underline the solemnity of the era but giving rise to endless stratagems to circumvent the curfew. While shirkers were harassed, foreigners were spied on, gossiped about and reported to the authorities. German immigrants of long standing and of faultless citizenship were abused, sacked from jobs

and had property vandalised, even when they avoided imprisonment. A highly successful German farming community in the hills
near Hobart had the name of their district changed from Bismark to
Collinsvale. There was an endless outpouring of invective about the
putative characteristics of the so-called Hun who was, by nature,
violent, brutal and cruel. Still more political tension emerged within
the labour movement, greatly exacerbated after the Easter Rising in
Dublin in 1916, reactions to which divided families, congregations
and communities There was also the conflict between the trade
unions and the political movement, particularly during the early
war years when a cautious Labor government led by John Earle
showed scant regard for the more contentious planks of the party
platform and refused to give preference to unionists in government
jobs.

The latent tensions burst into uncontainable conflict following
the decision of Labor Prime Minister W. M. Hughes who, given
his inability to win over a majority of the party or his own colleagues who had control of the Senate, put the issue of conscription
to the people in a referendum. It gave rise to one of the most bitter and divisive political campaigns in Australian history. Tasmania
did not escape the anger and bitterness that forced the community
into two irreconcilable camps dividing husbands and wives, siblings and long term friends. It was almost impossible to find any
middle ground whereon to stand. There was no compromise available between the stark alternatives of a continuation of volunteering
or of compulsory military service. Each side questioned the other's
integrity, honesty and patriotism. Pre-existing divisions relating to
class and religion were ripped apart in the intense campaigning.
Extremists on both sides found for the first time, willing listeners
and new followers. Conscriptionists detected an underlying plot
by the Catholic Church, masterminded by the detested Archbishop
Mannix, to undermine the empire in league with Irish republicans
funded by German gold. Union leaders detected a desire in Hughes'
heart to use conscription to crush the union movement and to introduce cheap foreign labour, thereby destroying the White Australia
Policy. The prime minister's increasing authoritarian use of special
war powers granted him by the Constitution increased the hatred
he evoked. The point of no return was reached when Hughes led his

supporters out of the Labor Party and formed a coalition government with his erstwhile conservative opponents. In Tasmania the long term parliamentary leader, Jack Earl, resigned from the party declaring it was a worse enemy than the Hun. Shortly after, he was appointed as a senator and supporter of the Hughes government.

The pro-conscription cause was supported by all the leading figures in the professions, the business community and the churches, including many of the Catholic clergymen. All the major newspapers supported Hughes with the exception of the labour paper the *Daily Post*. It also attracted the increasing body of returned soldiers who helped disrupt the meetings of the anti-conscriptionists. Regardless of the cause, meetings were chaotic and speakers often drowned out by the shouting of opponents. Passions were too great to allow for quiet deliberation and orderly argument. When the results were counted the conscriptionists had won but not by the margin that might have been expected given the organised support for the prime minister. The margin of victory was 10 000 – 48 000 yes votes to just under 38 000 no votes. Tasmania's yes vote was the strongest in Australia, but when a second referendum was held in 1917 the yes vote fell away, declining by just under 10 000. The majority for yes was fewer than 400 votes. Still, the vigour of the labour movement's opposition to conscription could not cloak the loss of electoral support at the federal and state levels and the growing ideological tension between traditional supporters and radicals enlivened by calls for direct action and those who were inspired by the revolution in Russia. Meanwhile the dramatic events in Ireland deeply troubled Labor's Catholic heartland.

11

Between the Wars

As did people all over the world Tasmanians greeted the armistice that silenced the guns on the Western Front with relief and thanksgiving. For some there was the sweet taste of victory and vindication of personal belligerence; for the many families with young men still overseas it brought benign relief from abiding anxiety. The community celebrated in what had become by 1918 routine ways, with church services to thank the almighty for the confirmation of Allied righteousness and civic meetings at which public men repeated what had become much-eroded rhetoric. Audiences sang the national anthem and 'Rule Britannia', expressing yet again Tasmania's loyalty to the king. Returned men were feted and children were given a holiday to help reinforce the magnitude of the moment. But all was not well with the world. Russia and Eastern Europe were in turmoil. Chaos threatened in all the lands trapped in the wreckage of the ancient empires of Hapsburg, Hohenzollern, Romanoff and the Ottomans. US President Woodrow Wilson talked of a league of nations; his preeminence intimated that the British empire itself was about to be eclipsed. The dramatic events in Ireland were followed more closely in Tasmania than those in any other part of the world and widened even farther the divisions first opened up by the rebellion of 1916 and the following referenda about conscription. To the many empire loyalists the Irish nationalists were traitors who deserved execution. To families of Irish extraction they were patriots seeking no more than the rights of small nations that had been proclaimed over and over again in wartime rhetoric or the self-determination promised to the world by Woodrow Wilson.

Tasmanians hoped that with the end of the war they would see better times. The war had been accompanied by reduced living standards, poverty and industrial strife. While there was much optimistic talk about the future the island was dogged by difficulties, which had their origin well back in the 19th century. Peace renewed the attention that had to be given to domestic problems, some of which were related to the war. The returned men had to be reabsorbed into families and community, found scarce jobs and settled on farms. But the more difficult problems were old ones. There was no longer an anxious looking back to the era of chains and the lash about which there was now an embarrassed silence but there was the problem of isolation and dependence on expensive and often disrupted shipping, the continuing difficulty of slow growth and persistent loss of people by migration, compounded by the difficulty of financing the government exacerbated by continued resistance to new taxes in the conservative Legislative Council. Touching everything else was the sense of being left behind combined with a deep attachment to place that often affected members of the diaspora as well as those who stayed at home.

One of the immediate problems arising from the war was the visitation of the so-called Spanish influenza, which had swept the world in 1919 killing as many as 20 million people. The virus first became apparent in Australia late in 1918, probably carried by returning soldiers. Tasmania watched with anguish as the epidemic spread on the mainland. The delay in it crossing Bass Strait enabled authorities to make advanced preparations, including establishing isolation hospitals in Hobart and Launceston and setting aside schools in other communities. During the early months of 1919 Tasmanians prided themselves in remaining free from the epidemic. But with the onset of winter there was a severe outbreak of ordinary seasonal influenza which caused anxiety about the killer strain to intensify. When the first cases were confirmed panic set in, a *Mercury* reporter observing that chemists' shops were besieged by anxious customers seeking medicines. Traditional remedies soon sold out, as did thermometers. People working in public positions wore face masks and anyone coughing or sneezing was carefully avoided. Doctors' surgeries were besieged with the ailing and the anxious. Schools were closed for two months and church services could only be held in the open air. It is thought that as many as one-third of the population contracted the disease during a seven week period and 171 of them died. One unexpected result of the epidemic was the attention focused on the depth of the poverty in the poorer parts of Hobart leading to important developments in public housing policy.[1]

A more enduring problem was the return of the soldiers from overseas and the desire to recognise their service. Once the marches were over and the speeches delivered, jobs fit for heroes had to be found in a depressed labour market. Tasmania had agreed during the war to participate in a federal–state scheme to settle soldiers on the land, a policy that combined the ideas of reward, therapy and economic development, so a board was established to select suitable land and find the ex-soldiers willing to become small farmers. Tasmania found itself tangled up in problems common to all Australia. Small farming was never an easy option. There was always the problem of determining how big a selection was required to allow for the achievement of self-sufficiency with modest industry in a reasonable period of time. The answer to that problem differed from state to state, even district to district. And then there were the associated difficulties of finding markets that would provide a return to cover the cost of production. There was as well the additional problem of soldiers with no farming experience, who, even when advised by officials, found they had no talent for or even desire to continue with the arduous, plodding work. War service probably rendered success less, rather than more, likely. Many men had come home with wounded bodies and troubled minds. Tasmania had a further difficulty of its own. There were no large reserves of Crown land with potential for development. Much of the land required was purchased on the open market, a venture of such an unusual scale that it drove up the price of rural land. Even as the difficulties mounted and angry and disappointed veterans walked off their selections it was still difficult to admit how bad things were. The mystique of the returned hero militated against rational and timely assessment. The scheme ran into a multitude of difficulties all over Australia but the failure was more complete in Tasmania than anywhere else. For the ex-soldiers a strong sense of entitlement clashed with economic reality. At a large protest meeting held at Penguin in April 1926 the majority of speakers 'deplored the treatment being meted out to men who had been prepared to sacrifice so much to ensure the freedom for their country, and it was claimed that they should be given a much fairer deal'.[2]

At the end of the 1920s, when there was an overall assessment of the scheme, it was found that there had been 1976 aspiring settlers, just under 40 per cent of whom had failed to succeed as farmers. The total loss to the state was £1.3 million, an enormous amount for a small struggling economy.

The labour movement, both unions and party, felt the force of the currents of change more emphatically than any other local institution. Two quite distinct developments disturbed accustomed patterns of thought and behaviour. The dramatic events in Ireland encompassing rebellion and repression had a direct impact on the Catholic community and necessarily, too, on the Labor Party and its electoral standing. For many Tasmanians the issue was clear: support for Irish independence implied rejection of king and empire in whose cause so many young lives had been sacrificed. Growing left wing radicalism added to the turmoil. In Europe and the USA unionists were attracted to the idea of direct action initiated by large consolidated organisations, and ideally the so-called One Big Union, no longer dependent of compromising politicians. The Russian revolution gave even greater emphasis to the need for and desirability of direct action. Activists all over the world were exhilarated by Lenin's call for global insurrection. For a few years labour leaders in Tasmania toyed with the idea of radical transformation. In a speech on the Domain in Hobart in 1921 the parliamentary leader of the party, later premier and eventually Conservative prime minister, J. A. Lyons declared:

The time has arrived when a momentous decision must be reached quickly whether the old order of affairs would prevail in the future as in the past...The distinction between wealth and poverty was daily growing more marked.

There was more poverty, more misery, more suffering, more privations...

There would be injustices and strikes while the present system of capitalism remained...The world is on the threshold of a complete change in the social system.

The time has arrived in Australia when the old order of affairs must go.

As the historian of the early labour movement M. D. McRae observed, never before had a local labour politician advocated such militant views.[3]

The electorate was unimpressed by such radical ideas or by the constant conflict between the party and the trade unions. The war and the conscription campaigns undermined the political support that had been gradually mobilised between 1901 and 1914. The decline of support was most clearly seen in the Tasmanian vote in the six federal elections between 1914 and 1928. In 1914 Labor received 52 per cent of the vote in the House of Representatives and won seven of 11 available seats in the two houses. In 1917 the party failed to win a seat, a result repeated in 1919 and 1925. Of 40 seats contested in five federal elections between 1917 and 1928 Labor won only three. But in 1923 the party returned to government in the state parliament in unusual circumstances although lacking a majority in the House of Assembly due to conflict between two competing conservative parties that resulted from the emergence of a local branch of the new Country Party, which had won the balance of power in the elections of 1922. Lyons formed a minority government, and then went on to win the election in 1925 and govern until 1928. It was a repeat of the situation facing the Earle government in 1914 with a minority on the floor of the House and hostility from the Legislative Council. Lyons proved to be an effective manager of a difficult situation, developing good personal relations with his opponents and adopting the mildest of measures crafted to win general support. The exigencies of the situation in 1923 and 1924 help explain the caution and conservatism of the administration but equally important was the start of Lyons's slow drift from young radical to elderly conservative and United Australia Party prime minister from 1932 to 1939. In her reminiscences Enid Lyons observed how the young Irish republican became a devoted monarchist and turned sharply against his earlier belief in socialism. She recalled an event of great symbolic importance that had occurred some time in the 1920s,

when the older children had begun to read beyond the limits of school requirements, I had suggested that we cancel our subscription to the *Australian Worker*, journal of the A.W.U. to which he had been devoted all his adult life. I thought it too bitter in its denunciations, far too intolerant and biased in the expression of its views. I did not want the children to cut their political teeth on a diet tinctured with the poison of class hatred. Joe had acquiesced. He agreed that we could not teach them love and hate together. If religion mattered at all, it mattered in every department of life.[4]

It is unlikely that Lyons had much time for thought about political philosophy during his years as premier. He was forced to engage in a persistent struggle with purely local problems that dated back more than half a century. After the war Tasmania entered into a period of depression as deep as that which had haunted the island in the middle years of the 19th century. Once again there was that nagging sense of being left behind by the larger, more prosperous states on the mainland. Hundreds of Tasmanians, usually young people in the prime of life, the women in the middle of their child bearing years, left the island, often with regret and with tears in their eyes, and settled elsewhere. The Tasmanian diaspora grew larger every year. So despite a high local birth rate the population stagnated yet again with a level of growth far below that of the other states. Many of the established industries stood still either through lack of investment or of initiative. The postwar slump in metal prices forced the closure of established mines and threw men out of work. West coast communities faltered and never recovered their earlier dynamism. Geographical isolation continued to burden the economy. Industrial conflict on the waterfront in Melbourne or Sydney often had dramatic consequences leaving tourists stranded and goods backed up on both sides of the Strait. Federal legislation aimed at protecting local shipping infuriated Tasmanians because it prevented overseas ships servicing the island. More than ever before Tasmania came to depend on Melbourne from where both exports and imports were trans-shipped. Also, the state government was desperately short of money. The tax base was much smaller than was the case in the other states and the level of debt was cripplingly high, the result often of imprudent development of railway lines that never ran profitably. As a consequence Tasmanian services were far poorer than what was taken for granted in other parts of the Commonwealth, which added to the incentive to buy a ticket on the steamer sailing for Port Melbourne.

Many Tasmanians concluded that the main problem was the federation itself, that they did not receive a fair share of Commonwealth revenue or benefit from the tariff protection that supported the manufactures in the other states. Older people recalled the dire warnings about the financial dangers of the federal union presented by Johnston in 1898 and there were many serious discussions about the possibility of secession. The premier warned the federal government that Tasmania might be forced by financial stringency to withdraw from the federation.[5] The call for secession came from many directions during the 1920s, from community groups, industry associations and the major newspapers. The *Mercury* demanded the 'complete dissolution of the Federation', while the *Launceston Examiner* declared that Tasmania might have to become 'the Ireland of Australian politics'.[6] In 1925 a Tasmanian Rights League was formed; it demanded 'justice for Tasmania or secession'. Dissatisfaction with the federation had been apparent from the early years of the century. Delegations of local businessmen and politicians had made many journeys across Bass Strait to lobby federal ministers in Melbourne. Tasmanian members of the national parliament often suspended their party differences to support their fellow islanders. In the state parliament both sides of the House joined to support demands for more financial aid. Motions pressing the federal government for ever-more assistance passed unanimously. Visiting federal ministers were besieged by advocates for reform. Committees were established and royal commissions deliberated and pored over the relevant financial information. Tasmania managed to extract many concessions and, from 1912, special grants to assist the state's finances, but it never seemed to be enough to meet the budgetary shortfalls or alleviate the old and abiding sense of grievance about not being able to keep up with the mainland.

Advised by Giblin, at the time a senior Tasmanian bureaucrat, Lyons decided to prepare yet another report called *The Case for Tasmania*, which he jointly wrote with the young, able and ambitious attorney-general, A. G. Ogilvie.

The report followed well-worn tracks, outlined yet again island disabilities and demanded annual grants of over $500 000. The federal government responded by appointing a special investigator, Sir

Nicholas Lockyer, to assess the islanders' claims, which he generally upheld. He recommended an annual grant of $300 000 and an interest free loan of $1 million. It was not enough to appease Tasmania's appetite for federal assistance and agitation continued. The enduring dissatisfaction of the small states led to the setting up, in 1933, of the Federal Grants Commission to distribute the financial resources of the Commonwealth to provide for a greater degree of equality between the states or, as the Commission declared, to allow each state 'by reasonable effort to function at a standard not appreciably below that of other states'.[7] It was an important milestone in the history of federation and of profound importance for the faltering island economy. Tasmania's incessant nagging of federal authorities clearly played a part in the evolution of the new institution. More specifically, the Grants Commission was an initiative of Lyons, now Conservative prime minister, and L. F. Giblin, who had become the professor of economics at the University of Melbourne.

Having struggled with Tasmania's financial plight and the continuing resistance of the Legislative Council the Lyons government lost the 1928 election by a small margin to J. C. McPhee, who led his recently united Nationalist Party into office. But as other governments of the time found, it was a good moment to be in opposition as administrations everywhere had to deal with the ravages of the Great Depression, which dated from the collapse of the New York Stock Exchange in October 1929. But the Nationalist government showed surprising resilience and won a resounding victory in 1931, skilfully exploiting the deep divisions within the whole labour movement and the perceived incompetence of the federal Labor government of J. H. Scullin. Lyons' resignation from the government and the party in March 1931, just two months before the state poll, added to the problems of the Labor opposition now led by A. G. Ogilvie. But the deflationary policies pursued by federal and state governments, while shaped by the financial orthodoxy of the time, did little to ameliorate the impact of the depression, although Tasmania was more inured to economic malaise than the hitherto more financially robust mainland states.

The problems created by the depression dominated Tasmanian life until well into the 1930s. As a result of low prices and shrinking demand trade withered. Government revenue fell away, even after injections of money from the Commonwealth. Yet not everyone suffered. Men with permanent jobs may have been better off as a result of prices falling more sharply than wages. The poor and the unskilled suffered first and longest; they had few resources to fall back on when they lost their jobs. Unemployment was already endemic during the 1920s, but it rose dramatically in the late 1920s and the early 1930s, from 10.6 per cent in 1928 to a peak of 27.4 per cent in 1931. It returned to its pre-depression level in 1937. The government provided meagre assistance in the form of rations, and then put men to work to earn the dole. Private charities worked among the swelling ranks of the jobless providing second-hand clothing and footwear and setting up soup kitchens. But they could not escape the self-righteousness that went hand in hand with charity. The poor were expected to be deserving, deferential and humble, attitudes that did not commend themselves to the grandchildren of convicts. Further, to the concern of the respectable, many of the unemployed joined radical organisations where they heard from communist party members that they were blameless victims of capitalism. The contribution of the charities to the poorest families in the two cities was of great significance. The Salvation Army's soup kitchen in Hobart provided soup and bread every day to 250 families, including 1500 children as late as 1938 by which time conditions had much improved. But the assistance of government and of charities was never enough to ward off hunger in the short term and malnutrition in the long run. Reports from medical personnel who examined school children thought that over 10 per cent of children showed evidence of malnutrition.[8] As the depression dragged on, men who were fit enough were expected to work on relief projects or go into the country to help harvest crops such as apples, hops and berry fruit. Urban dwellers did not always appreciate the expectation to work long hours for little pay. One expressed his dissatisfaction in a piece of doggerel published in the *Mercury*, which ran:

> I don't see why the Gover'ment
> Should take me off the dole
> And send me pickin' rasb'ries

In some God-forsaken 'ole.
From early in the morning till
The black mags roost at night;
You've got to go flat out they say
To get your 'undred w'ight.
And seven bob a 'undred is
The price the blighters pay –
So what's the union going to do
About our eight hour day?[9]

The election of 1934 was a political watershed of great significance although no one knew it at the time. Like so many local elections using the Hare-Clark system the result was very close, the Nationalists narrowly outscoring the Labor Party in the popular vote. But after the distribution of preferences two left leaning independents secured the balance of power and gave the nod to Ogilvie, who became Labor's third premier. When he received his commission from the governor it was the beginning of a long period of political dominance that lasted without break for 35 years until 1969. Labor won 10 elections in a row, some of them with a commanding majority of the popular vote. The Tasmanian experience was remarkable but not unique. The parties in power as Australia climbed out of depression had long terms of office in several other states. This was true for Labor in Queensland and Western Australia and for the Liberal and Country League in South Australia. The foundation on which Labor's success was built was very much the work of Ogilvie who emerged as one of the most remarkable political leaders in 20th century Australia during his five years as premier before his premature death at 49 in 1939.

Ogilvie was born in 1890, the grandson of Irish Catholic convicts. His father, who died soon after his son's birth, was a successful and popular publican. Ogilvie received his secondary education at a Catholic college in Ballarat and graduated in law from the University of Tasmania. He was successful at the bar and was engaged in labour politics from an early age; at the age of 28 he won a seat in the House of Assembly in 1919. In 1923 Lyons appointed him to be attorney-general in his ministry but there is no doubt that he found it difficult to contain Ogilvie's driving ambition. He seized the opportunity to demand Ogilvie's resignation in 1927 as he sank into the mire of a complex scandal involving his legal firm. A royal commission was set up following allegations of improper dealing between the firm and the public trustee, an authority that came under the aegis of the attorney-general. Ogilvie's partner was found shot in his office. He had apparently suicided. The commission found that Ogilvie, while not directly involved in illegal practices, had helped hide the true state of the accounts. It cast a deep shadow of suspicion over his career. The Law Society tried, without success, to debar him from practice, and then he was found guilty of contempt of court as a result of criticising the royal commissioner. It was a setback that might have destroyed many careers, but Ogilvie bounced back and received a massive personal vote from the electors of Franklin in the 1928 election. Lyons departed for federal politics; despite his best efforts, he was unable to frustrate Ogilvie's drive to become the leader of the party.

There is no doubt that Ogilvie combined many of the attributes that contributed to political success. He was obviously able, had driving ambition and supreme self-confidence. He was also tough and ruthless, practising what the *Mercury* called 'the politics of push', and he had no time for the old Tasmanian establishment, a sentiment richly reciprocated. A lot of history informed attitudes on both sides of that divide. Eminent Tasmanian historian Michael Roe has suggested that Ogilvie, with his coarse egalitarian vigour, embodied much of the spirit of old convict Van Diemen's Land. Be that as it may he was a man who attracted epithet and adjectives. He was called the Trotsky of Tasmania, the stormy petrel of politics and compared with F. D. Roosevelt. Perhaps the most surprising assessment of his career came from the highly conservative *Launceston Examiner*, which conceded that Ogilvie had given the state a sense of purpose and helped it to overcome its feeling of inferiority.[10] He took the unusual step of not holding any portfolio but clearly watched over all of them, driving his ministers and senior bureaucrats to measure up to his own overwhelming sense of purpose. A necessary precondition of his success was to gain control of the party and the labour movement generally. He built up the party branches to overcome union recalcitrance, managed the media in a way not seen before in Tasmania and used the radio to directly address the electorate. They liked what they heard. The 1937 election was an Ogilvie triumph. He won a massive personal vote and there was a swing to Labor of just under 13 per cent, which gave the government 18 of the 30 seats in the lower house. This was the achievement that set Labor up for its long hegemony.

Ogilvie was one of that small group of political leaders of the 1930s who eschewed the orthodox economic thinking of the time which prescribed reduced spending and balanced budgets to deal with the depression. He sharply increased public spending, borrowed more money and expanded the role of government. Some of the developments he fostered were innovative, but more often they built on what previous governments – Labor and non-Labor – had previously initiated. This was particularly the case with the generation of hydroelectric power. His opportunistic brilliance was strikingly apparent during the 1934 election campaign. The incumbent Nationalist government had nurtured plans to develop a new power station on the upper Derwent River. The Hydro-Electric Commission had completed the necessary planning but its work had been kept from the public.

Receiving a leak from a sympathiser in the bureaucracy Ogilvie made the project a centrepiece of his opening campaign speech, leaving his opponent Sir Walter Lee floundering in his wake, complaining that Ogilvie had not behaved like a gentleman. But having won the election Ogilvie pushed vigorously ahead with what became known as the Tarraleah project. With abundant loan funds work got underway with a large workforce, often suffering from the arduousness of the work and the inhospitable climate on the alpine Central Plateau. The scheme, which required sophisticated planning and engineering skills, doubled Tasmania's generating capacity. It was officially opened in February 1938.[11]

Nature provided Tasmania with all the preconditions for hydroelectric projects. The Roaring Forties brought abundant and reliable rainfall to the west coast and Central Plateau where it collected in hundreds of lakes scattered across the glaciated landscape. Deep narrow valleys provided dam sites and rivers tumbled down steep inclines onto the coastal plain with sufficient force to drive turbines. In the late 19th century a power station on the South Esk River at Duck Reach lit Launceston's streets and several

Image 11.1:   Hydroelectric Generators at Tarraleah Power
Station, 1956. (*Source:* Archives Office of Tasmania.)

mining companies established their own plants. The island's potential attracted investors anxious to find sources of cheap power for
the new methods that used electricity in metallurgical processes. In
1910 a mainland company secured the right to build a power station at Waddamana to provide power for the production of zinc,

but when the company was confronted with the problem of raising sufficient capital it sold the project to the state government, which set up a new department and completed the project, which began generating power in May 1916. It was an opportune moment to have bulk power for sale. The war had created a problem of what to do with zinc residues left over from the complex ores mined at Broken Hill once the lead and silver had been extracted. Before 1914 the residues had been sent to plants in Germany. To add to the conundrum zinc was urgently needed in the production of munitions for the Allied war effort. After complex negotiations involving the Commonwealth government and large Melbourne-based companies the decision was made to establish a plant in Tasmania to use power from Waddamana to refine zinc from ore shipped in from Port Pirie. The contract with the government was signed in July 1916 and the Electrolytic Zinc Company began work on the site at Risdon on the banks of the Derwent in November under the direction of dynamic industrialist H. W. Gepp. When work began:

There was no fanfare; five men and a typist arrived at the site, which consisted of apricot orchards and paddocks of crops. Beside the river was an old inn, and here the office was set up. Occasionally a visitor would drop in for a drink, not knowing of the changes about to occur. A reaper and binder was put through the crop, and carts and drays began to deliver building materials.[12]

In January 1917 Gepp arrived with his selected team of US metallurgists, tests began and the first zinc was produced a month later. Overcoming an array of problems with the process, infrastructure and delivery of essential equipment, the plant was producing 100 tons of zinc a day by 1922. A key moment in the island's industrialisation was to see the mobilisation of labour and capital on a scale that had previously occurred only on the isolated west coast. Gepp also introduced his own distinctive form of authoritarian welfare capitalism. He fought against interference by the Commonwealth Arbitration Commission and by trade unions while providing subsidised medical and dental services, company housing, and social and sporting clubs. But it was a feudal rather than a friendly embrace and for that reason not always welcomed.

At much the same time Cadbury's was establishing its plant on a similar site on the river just north of Risdon. It, too, was attracted by the availability of cheap power, low land prices and a ready supply of labour. The Quaker families who controlled the company also introduced traditions they had developed at their British head-quarters at Bournville. At Claremont a garden suburb was built for workers, and clubs and societies subsidised. After the war British firms also invested in textile mills in Launceston. Kensall and Kemp, and Patons and Baldwin built large factories to weave and spin local wool utilising cheap power and abundant supplies of soft water. Both enterprises employed large workforces. This pattern was followed in the 1930s when the Ogilvie government attracted large paper mills to the island. Various companies had shown interest in Tasmania's forests and the availability of abundant electric power. In 1936 Ogilvie announced that Australian Pulp and Paper Manufacturers intended to establish a paper mill that would produce fine paper at Burnie using timber concessions in the hinterland. Production began in August 1938 and for the next 50 years the pulp dominated life in the town, physically and economically. By 1940 the mill was working 24 hours a day and employed 850 hands. In the south a paper mill was established at Boyer where eucalypts were used to produce newsprint. It began production in the early war years.

Tourism was another one of Ogilvie's interests. It had an even longer local history than the generation of power or the establishment of heavy industry. The desire to present an attractive image to the outside world was apparent from the earliest colonial years although the initial purpose was to attract settlers rather than travellers. Two themes were immediately apparent in promotional literature – the salubrious climate and the picturesque landscape. They were obvious selling points, the more appealing because they might divert attention from the hated stain of the convict system. Tasmania was promoted as a place rather than a society. Even so, to the perpetual disappointment of the island's promoters, attempts to attract migrants were never very successful until, with the development of steamships and railways in the late 19th century and the growth of a class of well to do would-be travellers in the burgeoning mainland cities, tourism came to be a distinctive pursuit. Visiting Tasmania became a serious option for families with a few weeks holiday and enough money to leave their own neighbourhood. The island's backwardness and slow pace of life became quaintly attractive to mainlanders; so, too, was the cool climate to a generation who still found the summer heat alien and oppressive. Tasmania's dank, fern-filled mountain glens and sparkling waterfalls became famous for over-dressed ambling, sketching and photography. Leaping trout lured adventurous anglers farther afield. The surviving relics of the convict past produced frisson among mainland visitors familiar with Marcus Clarke's best-selling classic *For The Term of his Natural Life* rather than the embarrassment still felt by locals.[13] For several decades in the late 19th century, Hobart's season in January and February attracted leaders in business and politics from Melbourne and Sydney to the better hotels and genteel boarding houses. They met and mingled with Tasmania's old established families.

The first attempt to set up a professional tourist organisation resulted from the initiative of Henry Dobson, Conservative premier between 1892 and 1894, and native-born son of one of the colony's most prominent professional families. In May 1893 he called a public meeting in Hobart to create a society to 'conserve, make known the numerous beauty spots of the island' and spread information about them and the climate of the island in order to 'attract visitors from all parts of the world'.[14]

The meeting created sufficient momentum to see the establishment of the Tasmanian Tourist and Improvement Association and the attraction to the island of a Thomas Cook's Tourist Agency office, the premier travel company in the empire. The association and the company produced new booklets and pamphlets; Cook's also provided an array of packaged tours that encouraged local service providers to raise their standards to an acceptable international level. In 1898 a Northern Tasmanian Tourist Association was established to emulate and compete with the older Hobart-based organisation. Operating with only a small government subsidy the reach and professionalisation of the associations was too limited to underpin a modern tourist industry. The state government created a tourist office in 1914, which was placed under the control of the Railway Department. So when Ogilvie came to power the importance of tourism was generally recognised, as was the necessity of direct government engagement with the industry. His contribution was to add his own dynamism and a keen appreciation of the importance of professional promotion. He worked closely with E. T. Emmett who he appointed director of the new independent tourist bureau established in 1934. Emmett was an irrepressible enthusiast for the Tasmanian landscape through which he had walked, skied and cycled for most of his long life. With the premier's energetic backing and greatly increased funds he established offices in the mainland cities and commissioned high quality posters and films, which were distributed confidently throughout the world. Gangs of unemployed workers were used purposefully to develop roads to service the industry, most famously the road to the summit of Mt Wellington. During the 1930s visitor numbers increased every year; on the eve of the war there was no doubt in anyone's mind about the importance of tourism for the Tasmanian economy.

During his period as minister of education in the Lyons government, and then as premier, Ogilvie was an advocate of wider educational opportunities. He gave strong support to the creative director, G. V. Brooks, who was in office from 1919 to 1945. Ideas that were foreshadowed in the 1920s came to fruition in the following decade. Ogilvie campaigned in 1934 for the removal of school fees and acted on the promise immediately. The most innovative reform during his five years in office was the establishment of centralised area schools in rural districts to replace a multitude of small, often one teacher schools, and to use buses to bring the children to lessons each day. After some initial resistance from country parents the schools became very popular, providing greater opportunities and at least some vocational and secondary schooling in districts where they had not previously been available. The first two schools were opened in 1936 and nine more were established by 1939. Ogilvie also appreciated the value of the university, which, however, remained a small impoverished institution until the 1950s. He worked closely with Professor of Philosophy and Psychology E. Morris Miller to introduce psychological testing in schools, but the most creative partnership was with the Economics Department as it had been throughout the interwar period. A series of talented academics gave expert advice to the state governments, including Giblin, D. P. Copland, J. B. Brigden, E. R. Walker and T. Hytten, who travelled overseas with Ogilvie and his ministerial colleague S. Gaha in 1935.

Many people have speculated as to what Ogilvie would have done if he had lived until retirement – the long term premier, the Supreme Court bench or federal politics. His legacy to the state and to the Labor Party was extremely important and the direction he had taken was followed by those who succeeded him, particularly Robert Cosgrove who took the premiership in December 1939 and held it with a short break for 20 years, winning six elections in a row. He came into office just a few weeks after the outbreak of war.

Tasmania's experience of war during the 1940s was very different from that which older islanders remembered of the First World War. Far fewer islanders died but the demands of modern war were felt at home in a way not known between 1914 and 1919. Thirty thousand Tasmanians served in one way or another, 16 000 overseas, including 200 women. Women also worked in the Land Army and many others were drawn into the areas of the economy drained of labour. An unknown number of islanders worked in the wartime industries on the mainland. Eleven hundred Tasmanians did not return: 700 died in the army, one-third of them while prisoners of the Japanese, most of them members of the 2/40th battalion captured on Timor. Three hundred airforce personnel lost their lives, more than half in flights over occupied Europe. One hundred and forty Tasmanian sailors went down with *HMAS Sydney* and *HMAS Perth*. While the loss of so many young men and women was devastating for Tasmania's closely knit extended families, the effect was not as great as the losses on the Western Front or at Gallipoli because the impact of modern war had been so unexpected among a community innocent of the horrors brought by the total war of the new century.

Like their fellows on the mainland Tasmanians had to come to terms with the vast expansion of the powers of the federal government, fortified by wartime regulation and used with determination by a confident, if anxious, Labor administration. The island's isolation was accentuated by the shortage of shipping and the dangers from mines and submarines in Bass Strait. Tasmanian officials had to constantly remind their federal colleagues of the need to maintain supplies of wheat, sugar, petroleum and the innumerable other articles not made on the island. The nighttime crossing of the Strait in the *Taroona* from Beauty Point in the Tamar's mouth to Port

Melbourne became an interval of anxiety in which there was always the fear of that vast explosion that would crash through the regular whip of wind and water. The Holyman family's Australian National Airlines flew regular flights over the Strait but seating was limited and expensive and several crashes in the 1930s had underlined the uncertainties of early aviation. The island's economy was boosted by wartime demand and the interdiction of supplies from overseas. Farmers, hindered by the shortage of labour, turned up pasture to produce vegetables and fruit. Their sons were often frustrated because the authorities thought them more use down on the farm than in uniform. Young city women joined the rural workforce after brief training and orientation courses. Over 900 Italian prisoners of war worked on farms and orchards bringing skills, cuisine and music from their peasant villages. New factories were built and manned to process tinned and dried fruit and vegetables. The mines on the west coast worked overtime to meet the demand and Launceston's textile mills won lucrative government contracts that required extra shifts and more hands. Munitions factories, which were established in several locations, drew in young women from home duties and domestic service. The university employed skills developed in the construction and maintenance of scientific equipment to produce high quality lenses and prisms. Under the inspired direction of Eric Waterworth 200 workers were trained to produce high precision articles of critical importance for the war effort that had before always been imported from overseas. Large scale building of wooden boats returned to the Derwent and the Tamar.

Anxiety about the war mounted with the Japanese attack on Pearl Harbour, which was followed soon after by the fall of Singapore and the bombing of Darwin. Preparations for a feared air attack intruded into everyday life. Industrial plants and fuel depots were camouflaged and defended by armed guards. Windows were papered over and lights cloaked with black fabric shades. Households were issued with large wooden scoops to dispose of incendiary devices and air raid wardens called on houses emitting any unnecessary light. Searchlights criss-crossed the night sky seeking the enemy planes that only ever came once. Young boys learnt how to recognise war planes from reproductions of their silhouettes. Trenches were dug outside offices and schools. Children trooped out in practice and were taught how to crouch down in the trench. More anxious or more energetic families built air raid shelters in their gardens. The port hosted warships of all sizes and when the US troop ships arrived unannounced Hobart was overwhelmed with thousands of khaki-clad, fresh-faced, white Americans. Local children were amazed when they were handed icecreams by young men at the end of a human chain that began at the counter where frantic shop girls tried to keep up with the unprecedented demand. Many families took young men in for meals. Some from the small towns of the midwest said they had never before seen a city as big as Hobart. The usual stories flew around of young women throwing themselves at the Yanks, of pub fights and the brutality of the military police. US officers from all services in elegant tailored uniforms took up all the rooms in the recently opened luxury hotel on Wrest Point.

But it was not the shortage of hotel suites that vexed Tasmanians; it was the rationing of such basic commodities as sugar, butter, tea, meat and eggs, as well as clothing and footwear. Ration books and their coupons became an essential complement to the shopping list. People made do with new, more sparing recipes, or old ones from meaner times in the past. Knitting and sewing and improvising kept families clothed. And there was a firm egalitarianism in it all – money could not buy you more unless you used the ever-present black market. Any display of unnatural abundance risked prosecution and social opprobrium. With almost no toys in the shops children made their own with scraps of wood, leather from old shoes, cast-off tins and tyres and rubber bands. They helped their families hoard paper bags, string and the increasingly rare silver foil. Jelly crystals took the place of lollies except when some saved sugar could be transformed into homemade toffee. Children were also asked to collect old aluminium pots and pans to send to Britain and even tins of dripping that every family carefully preserved. The lack of new cars and the strict rationing of petrol meant that many vehicles were put up on blocks in family garages. Tradesmen used horses and carts and almost everyone caught trams and trolley buses. Children took over the empty streets and played cricket, rounders and hopscotch and regarded the occasional car as an unwelcome intrusion.

The detailed controls exercised by wartime governments predisposed them to engage in postwar planning once the intimations of an Allied victory became more certain. The Tasmanian Labor government worked in parallel with its fraternal federal administration to both prepare for the demobilisation of defence personnel but also to plan for a world that would avoid the disaster of the Great Depression. Plans were put in place for the mass construction of houses, for new roads to cater for the anticipated return of the private motor vehicle, for further hydroelectric projects and for the retraining of the servicemen in schools and at the university. A new program of soldier settlement was launched with safeguards that, it was hoped, would avoid the failures of the earlier scheme. Like the federal government the Tasmanian administration made plans to ensure that full employment would be maintained, something that the war with its high expenditure and detailed economic planning had facilitated. The transition from war to peace was much easier in 1945 than it had been a generation earlier.

12

Postwar Tasmania

In the first few months of 1969 the Tasmanian government was the sole surviving Labor administration in the country. It had been in power since 1934 and had won 10 elections in a row. It was more enduring than any other government in Australian history. In that time three premiers – Ogilvie, Cosgrove and Reece – had dominated the political scene. They often had to deal with the wafer thin majorities delivered up by the Hare-Clark system, fractious critics on the Left and the Right within the broader labour movement and, as ever, the ancestral opposition of the Legislative Council. The May election produced a typical Tasmanian result. Labor outvoted the Liberal party by 7000 votes but both parties gained 17 seats. The balance of power was left in the hands of Kevin Lyons, son of Joe and Enid, who had left the Liberal Party to run as leader of the new and short-lived Centre Party. Lyons became deputy leader in a coalition led by W. A. Bethune, descendant of an old gentry family. The end of Labor's dominance reflected the dramatic developments that were taking place in Australia and in the wider world and which themselves grew out of the many changes that reshaped Western societies during the long postwar boom.

Tasmania became far less isolated during the postwar generation, a development welcomed by most islanders but regretted by some. Air travel became a common experience and by the 1950s returning travellers were no longer asked endless questions about what it was like to fly. Hobart's new airport at Llannherne was opened in 1956. The introduction of new vehicle and passenger ferries, beginning with the *Princess of Tasmania* in 1957, greatly increased the two-way traffic across Bass Strait. Melbourne, which offered sophistication and big city excitement, remained a promised land for young Tasmanians. Television, which arrived in Hobart in 1960 and Launceston two years later, was keenly taken up and by 1969 nearly 90 per cent of homes in the viewing area were connected. Tasmanians travelled more widely within the state itself; cars began to crowd the roads and motels and caravan parks proliferated. Children growing up in the 1950s were no longer able to commandeer the local streets for day long, albeit occasionally interrupted, cricket matches. Registered vehicles increased dramatically from 46 000 in 1950 to over 104 000 a decade later. The struggling railways found it even harder to operate profitably. Large losses every year dispirited the service and angered Treasury officials. Branch lines were closed and services curtailed. Passenger services struggled with the insurmountable problems of narrow tracks and mountainous terrain, the trip from Hobart to Launceston taking several hours longer than a comparable excursion by car. In the two cities the efficient and regular service provided by electric trams and trolley buses were deserted by a new generation in love with their cars; services and passenger numbers declined together. By 1968 trams and trolley buses were superseded in both cities by petrol powered replacements. Tasmanians walked less and less. Children were ferried to school in the family car. The traditional walk to and from the tram and to the corner shop became increasingly lonely. The clusters of local shops thinned dramatically as customers drove to new and larger establishments. The first supermarket opened in 1958. Drive-in cinemas were established on Hobart's outskirts, Launceston and the northwest coast towns.

Hobart and Launceston grew more rapidly in the postwar period than at any time since the 1880s but the expansion was on the ever-expanding outer fringes. Hobart spread out north and south along the banks of the river and across it to the eastern shore, development facilitated by the unique floating bridge completed in the war years and later replaced with the high arch Tasman Bridge. The once popular ferries that had serviced the eastern shore lost patrons and were taken out of service in 1963. Launceston grew away from the old city in three directions – south into the farmland in the valley of the North Esk and northwards along both banks of the Tamar. Immediately after the war most new suburb houses were built of weatherboard but increasingly the larger houses that superseded them were constructed in brick. The terrain surrounding both cities meant that most new subdivisions boasted wide vistas of river or mountain, or both. Hobart and Launceston, still small cities, were marked by strong class segregation. The citing of public housing in both cities after the war accentuated this characteristic as did the concentration of industry in Hobart's northern suburbs. As the suburbs grew Hobart and Launceston became more and more like other Australian cities despite their distinctive localities and inimitable history. Long periods of stagnation, even of decline, left an unmistakable legacy of old buildings that would have been replaced in more dynamic communities. Even the drafted plans for redevelopment were shelved due to lack of finance to carry them out. Old slums slated for demolition survived and eventually became sought after heritage neighbourhoods. The shabby became picturesque. Both cities had a unique stock of housing that included fine examples of every style fashionable in Australian domestic architecture since the 1820s and 1830s. Hobart's central business district retained many sandstone and brick buildings that were there in 1836 when George Arthur left the town. A survey of 1962–63 found that in inner Hobart there were over 2300 buildings that were built before the 1840s.[1] Almost one-quarter of the structures from that era remained standing. Launceston's streetscape was dominated by the stately Victorian buildings that dated back to the mineral rich era of the 1880s and the colonial churches still dominated the skyline overshadowed by only a handful of tall postwar structures. The more dynamic go-ahead decades of the postwar period also coincided with the emergence of a strong current of concern for Tasmania's unique heritage, which tempered the zeal for redevelopment. A Tasmanian branch of the National Trust was established in Launceston in 1960.

The postwar period was also unusual for Tasmania because it shared in the nationwide growth and prosperity instead of being, as in the past, an envious spectator of the other states' good fortune. Islanders still left; at the 1954 census 20 per cent of people born in Tasmania were living out of the state. But the overall population grew more rapidly in the late 1940s and 1950s than it had done at any time since the convict era, and for the first time since the 1880s more people arrived than left the state. What made the change manifest was that many of the newcomers were from overseas and that was a new experience for most Tasmanians. The lack of immigration for much of the time since the convict transports tied up at New Wharf meant that the Tasmanian population was remarkably homogeneous for a New World society. Most people were of British origin but their families had already been in the state for generations. There were small communities of Chinese families whose local progenitors had come to the tinfields in the northeast in the 1880s. There was a small number of people of German and Scandinavian extraction and a couple of prominent Greek families. But when the first postwar migrants arrived Tasmanians were often startled by the experience and became curious or hostile when, often for the first time in their lives, they heard foreign languages spoken in their streets and on their trams and buses. People stared at young, foreign men with unfashionably long hair wearing such exotic items as corduroy jackets and suede shoes. When migrant children turned up at local schools for their first day they were followed around the playgrounds by small, curious crowds. British migrants were exotic enough but in the late 1940s and early 1950s Tasmania received an unprecedented array of immigrants from all over continental Europe, including, in the late 1940s, a sudden influx of displaced people from Europe's refugee camps. Men from Poland, Germany, the Ukraine and the Baltic states arrived on contract to work on large engineering projects, particularly those of the Hydro-Electricity Commission in the Central Highlands and on the South Esk River near Launceston. The large multicultural communities who grew up near the work sites were a source of wonder and fanciful speculation in Hobart's monocultural suburbs. At much the same time Dutch immigrants arrived and established closely knit communities in several localities. But British migrants always outnumbered those from other parts of Europe and by 1961 over 12 000 had received assisted passages and settled on the island.

As in other parts of Australia Good Neighbourhood Councils were established in 1949 to assist in what was assumed would be the process of assimilation. But most migrant groups established their own institutions and in the late 1940s and early 1950s ethnic clubs were founded and club rooms opened where social ties were strengthened, friendships cemented and classes formed to teach language and culture to locally born children. Soccer clubs, scout and guide packs, dance troupes and choirs were founded. Churches were built by German Lutheran, Greek Orthodox and Italian Catholic congregations. Many of the immigrants who came under contract stayed on in Tasmania after their two year term but there was always a tendency for those with mobility to leave the island to join the far larger communities of countrymen and women in the mainland cities. It all added colour and diversity to a hitherto homogenous society but Tasmania was bypassed by the great wave of migration that, in the 1950s and 1960s, was transforming the country. While Tasmanians talked of their new cultural diversity Hobart and Launceston remained among the most monocultural cities in Australia. At the census of 1961 only 9 per cent of the population was born overseas and over half of them were from the United Kingdom. By then the mainland cities had twice the percentage of overseas born residents. Tasmania clearly had changed as a result of postwar migration but it had not changed as much as mainland Australia and that, in itself, added to island distinctiveness.

Tasmania became culturally richer in the postwar period. The impoverished condition of public libraries was outlined by an inquiry carried out in 1943 by an officer of the National Library. There were very few libraries in the country towns and those in the two cities were run down and impoverished. Responding to this dispiriting picture the government established the State Library of Tasmania in January 1944. Municipal libraries were established all over the state, each with its own small collections supplemented by regular exchanges of books from an extension service based in Hobart. The State Archives was also established by legislation in 1943 and tasked with the preservation of the state's treasure trove of records. In 1948 the Tasmanian Symphony Orchestra was established as a result of a partnership between the state government and the Australian Broadcasting Commission. The gala opening concert, held in City Hall, featured Tasmanian born pianist Eileen Joyce, and was broadcast nationally. At much the same time the government passed legislation paving the way for the purchase and restoration of the Theatre Royal, which had been lauded by Laurence Olivier and Vivien Leigh who played there during the Old Vic Company's triumphant 1948 Australian tour.

Adult education was another initiative in the immediate postwar years and from 1948 the small staff of the new board began to initiate a broad program of cultural and educational activities. But it was secondary education that experienced the greatest changes during the two decades after the war. The leaving age was raised to 16 in 1945 and an extra year added to the curriculum. The tripartite system of schools – academic, technical–commercial and modern – that streamed children once and for all by means of an ability test taken at the end of primary school was transformed. District comprehensive schools were established; they catered for all students in a given geographical area regardless of academic attainment. Streaming was to be implemented inside each school rather than between them. As a result new schools were built all over the state at an unprecedented rate. The four academic high schools in Hobart, Launceston, Devonport and Burnie were gradually run down and replaced with senior matriculation colleges that were designed to provide a bridge between secondary and tertiary education. At the time they were unique in Australia, but the retention rate of students to Year 12 remained low by national standards. In the immediate postwar period the university was small, poorly funded and inadequately housed in a few old buildings on a site overlooking the town and in temporary huts on a constantly muddy, disused rifle range near the river at Sandy Bay. More than any of the other state universities the Tasmanian campus was saved by federal funding that followed the *Murray Report* to the federal government in 1957. By then though, the university was embroiled in the Orr case, which elevated the institution out of its unsurprising obscurity but not in the way that any of its well wishers would have wanted.

Sydney Sparks Orr, a slightly built, quietly spoken Irish philosopher, was an unlikely figure to be swept up in a political and legal maelstrom of international significance. The background to the conflict was all important. Many of the academic staff were deeply and justifiably discontented with their working conditions and the high-handed way they were treated by the University Council. Neither their material circumstances nor the institution's administration accorded the respect that highly qualified academics might have reasonably expected. A decisive moment arrived when Orr and 35 colleagues sent an open letter to Premier Robert Cosgrove outlining the unsatisfactory conditions within the institution. The letter was published in the *Mercury* in October 1954 ensuring that university politics spilled out into the public arena. After that it was impossible to contain the tensions within the ivory tower. A month later the government set up a royal commission to investigate the contending claims and complaints. It was a humiliating development for the council and the administration, exacerbated for many by the experience of facing searching cross-examination under oath. This was particularly so for the academics who had to cope with the unrelenting assault of the combative senator and barrister R. C. Wright who was acting for the university. Conciliation was now out of the question. The council struck back at Orr and set up a committee to investigate four complaints that had been levelled at the hapless philosopher. Three of them were minor matters scarcely warranting investigation. But the accusation of sexual predation by Suzanne Kemp, one of his students, was altogether different. It was an accusation that whetted the public's salacious imagination that gave birth to titillating jokes, dirty ditties and scandalous fast-flying rumours. Everyone had an opinion on the matter but the true nature of the relationship was never definitively established.

Another turning point in this drama had been reached. Orr offered his resignation. It was refused and he was summarily dismissed. It was a fateful, intemperate decision suggestive of persecution and retribution. It also drew attention to a matter of the highest principle, which had far more purchase than the particular details of Orr's predicament. Individuals with varying opinions about the philosopher himself united on the question of academic tenure and their rights as highly skilled professional men and women. Orr pursued his case for wrongful dismissal in the Tasmanian Supreme Court and the High Court, without success. He gathered supporters from Tasmanian church leaders and from the wider academic community and in continuing to fight ensured that the growing audience was inevitably aroused by such a cause célèbre. For his supporters Orr had become a martyr, the victim of powerful forces within Tasmania's insular, self-righteous establishment. Orr suffered grievously, but so too did the university. The Australian Association of Philosophers imposed a ban on Orr's chair, which they maintained for 10 years. The Federation of Australian Staff Associations strongly attacked the university over its attitude to academic tenure. It was disastrous for the university's reputation. In 1963 the council offered Orr the sum of £16 000 and negotiated a new agreement that greatly improved academic tenure, set up a formal structure when cases of incompetence or impropriety arose and ended the situation in which academics were treated as servants of the council. Orr reluctantly accepted the settlement but died soon after, a broken man, at the age of only 52.

The 1950s and 1960s was a time of greatly increased spending on education but the bulk of Tasmania's generous loan funds went to the Hydro-Electric Commission or the 'Hydro', as it was called. It was the heroic age of what became known as hydroelectric industrialisation, which had been a central objective of all governments since the First World War but was especially associated with the Labor Party. The Earle government purchased the first power station at Waddamana in 1916 and Ogilvie campaigned in 1934 with a promise to build its successor at Tarraleah. As in so many other areas of policy Ogilvie surveyed and set the course that Labor governments followed for a generation. Cheap electricity had attracted industry to the state and appeared to be the panacea that would overcome the inescapable disadvantages of a remote location and a small domestic market. The expansive economic climate after the Second World War provided the optimistic conditions for the rapid expansion of generating capacity. Demand from industry and domestic consumers was increasing every year and was reasonably expected to continue. In 1944 the decision to build an aluminium smelter at Bell Bay at the mouth of the Tamar greatly increased the notional need for power and resulted in the building of a new dam and power station on the outskirts of Launceston. In 1946 A. W. Knight became the commissioner or managing director of the Hydro and remained at the helm until his retirement in 1977. A graduate of the University of Tasmania, Knight was an outstanding engineer and a man of great drive and determination. Under his direction the Hydro recruited a large cadre of highly skilled workers from a variety of disciplines, including 300 engineers. It had a greater concentration of expertise than was available anywhere else in Tasmania in either the public or private sectors. It was a formidable organisation by national, even international, standards and it had developed highly prized skills in the construction of dams and the transmission of power. By the time Knight retired the Hydro had built 26 power stations and 39 dams, electrical capacity had increased from 172 to 1515 megawatts and the workforce from 1000 to 5000, and in a small state such as Tasmania most people knew someone who worked there.

The Hydro received strong support from politicians on both sides of the parliament, particularly from Labor Premiers Cosgrove and Reece who ran the state from 1939 until 1969. Reece's embrace of hydroindustrialisation was so ardent that he earned the nickname 'Electric Eric'. Until the 1970s the Hydro was largely admired. In many high schools students spent weeks on projects with titles such as 'Power from the Plateau' and teachers were encouraged to take their classes on conducted tours of the dams and power stations. But there were always critics who were concerned about the lack of ministerial or parliamentary oversight of the Hydro's operations and a general absence of accountability. There was often criticism of the way in which it usually captured the great bulk of Tasmanian loan funds to the detriment of schools, roads and hospitals. There was also an abiding suspicion that the large industrial concerns were getting their power at uneconomic rates and being subsidised by increasingly electrified family homes. Frustration mounted because the details of industrial tariffs were always hidden away behind the rubric of commercial confidentiality. But as the historian W. A. Townsley observed:

A later generation grew up to criticise, scoff at and even denigrate the Hydro. To the people of the 1960s, particularly to those who grew up in the harder days of the 1930s, the Hydro was the pride of Tasmania, its greatest achievement.[2]

Criticism of the commission emerged in the 1960s as its engineers, surveyors and hydrologists searched farther afield for new rivers to dam in expectation of ever-increasing demand. A prolonged drought in the late 1960s, which necessitated power cuts, seemed to under-line the need for further expansion, but the problem was where to turn for new schemes. Until the 1940s the focus of development was on the water that ran from the Central Plateau in a southerly direc-tion in the Derwent and its tributaries. The next major development harnessed the rivers flowing north, which powered six stations on the Mersey, Forth and Wilmot Rivers. Water from the Great Lake was diverted northwards to drive the turbines in the underground power station at Poatina. It was when the Hydro made plans to dam the rivers in the little known country in the southwest of the state – the Gordon, the King and the Franklin – that sporadic dis-quiet about the Hydro's operations and ambitions intensified into a protest movement that changed Tasmania forever. In retrospect it was not surprising because interest in the wild mountains of the west coast was quite as old and equally deeply rooted as the desire for material progress.

Mountains were inescapable in Tasmania. The Wellington Range brought the alpine country to Hobart's back door. In Launceston the Ben Lomond Plateau defined the eastern horizon. Travellers between the two towns skirted the Central Plateau and the road to the west ran parallel with the wall of the Great Western Tiers. The settled districts from the Huon valley in the south to Circular Head in the northwest embraced the mountains like a cupped hand. The early settlers arrived with sensibilities attuned to the picturesque and walking in the mountains became a popular pastime.

The more adventurous gentlemen ventured farther afield but had usually been preceded by bushrangers, stockmen and hunters. John Glover climbed to the top of Ben Lomond and the second generation of colonial painters, men such as the colonial born W. C. Piguenit, ventured into the western mountains to sketch and seek inspiration from untamed nature. Pioneer photographers followed the same rough tracks carrying the heavy equipment and founding Tasma-nia's distinguished and continuing tradition of nature photography. Tasmania's distinctive history as a penal colony gave an added local fillip to the 19th century's romanticism. The purity of wild nature was juxtaposed with the depravity of the towns and the penal settle-ments. Colonial patriots shunned the tainted society and identified with the land with a concomitant fervour. Painting and especially

Image 12.1:   Photograph of Russell Falls taken by John Watt
Beattie. (*Source:* Archives Office of Tasmania.)

photography allowed a much wider audience to appreciate Tasmania's lakes, waterfalls and mountains. The scenic landscapes of men such as J. W. Beattie, who became Tasmania's official photographer in 1895, were widely employed in tourist promotion.

His images were used as postcards, glass plates for lantern slides and for six of the eight pictorial stamps issued by the government in 1899. The Tasmanians formed clubs to facilitate excursions into the mountains and to promote conservation. The Field Naturalist Club was founded in Hobart in 1904 and a Mountain Club in 1911. The government responded to the lobbying of the many walkers and the influential members of the Royal Society by creating the Scenery Preservation Board in 1915 and the gazetting of national parks at Mount Field and the Freycinet Peninsula in the following year.

The impending struggle between development and conservation was foreshadowed in the late 1930s when there was considerable opposition to the Hydro raising the level of Lake St. Clair, thereby flooding the beaches and drowning islands. But the questions touched on then re-emerged with great intensity with the growing public realisation in the 1960s that the Hydro's Gordon River scheme involved damning the Serpentine river and thereby flooding Lake Pedder. It was unique and for a growing number of Tasmanians a very special place although until the 1960s only visited by experienced bush walkers.

Its shallow waters covered an area of 9 square kilometres. On its eastern shore it was fringed by a unique 3 kilometre long beach of pale pink quartzite sand and was framed by a range of jagged peaks. There was general agreement that it was a beautiful place, even among those who supported the plans of the Hydro, and for that reason it had been incorporated as a national park in 1955. But even then the Hydro was already carrying out extensive exploratory work and building access roads into the area while the state government received special funding from the federal government for the project long before there had been any parliamentary consideration of it. Clearly, the Hydro was planning to flood the lake years before there was any public acknowledgement of what was to happen, confirming latent suspicions that it was able to commit large loan funds in whatever way it wished on the assumption that ministers and the parliament as a whole would retrospectively fall into line and rubber stamp whatever had long before been determined. By the mid 1960s public disquiet began to grow and the campaign to save the lake slowly built up momentum. It was 'initially polite, hesitant, hopeful that reasonable concerns would be addressed'. Letters from ministers and the Hydro responding to concerned electors were 'conciliatory, yet designed to mislead by a deliberate paucity of precise information'.[3] A South-West Committee, representing 12 interested community organisations, was established to lobby for an extended national park in the region. But the drive to undertake the project was relentless. Enabling legislation was approved by the House of Assembly but was held up by the Legislative Council which appointed a select committee to look more closely at the scheme. While the ensuing report expressed deep regret about the impending flooding of the lake, it nevertheless gave its approval and the Bill quickly passed. There was a general sense that the project was already too far advanced to halt its impetus.

The defeat of 'Electric' Eric Reece at the 1969 election brought little change. Both parties supported the Hydro and the policy of further expanding generation. The power shortages of that summer weighed heavily on the official mind. In his policy speech Liberal leader Bethune promised that his government would 'see to it that never again are Tasmanian industries and workers placed in jeopardy by shortages of electric power'.[4] As the work on the Serpentine Dam progressed towards completion, the flooding of the lake loomed. When the gates on the dam were closed on 2 December 1971 the process had reached its final stage. Anger grew among the lake's defenders and began to spread more widely. A new more inclusive and radical Lake Pedder Action Committee was formed and the decision was made to take the campaign offshore. The campaign used all the traditional techniques of lobbying – public rallies, petitions, the printing and distribution of pamphlets, letter writing and the insertion of paid advertisements in the press. Parties flew down to the lake in light planes and walked along the doomed beach. Painters and photographers paid tribute to the imperilled beauty and displayed their works in exhibitions or used them to illustrate the point at public addresses. Scientists presented papers that outlined the distinctive flora and fauna of the lake and warned that their survival would be threatened in the new evolving environment. Yet all that energy, creativity and enthusiasm failed to shift the resolve of the politicians or to turn back the encroaching waters. The deep and enduring emotions evoked by the drowning of Lake Pedder and its impact on the activists is difficult for people who were not involved to fully appreciate. Activist and botanist Dick Jones wrote in lyrical terms of his first visit to the lake:

I was surprised by my reaction to Lake Pedder. Really was surprised at the impact that had on me as a physical place. The whole combination of flying in – the place was filled with cloud, the sun was shining brightly above – we circled a couple of times and then dived down through this cloud to this incredible beach. Then being on the ground looking at swirling mists around me, the mountains and the water and the native vegetation. It seemed to be all there in one little place. Not only that but the moods were so ephemeral, they came and they went so that you could get enormously different experiences in the one place. You could go back to it again and again.[5]

An unexpected opportunity for activism arose in early 1972 when the Liberal government unexpectedly fell and an election was called. The common front of the two major parties on the fate of Lake Pedder encouraged the Action Committee to consider running candidates in the impending poll. Because the Hare-Clark system offered a reasonable chance for minor party candidates, success in even one seat had the potential to deliver the balance of power. At a public meeting in March 1972 it was decided to form the United Tasmania Group and run candidates in four of the five electorates. Dick Jones became the party spokesman. The claim that it was the world's first green party is not unreasonable. The campaign was hampered by a lack of funds and the difficulty of receiving attention from the mainstream media. The overall vote in the state was just under 4 per cent but was higher in the two southern electorates. Retired Labor Cabinet minister Sir Alfred White defected to the party and fell short of election by only 150 votes. While the party adopted largely conventional electoral methods its program was distinctly radical. Candidates campaigned on the slogan 'Neither Left [n]or Right, Just Out In Front'. Jones and a colleague drafted a platform entitled 'A New Ethic', which presented ideas the like of which had never before been promoted in an island election. The group undertook

To husband and cherish Tasmania's living resources so that we do minimum damage to the web of life of which we are part while preventing the extinction or serious depletion of any form of life by our individual, group or communal actions;

And we shall . . . Change our society and our culture to prevent a tyranny of rationality, at the expense of values, by which we may lose the unique adaptability of our species for meeting cultural and environmental change.[6]

Of more immediate utilitarian concern the UAP argued that the policy of hydroindustrialisation had run its course and that the island needed to attract smaller labour-intensive industries fuelled by creativity rather than kilowatts. Intervention on behalf of the lake from the Australian Conservation Foundation, prominent public figures and the offer by the new Whitlam administration to compensate Tasmania failed to bend the will of the Reece government, triumphantly returned in 1972, or to turn back the encroaching tide. But the environmental movement had learnt a very important lesson about the use and abuse of power, which taught them to be more creative and more cunning. In the next confrontation with the Hydro they eventually outplayed their once all-powerful opponent.

The emergence of the environmental movement was only one of the local developments that reflected the dramatic intellectual and cultural changes of the turbulent 1960s. Many of these changes troubled the Tasmanian labour movement. The old men who dominated party and trade unions found themselves having to cope with new, young, tertiary educated members who flooded into the party in the late 1960s and early 1970s, often as a result of their opposition to the Vietnam War. New branches in affluent suburbs, with their insistence on discussing such questions as women's rights, abortion and racial issues relating to Aborigines and the White Australia Policy, upset the traditionalists. On both sides of the fence there were the misunderstandings that grew from generational difference and the greatly varied life experiences of those who grew up in the mean years of the depression and the younger people who had known only the abundance of the postwar boom. There were also class prejudices on both sides: thoughtless arrogance from the young, and angry reactions from men and women who felt they were being patronised – and often were – in part because they often had only a primary education and had learnt much of what they knew from what they called the university of hard knocks. Many members of party branches espoused the new green sensibility and worked within to turn the party around. It was from this time that progressive Tasmanians found themselves torn between the Labor

Party and the Greens, who appealed to those people who were uneasy about Labor's close association with the unions and the strong working class presence in the branches.

Radical feminism emerged at much the same time as green politics and the movements often shared personnel. Students formed the University Union Women's Liberation Club in 1971 and in the following year the Hobart Women's Action Group added intellectual rigour to the movement. Both groups lobbied for a range of practical reforms but reached beyond amelioration to espouse deep cultural change facilitated by conscience raising sessions. They often alarmed conservative islanders but pressed forward with the heedless zeal common to bearers of a New World view. Later in 1972 more conciliatory feminists set up a local branch of the Women's Electoral Lobby with the intention of actively involving themselves in electoral politics. They participated enthusiastically in the federal election of December 1972 quizzing candidates on their attitudes to women's issues. Local branches of the National Council of Women, founded at the turn of the century, remained active and influential, having the ear of local and state politicians. Dorothy Edwards, the leading figure in the council was an alderman on the Launceston City Council from 1949 to 1964 and mayor of the city in 1956–7. Several other women were politically prominent at the time. Phyllis Benjamin led the Labor Party in the Legislative Council and in 1952 Mabel Miller was the first woman elected to the Hobart City Council. In a 20 year municipal career she served two terms as deputy mayor. She won a seat for the Liberal Party in the House of Assembly in 1955, the first woman to do so. But the doyenne of Tasmania's politically conservative women was the redoubtable Enid Lyons, who remained active in the community until her death in 1981. She had managed to have it all in a way that the young radical feminists could only theorise about. As well as having 12 children she worked closely with her husband Joe and, in 1943, four years after his death, took his seat in the House of Representatives, the first woman to enter the chamber. Pioneer female cabinet minister Enid Lyons retired in 1951. The 1960s was a moment of rapid change for Tasmanian women. The age of brides rose, there were fewer marriages and many more divorces. In 1966 equal pay was awarded in the state public service and in the following year the marriage bar, which required women in the public service to retire when they married, was removed. Between 1966 and 1981 the number of women in the workforce increased by 50 per cent while the number of men remained almost stationary. Young women flocked in increasing numbers into the expanding, federally funded university.

Aboriginality was another question that emerged in this period, to the surprise of many Tasmanians. People were aware of the contemporary public discussion about the traditional societies in the centre and the north of Australia, but for generations Tasmanians had been told that there were no Aborigines in the island. There was some awareness that there were people known as 'half caste' living on the islands in Bass Strait, but few people from mainland Tasmania had ever been there or met any of the local people. They were more often thought of as Islanders or Straitsmen rather than as Aborigines and that was how many of them identified themselves. They were strongly aware of their unique history and way of life and of their family histories. Anthropologists who visited the islands in the 1930s were astonished at the detailed and precise knowledge of their genealogy, which all the older members of the community possessed. This understanding extended into the present, which enabled the community to preserve their knowledge of the complex web of kinship that embraced all the families from the islands, even when many of them had left to settle in Launceston or Hobart. The strong sense of community was enhanced by the continuing identification with the islands as an ancestral homeland associated with a rich tradition of stories and memories. Many families who had left the islands returned to participate in the mutton bird season when the birds were gathered and processed in a collective, bonding enterprise. Solidarity and identity were enhanced by discrimination, which was often intense to the point of persecution on Flinders Island where everyone knew which families were half-castes and which were not, regardless of similarities of appearance and contemporary lifestyle. Discrimination followed families to Launceston where many of them settled in the poorest suburbs. Tasmanian Aborigines had experiences common to Indigenous Australians all over the country in the 1950s. While governments spoke of assimilation and urged Aborigines to become part of the nation, racial hostility in schools, on streets, in shops and pubs maintained a caste barrier that made that venture very difficult, even when it was considered a desirable one.

Tasmanian officials had great difficulty dealing with the Aborigines. This arose partly from their conceptual confusion about what was a quite unique society. By the 20th century many of the mixed descent people looked more European than Aboriginal although that was not always the case. They spoke English and were nominally Christian. What they still knew about the tribal ancestors was often deliberately kept from inquisitive visitors. But while the islander families reflected a blending of their Aboriginal and European heritages there were characteristics that had emerged from the experience of living in a distinctive and isolated environment for 100 years. Also, while life on the islands was often hard and impoverished it provided a supportive environment that people might want to improve but not abandon. While islanders had a heritage that was culturally mixed in the manner typical of mestizo peoples all over the world they were politically Aboriginal with a strong sense of their tribal ancestors' terrible and tragic history. Memories of loss of land and betrayal remained insistently alive as enquiring officials, clergy and teachers found to their often amazed consternation. The Aborigines had a better grasp of Tasmanian history than their much better educated inquisitors. This was a history lesson that had to be repeated again and again. For generations the Aborigines argued that they had a moral and legal right to the islands in Bass Strait, which they viewed as compensation for their ancestors' loss of mainland Tasmania. They also made it clear that they felt under no obligation to the government and refused to concede anyone's right to tell them what to do. They combined the moral righteousness of the dispossessed with the rebellious, irreverent spirit of old Van Diemen's Land.

In 1883 the leading members of the Bass Strait community wrote to the *Launceston Examiner* asserting that

We are under no obligation to the government. Whatever land they have reserved for our use . . . is a token of their honesty, in as much as it has been given in lieu of that grand Island (Tasmania) . . . which they have taken from our ancestors[7]

Thirty years later a visiting official reported that the ancestral dispossession was their 'ever present thought'. They kept uppermost in their minds the conviction 'that their aboriginal fore fathers were deprived of their original inheritance . . . by the treachery, robbery and blood thirsty actions of the first white settlers'.[8] A visiting clergyman from the Australian Board of Missions was shocked by the islanders' assertiveness. They told him the Tasmanians should be paying them rent for the land that had been taken. It was, the missionary declared, 'an utterly foolish expectation of favoured treatment'. He concluded that the islanders were not suitable human material for the mission's patronising charity.[9] But the sense of entitlement was expressed again and again. A visitor to Cape Barren Island in 1929 observed that the Aborigines believed they had a claim on the state because their country 'had been taken away from them by the whites'.[10]

After the war, even though many families left Cape Barren Island and settled on nearby Flinders Island or farther afield in Launceston or Hobart, they maintained their identity, their strong sense of kin and their distinctive view of history. While they sought employment, access to education and better services, they strongly resisted the persistent attempts to assimilate them. The crucial step in the community's political development was to merge the strong local identity as islanders with the movement all over Australia for people of mixed descent to merge their own sense of who they were with the ascendant pan-Australian Aboriginal rights movement. The reassertion of Aboriginality was a matter of great personal importance and although not everyone made that transition, many did. The number of Tasmanians formally identifying themselves as Aboriginal in the census jumped from 671 in 1971 to 2942 in 1976.[11] By 1978 it was officially estimated that there were between 4000 and 5000 Aborigines living in the state, mainly in Hobart and Launceston; only 58 remained on Cape Barren Island.[12] It was a change of great significance.

Urged on by the Flinders Island Municipal Council and assisted with federal money to build houses on mainland Tasmania the Tasmanian government made strenuous attempts to remove the remaining Aborigines from Cape Barren Island in the 1960s. But the islanders resisted and received support from the University Students' Union, which, through its affiliated society Abschol, organised a conference of Aboriginal families in Launceston in August

1971. It urged government to create employment opportunities for Aborigines and, more radically, unanimously passed a motion that the Government 'acknowledge the land rights of the Aboriginal owners of Tasmania'.[13] An Aboriginal correspondent wrote to the *Examiner* a few years later, declaring that 'We are claiming land rights... What is wrong with that? It is our ancestors calling from their graves. Claim what is rightfully yours.'[14] Leading activist Jim Everett recently recalled the experiences of the young activists who gave rise to such consternation among the general Tasmanian community who had lived for so long with the comforting thought that there were no local Aborigines to remind them about their own history. In Tasmania, he wrote,

the Aboriginal movement's major objective was to be formally acknowledged by white Tasmanians as a living Aboriginal community. Not as descendants, not as part-Aborigines but as Aborigines. It was a fierce political struggle, with a strong Aboriginal community prepared to do anything in a peaceful struggle to end the widely held attitude of dismissal. Tasmanian Aboriginal identity had never been abandoned by the people, a fact that ensured our objective would never be given up. Tasmanian Aborigines were breaking down the official barriers of government, and gaining acknowledgement and acceptance of our Aboriginality and our rights to our heritage.[15]

The fate of Truganini's skeleton was one of the most important battles about heritage. The recently founded Tasmanian Aboriginal Centre sought the return of her remains from a reluctant Tasmanian Museum and Art Gallery, who had displayed the skeleton in a glass case in the entry to the museum until 1951, after which it was stored in a box in the basement. A century after her death her remains were cremated and her ashes scattered on the waters of D'Entrecasteaux Channel. It was not what she herself had sought. She asked to be buried beyond the mountains, but there was an abiding fear that even then her bones could once again be dug up in the interests of science or simply out of curiosity or malice.

The new and radical movements that had emerged in the turbulent 1960s had not disappeared by the concluding years of the century. If anything their impact on island society became more pronounced.

13

Towards the Bicentenary

The 1969 election was a political watershed. On one side was the long period of Labor rule. On the other was a quite different era with more rapid change of government and the emergence of a mass environmental movement and ultimately the creation of the Greens Party, which, by the bicentenary year, had become a permanent feature of Tasmanian political life. Other things remained the same. The Hare-Clark system continued to distinguish Tasmanian elections and characteristically produced governments with tiny majorities. Further reform took away the power of party organisations to present lists of candidates, which ensured success for those most favoured by the party. Ballot papers were printed with a random selection of candidates so that everyone appeared at the top of the ballot paper an equal number of times. The parties could no longer hand out how to vote cards with their pre-arranged hierarchy of candidates. The innovation pitted electoral aspirants against their party colleagues as well as their political opponents. It was a welcome reform because it transferred power from the parties to the people who often used it with fine judgement to reward the conscientious local member and punish those who had taken the electorate for granted. The Legislative Council continued to trouble governments and despite endless talk of reform it remained, as it had been since 1856, one of the most powerful upper houses in the democratic world. The members eventually accepted the inevitability of universal suffrage and so shed the image of being a bastion of wealth and privilege. Electors in the periodic council elections continued to vote for independents, although the Labor Party made many attempts to capture an ever-elusive majority.

The victory of the Liberal Party in 1969 was not as members of the new government might have hoped, a prelude to an era of conservative hegemony. The Centre Party's Kevin Lyons resigned and brought the government down. The ensuing election in April 1972 brought Labor back with a resounding victory as Tasmania reflected the national movement for change that was to bring the Whitlam government to power at the end of the year. A swing to Labor of 7 per cent gave the party an almost unprecedented majority of seven in the 35 member house. Even though it was a moment of triumph for 63 year old veteran Eric Reece, his own Labor colleagues gave him more trouble than the enfeebled Opposition. His autocratic style made enemies and to the young university educated members he seemed to be a man out of his time, reflecting in his style and manner a world that had passed away. He was eventually humiliated at the February 1975 party conference in Launceston. His opponents spent months planning his demise and without warning introduced a rule change that required politicians to retire at the age of 65. The motion, which was put late at night after many delegates had left for the evening, was passed with an overwhelming roar of approval while Reece looked on in stony silence. The master tactician had been out-manoeuvred. He asked a colleague to drive him back to his motel and during a sleepless night decided to resign, a decision he announced to the conference the following morning. It was a quiet, sad end to a lifetime's career in the movement and 30 years in parliament.[1] The succession passed to Deputy Premier W. A. Nielson, who had entered parliament with Reece in 1946 as a 21 year old though already a political veteran having attended party meetings from the age of 11. Generational change came two years later with Nielson's retirement. He was succeeded by D. A. Lowe who at 35 was the country's youngest premier. Lowe was a very popular leader who won a another victory for the party in the 1979 election. But by then tensions relating to the future of the rivers in the southwest were building up to a point where Lowe's preference for compromise and consensus was no longer viable. The environment became the overriding question of the time, dividing communities, families and friends. The union

Image 13.1:   Peter Dombrovskis' famous photograph of
Rock Island Bend on the Franklin River.
(*Source:* © Liz Dombrovskis, reproduced with permission
of West Wind Press)

movement and the Labor Party itself comprehended all these
competing forces.

Tasmania was facing a global problem of how to balance the competing claims of conservation and development. The region in dispute was the rugged little-known southwest of the state, especially
the rivers that joined the Gordon as it flowed towards Macquarie
Harbour. A land of incessant rainfall it presented an irresistible
attraction to the Hydro engineers and hydrologists who were committed to providing Tasmania with more power. The focal point
of contention was a tributary of the Gordon, the Franklin River,
which would be drowned by the planned dams.

Lowe sought to balance the conflicting forces. He set out to gain
greater ministerial control over the Hydro and accepted the advice
of an expert committee to greatly expand the southwest National

Park. The party, the unions and the caucus were torn between the two poles of opinion. Lowe came out in favour of an engineering compromise that would provide jobs in the short term and more power in the long run but which would avoid flooding the Franklin. Two proposals were endlessly debated – the Gordon below Franklin on the one hand, the Gordon above Olga on the other. Conflict in the party and between the two houses of parliament led to a referendum on the question, which increased Lowe's difficulties. His compromise scheme was massively outvoted by those who wanted no dams at all and those who opted for the larger and more destructive project. Lowe was increasingly vulnerable; he was overthrown by the hungry, impatient H. Holgate who had been a print and television journalist before his election in 1976. But the removal of the widely popular Lowe was a fatal miscalculation. Lowe left the party and was joined on the cross benches by another colleague, which removed Holgate's control of the House. A long recess over Christmas merely delayed the day of retribution. Labor lost a vote of no confidence, and then, in 1982, went down to a disastrous defeat in the election with a swing against it of 17 per cent. Robin Gray came to power and used it with authoritarian determination for the next eight years. The most successful Liberal leader of the postwar period he lacked that aura of inherited privilege that his predecessors had found hard to dispel. With a combative populism he was able to appeal to many of Labor's traditional working class supporters. Yet for all the drama in and around the parliament the most significant development of the 1970s and 1980s was out in the community in meeting rooms, pubs and family kitchens.

The Wilderness Society was founded by a handful of activists in June 1976. They met at a Liffey farmhouse that belonged to the Launceston-based general practitioner, Bob Brown.

Many of those present had been involved in the struggle to save Lake Pedder and been members of the United Tasmania Party. Few of them would have foreseen that weekend that they had founded what became one of the most successful lobby groups in Australian history, or that Brown would emerge as a major national political leader. The immediate concern of the fledgling society was the plans of the Hydro to build dams in the southwest. Brown had been

Image 13.2:   The young Bob Brown, current parliamentary
leader of the Australian Greens. (*Source:* The Greens.)

Image 13.3: The Franklin River upstream of the Irenabyss, taken in 1980 by Bob Brown. (*Source:* National Library of Australia, vn4660799-v.)

converted to the cause during an 11 day hazardous, albeit exhilarating, rafting trip down the Franklin a few months before the Liffey meeting.

He later described his experience of exultation while on the river:

We floated into the immensity of Serenity Sound, the second and deepest reach of the Franklin in the Ravine. Upstream, a mountain bank stood like a dome and from the rapids at the bend a pattern of white foam coursed around us on the deep amber water. Except for the occasional call of the bird in the forest, there was absolute quiet. For a time the grandeur of this monumental place flooded my mind. I lost awareness of all else – my raft, my friend, my obligations, myself. The process of thirty years which had

made me a mystified and detached observer of the universe was reversed
and I fused into the inexplicable mystery of nature.[2]

Brown's communion with nature was rudely disrupted when in the
latter part of the journey the rafters came utterly unexpectedly upon
a Hydro work camp doing preparatory work for the impending
dams.

Many Tasmanians would have understood Brown's exultation.
They have expressed similar sentiments from the earliest years of settlement, but what was dramatically new was that with the Greens
these sentiments became fused for the first time with a political
agenda. At the heart of the new sensibility was the belief that nature
itself had intrinsic rights that were not contingent on human valu-
ation of untapped resources, or as a source of spiritual renewal or
aesthetic wonder. Nature did not exist to serve humankind. Conservation or, more properly, stewardship, must take precedence over
development, and whenever development was undertaken it must
be judged not in respect to its immediate utility but to its long term
impact on the whole ecosystem. Brown summed up his political
agenda with the aphorism: ecology, economy, equality, eternity.
Ecology required understanding the planet and acting to protect the
Earth in all its diversity and interdependence. Economy implied the
careful shepherding of the world's resources. Equality meant shar-
ing the earth with other species and fellow human beings. Eternity
implied the necessity of considering the welfare of all life forever,
not just for 10, 100 or even 1000 years. Those at present living on
the planet had the role as baton holders in the relay of the ages.[3]

The great success of the Wilderness Society was not in philosoph-
ical speculation but in competent organisation, strategic thinking
and brilliant campaigning using the most sophisticated application of all forms of media. They also had the ability to motivate
and inspire activists from all over Australia, to attract generous
funding and to mobilise the talents of the most creative people
of a whole generation. Within a few years the Wilderness Society
had more members than the political parties and could campaign
with a sophistication unmatched by politicians, unionists or even
the public relations experts hired by industry. All these attributes
were brought together in the campaign against the plans to flood
the Franklin.

The issue reached crisis point in the summer of 1982–83. Robin Gray's government pushed ahead with the project from its first days in office, enabling legislation to pass through the parliament with bipartisan support. The Society's campaign had two distinct aspects: a large cadre of highly motivated, well-disciplined activists who set out to blockade Hydro worksites and to obstruct access along Macquarie Harbour and the Gordon River. The intention was to frustrate and delay the workforce but above all to provide brilliant political theatre set against an awesome backdrop that, in the evening, would fill screens in every loungeroom in Australia. The daily confrontations with police and Hydro staff and the hundreds of arrests provided ideal copy and innumerable photo opportunities for the accompanying media. The disciplined application of passive resistance and the refusal to respond to provocation won over many non-committed Australians who watched from the sidelines. Mass meetings and marches in Tasmania and mainland cities were incontrovertible evidence of the compelling power of the campaign to save the wild rivers and the extent to which the environment had suddenly emerged as a significant national political issue.

The eventual success of the campaign was due to a series of events beyond the control of the activists. The Lowe government had earlier gained the support of Prime Minister Malcolm Fraser to nominate the whole southwest for world heritage listing. Acceptance was declared by UNESCO at the height of the blockade. Then, in the early months of 1983 when the campaign was losing momentum and news value, Fraser unexpectedly called a federal election. The Wilderness Society initiated a campaign targeting marginal Liberal-held seats in and around the mainland cities and were able to call on a large enough troupe of activists to have an important influence on the campaign. The precise impact of the 'No Dams' campaign cannot be determined but it certainly helped Labor, led by R. J. Hawke, sweep into office promising to use federal power to halt work on the Franklin. The World Heritage listing was the instrument that allowed the federal government to intervene in what otherwise would be an area of legitimate state jurisdiction. The validity of the relevant federal government legislation and dependent regulations was immediately challenged by the Tasmanian government in the High Court. On 1 July 1983 the court upheld the federal legislation. The Franklin was saved, if by a very narrow victory: the bench divided four to three. Even then the decision was highly controversial. The majority validated the federal legislation by reference to the so-called external affairs power. The ratification of the World Heritage Convention allowed the federal government to override other sections of the Constitution that conceded power to the states. Committed federalists, regardless of their views on the issue of the dams, worried about the ever-increasing dominance of the central government.

The transition of the Greens from lobby group to active participants in parliamentary politics was underway before the Franklin campaign. Brown had made several attempts to win a seat as a member of the United Tasmania Party, but his entry into the Tasmanian parliament occurred in an unusual way and in improbable circumstances. While he was in prison after being arrested at the blockade site in 1983, the Australian Democrat Party member for the state seat of Denison retired. The Hare-Clark system required a countback of votes cast in the previous election rather than the more usual by-election. Brown had to sign nomination papers in his cell, accept the need to apply for bail, which he had previously refused, and a day later was declared the member for Denison. He remained in the Tasmanian parliament for the next 10 years. He took a highly successful team to the state elections in 1989. The Greens had been involved in a vigorous campaign, led by local school teacher Christine Milne, to prevent the building of a large paper pulp mill on rich farmland at Wesley Vale in the northwest. They carried the momentum into the election campaign and won a seat in each of the five seven-member electorates, with just over 17 per cent of the vote. Brown won almost one-quarter of the vote in Denison, an unprecedented result, not just for the environmentalists but also for any third party in local elections. The five members now held the balance of power as neither Labor or Liberal had won an outright majority. Melodrama followed. The powerful Launceston businessman, media proprietor and friend of Premier Gray, Edmund Rouse, attempted to bribe a newly elected Labor backbencher to cross the floor. It didn't work: the police were called and Rouse eventually went to prison. But the stalemate in parliament was resolved by an agreement – or accord, as it was called – between the Greens and the incoming Labor Premier Michael Field. After 15 months the accord broke down leaving a legacy of bitterness and hostility that lasted for years. Interpretations of who was mainly responsible for the rupture are still determined by partisan loyalties.

While Brown was elected to the Senate in 1996, the late 1990s was a lean period for the Tasmanian Greens, who faced their greatest challenge when the two major parties combined, making their task even more difficult. Carrying the populist banner of reducing the number of politicians the two parties conspired to reduce the House of Assembly from 35 to 25 members. This had the effect of significantly raising the barrier to any aspiring third party candidate or independent from a minimum of 12 per cent to 17 per cent of the vote. It was a cunning stratagem that appeared to make the Greens' task almost impossible, yet at the 2002 elections the party won 18 per cent of the vote and took seats in four out of five electorates. In Denison party leader Peg Putt won 25 per cent of the vote, outpolling the Liberal Party. It was a result that indicated that the Greens were a permanent force in Tasmanian politics. It was also portentous for the future of Australian politics as a whole: Tasmania was pointing the way to the future erosion of the essentially two party system that had dominated Australian politics since 1910.

While the environment overshadowed all other issues during the final decades of the 20th century, there were other contemporaneous reforms that helped change the image of the island. Tasmanian shed its tradition of homophobia. Anxiety about male homosexuality had been one of the driving motivations of the anti-transportation movement. Tasmania hung a man for sodomy in 1867, the last time this happened in the empire. During the early years of the 20th century, Tasmania had an unusually high incidence of imprisonment for consenting homosexual practice. Bob Brown was very courageous to come out as a gay man in 1986. The Tasmanian Gay and Lesbian Rights Group was formed in 1988, but strong local resistance to reform of the punitive 19th century legislation led activists to take their case to the United Nations Human Rights Commission. A judgement in their favour and federal legislation forced the hand of Ray Groom's Liberal government, which led to reform in 1997; in 2004 Tasmania became the first state to allow same sex couples to register their relationships.

The Aboriginal community was also active in the 1980s and 1990s. Having fought a battle to achieve recognition as members of Australia's Indigenous population they had to engage in further agitation to establish their right to land, even though they would have difficulty establishing those rights under the law as it was changed after the Mabo judgement in 1992. During the 1980s numerous Aboriginal organisations emerged to represent regional communities as well as cultural and sporting groups. The Tasmanian Aboriginal Centre (TAC), led by the talented activist and lawyer Michael Mansell, was by far the most prominent and professional body but was often opposed by the regional organisations. During the 1980s the TAC waged a long campaign to have all the Aboriginal remains held by the Tasmanian Museum and Art Gallery returned to the community. Eventually, the campaign was successful and the remains were cremated at ceremonies held at Oyster Cove, the site that became the home of the old people returned from Flinders Island in 1847.

Attention then turned to the large number of overseas institutions that held Tasmanian remains. As a result of a campaign that has been maintained for several decades, many of the institutions have been shamed into returning the material. The Field government introduced legislation in 1991 to return land to the community but the Bill was defeated in the Legislative Council. The Mabo case and the movement for reconciliation gave new impetus to the pursuit of a Tasmanian solution to the question. After complex and often contentious discussions the Groom government introduced legislation that returned 12 parcels of land to the Aboriginal community, including Cape Barren and other mutton birding islands, Risdon Cove, Oyster Cove and other sites of cultural significance, including Wybalenna on Flinders Island. At each census the number of people claiming Aboriginality increased, which led to a long and often angry debate about who could legitimately claim Indigenous identity. The matter became more complicated because state and federal governments applied different tests to establish Aboriginality. A legal case taken to the Federal Court did not resolve the matter. Internal dissension notwithstanding, the emergence of such a powerful Aboriginal movement would have amazed those generations who lived with the comforting illusion that there were no Aborigines in Tasmania. It is one of the most striking features of 20th century Tasmania. Perhaps more than any other Aboriginal community in Australia the Tasmanians can proudly declare: 'We have survived.' It is an achievement of international significance.

It was a constant backdrop to Tasmania's celebration of its bicentenary in 2004. The choice of 2004 was a strange one and it requires some explanation. The Labor government of Jim Bacon displayed a reluctance to do much about the historical milestone although it was obvious that something had to be done. Western Australia, South Australia and Victoria had all recently commemorated their sesquicentenaries and the national bicentenary of 1988 was still fresh in everyone's mind. The government appointed an advisory committee and an executive officer, but planning began far closer to the event than had been the case in the other states and the budget was very small. It was all done in a way that precluded the ambitious research, writing and publishing projects that had been undertaken in Melbourne, Adelaide and Perth, each of which had more money at their disposal than Tasmania. In the end though, what was really lacking locally was the desire, not the amount of available cash. It was a confusing brief for the members of the committee, whose greatest problem was the question of when the commemoration should begin. There was no doubt about the historical events. There were three foundational settlements – Risdon in September 1803, Sullivan's Cove in February 1804 and in November of that year on the Tamar. But the premier decreed that the commemoration could not begin until 2004; all the literature, letterheads, posters and advertising material referred to that year, not to 2003. Public criticism and the committee's disquiet had no effect. The premier was adamant, though no explanation was ever forthcoming. The settlement at Risdon had been air-brushed out of history The most plausible suggestion for this strange decision seemed to be that he acted out of concern for the Aboriginal community and in return they had agreed not to disrupt the proceedings or demonstrate against them. The most sensitive date – the day of conflict at Risdon Cove – was in April 1804, not in 1803. When the committee decided, in September 2003, that they must mark the day of Bowen's arrival at Risdon they were not permitted to hold the event in a government building and so chose the Anglican cathedral; government officers and Labor politicians were officially discouraged from attending.

The executive officer undertook extensive public consultation in the months leading up to the bicentenary, which enabled large numbers of Tasmanians to indicate what they thought should be commemorated. More than 2500 informants were consulted at public meetings, focus groups and by opinion polling. The lack of any large-scale government programs may have made it easier to tap into the historical awareness of the wider community.

So what, when left to themselves, did Tasmanians value about 200 years of European settlement and how did they think it should be remembered? They wanted to celebrate the achievements of ordinary people, not the work of major public figures. Their focus was intensely regional. They wanted to remember their own local stories. They did not value large gala events or fireworks. The feeling was that Aboriginal history should be respected but that the communities' involvement should be a matter left to their discretion. There was no interest in remembering the various voyages of European explorers. Nor did the community show any enthusiasm for celebrating the achievements of war heroes or the sacrifice of the dead, suggesting that such remembrance was seen as a specific form of commemoration that had its own public occasions and protocols. There was some interest in the convict legacy but not as much as might be suggested by the focus of professional historians and the tourist industry. Any sense of embarrassment about that aspect of the past appeared to have gone. There were several gatherings of convict descendants and the North Midlands Council established through Campbell Town a walkway lined with bricks, each one of which carried the name and other details about an individual convict. Respondents frequently wanted to focus on their own town or district. Many families had, after all, been resident in a particular area for generations. They were often surrounded by old buildings, historic patterns of land settlement and had access to collections of artefacts of all descriptions. It was easy to document change in such communities. So with the assistance of funding from state and local governments there were numerous displays and publications relating to subjects as diverse as cooking, farming, land use, public health, literature, painting and poultry raising. The year's activities

also emphasised that there was a great fund of regional historical knowledge and many local experts on the most specialised and
arcane subjects relating to steam technology, water and windmills,
old ploughs, trains, trams, trading ketches and jetties, blacksmiths,
potters and much else. Enthusiasts visited old mine sites, disused
railway embankments, traditional droving trails. They rebuilt old
boats, restored cemeteries, churches, clocks and organs, established
history walks, painted murals and replanted historic gardens.

What was almost completely missing from the celebrations was
any reference to politics. The subject was rarely mentioned by any
of the respondents. It was as though there was nothing to commemorate or, perhaps more correctly, no knowledge of what might be
worth remembering. This is not what politicians and activists of the
past might have expected. At every moment of significant historical
change – democratic reform, responsible government, cessation of
transportation, the rise of the labour movement – participants made
speeches about the significance of what was happening and how
future generations would remember and celebrate their achievements. Feminists celebrated the attainment of women's suffrage in
1903 at a boisterous banquet but the most surprising oversight was
that no one bothered to remember the birth of the Labor Party in
that same year, despite a Labor government being in office and the
party's long dominance of state politics.

The public consultation prior to the bicentenary provided an
insight into public attitudes to the island's past, but what do historians make of it? And how distinctive is it? Does it differ from
the histories of the other Australian states? In his history of 1852
John West declared that Tasmania was 'a type of the Australian
world'.[4] The parallel development of the colonies in the 19th century and their similar relationship with Britain eased the task of
federation and from that time the disparate destinies were braided
together. Tasmanians went to war with their interstate contemporaries and came home when they did. They suffered when the
continent was depressed and benefited, at least some of the time,
when it boomed. Federal financial arrangements generously subsidised Tasmania and evened up the standard of living. Islanders
generally remained poorer than mainlanders but not that much so.
The expanding reach of the federal government, the Arbitration

Commission and the High Court drew even the remotest parts of the continent closer to Canberra and imposed many uniformities. Increased coming and going across Bass Strait in the second half of the 20th century meant that more Tasmanians got to know the other states than ever before and mainlanders increasingly enjoyed island holidays. The national banks, insurance companies and retail chains imposed their own uniformities. Tasmanians who had never left the island, once quite commonly and often proudly insular, came increasingly to be seen as quaintly eccentric and worthy of a patronising after dinner anecdote. In writing the history of a single Australian state one is necessarily writing about the history of the nation, but it would be a mistake to think that Tasmania is no more than an offshore extension of Victoria. Distinctive geography and history have left their stamp on the island and its people.

The convict system was central to Tasmanian history. It had a greater impact than it did in New South Wales and, given that as many as 75 per cent of Tasmanians have at least one convict ancestor and some families have many more, was not as easily forgotten. Sensitivity about the past of the kind common in Tasmania had no parallel in the other colonies. Pride in the pioneers, which became a common feature of late 19th century Australia, was muted in the island and the accompanying image of the outback bushman had little local relevance. The experience of the system left a legacy of irreverence and rejection of deference passed on to children and grandchildren who may not have known the source of what became known as the Van Diemonian spirit. The free settler's fear of the emancipist working class influenced master–servant relations for a generation and helped shape political life for much longer. The Legislative Council was designed to inhibit the reforming zeal of the popular House and carried out that mission with great effect for over 100 years. But it was A. I. Clark's experience of growing up in Hobart, with its rigid system of caste, that inspired him to introduce the most democratic voting system in the world with its promise of according each vote absolute equality.

The fate of the Tasmanian Aborigines was repeated many times over in other parts of Australia but there was nothing comparable with the Black Line or the banishment to an offshore island.

Still, there were significant differences between the Tasmanian experience and that of the larger mainland colonies. The great majority of Tasmanian settlers were convicts who had not chosen to be in the land that belonged to the Aborigines. Nor did they willingly venture out into the remote districts of the colony where they came into conflict with them. Government policy was made in Britain; the settlers had no say on what happened. In Queensland, South Australia and Western Australia, democratically elected parliaments adopted policies that led to the violent dispossession of Aboriginal bands across the whole northern third of the continent. The free settlers were people who had made personal decisions to participate in the despoliation of the Indigenous tribes. In a moral sense the two cases were quite different.

Tasmania's economic history diverges from the common Australian pattern. The period of rapid growth and prosperity before 1850 was followed by prolonged depression interspersed with short periods of relative abundance. No other state has been so often in depression or experienced such a persistent loss of population. The sequence of growth followed by depression had the effect of preserving the buildings dating from the times of growth; in Hobart's case the 1830s and 1840s and in Launceston the 1880s. The struggling economy also limited the growth of the two cities, which were overtaken by the mainland capitals during the 19th century and never made up the lost ground. Hobart in particular is quite distinctive among capital cities in that it does not dominate the state in the way that other state capitals do. Launceston is distinctive as well in the sense that it is the only provincial city in Australia that has always been a serious rival, commercially and culturally, to the capital. Another consequence of slow growth and minimal immigration is that many Tasmanian families have been on the island for a long time and are part of dense networks of kinship and friendship that are among the most striking characteristics of Tasmania and are unusual in a New World settler society. It is certainly true that a small group of Tasmanians, hitherto unknown to each other, can, after a short conversation, find that they have mutual friends or at least acquaintances and even distant relatives. They often realise that they had ancestors who must have met one another at some time in the past. Some people find this demographic closeness oppressive but many others consider it comforting and it is one of the reasons they feel so completely at home on the island.

Bass Strait still matters. The coincidence of the state boundary with the encompassing shoreline reinforces the sense of separateness. The Strait is much mightier than the Murray or any other of the state boundaries. The scale of the land is quite different. Talk of a wide brown land means nothing in Tasmania. Every horizon is bounded and nearby hills enfold the spectator. Even the flat land lilts and ripples. The mountainous heartland pushes long forested fingers down into most towns and villages. The bush is a short walk away from the centres of the two small cities. The southern sky has movement and daily drama unknown in the high steady domes that arch over many parts of the continent. The extreme patterns of weather experienced on the mainland are moderated in Tasmania by the surrounding southern ocean and the seasons come and go with an easy regularity dramatised by the hundreds of deciduous trees, shrubs and flowers transplanted from the northern hemisphere. As we have seen above, the early settlers arrived with sensibilities receptive to Tasmanian landscapes, the picturesque wildness and the open grasslands. Their descendants inherited their appreciation and turned it into a distinctive tradition of island patriotism that passing time has not diminished. Tasmanians talk without embarrassment of their love of the island, and with an enthusiasm that might in other circumstances be kept for exchanges between consenting adults in private. When visitors declare they have fallen in love with the island, as they often do, the locals smile to themselves, quietly confirmed in their faith. It is not surprising that the most characteristic Tasmanian art forms are landscape painting and photography and that images of the land have played such a central role in tourist promotion and the campaigns of the conservation movement.

These considerations take us back to the early colonial period when the beauty and the purity of nature was juxtaposed with the degradation of the convict system. The two attitudes were mutually reinforcing in a way that was unique to Tasmania. Few people could feel proud of a large, open air prison. Governor Arthur spent 12 industrious years trying to induce in the convicts a sense of shame. The Anti-Transportation Movement transferred that sentiment to the whole society. Nineteenth century Tasmanians needed nature.

They sought out what they liked to think of as wilderness untouched by the spoiling hand of man. The exile of the Aborigines to Bass Strait and their rapid demographic decline enabled generations to innocently talk of pristine nature. They had no appreciation of the ways in which, over hundreds of generations, the Aborigines had shaped and humanised the environment they chose to call wilderness. The assumed innocence persisted. The high priest of the modern environment movement, Olegas Truchanas, was an influential exemplar of these attitudes. His biographer observed that

It delighted him to think of the undiscovered places he might visit. Every inch of Europe, he said, must have been trodden by some man at some time. In the South-West, he thought, he could perhaps find lakes, tarns, or a river he would be the first to see.[5]

The seeming innocence of the conceit disguises the politics implicit in the concept of the wilderness. Untrodden land was by definition a *terra nullius*.

Tasmanians became island patriots early in the history of the colony, although they thought of the island as a place rather than as a society. So when the community was asked to nominate those things they wanted to commemorate they felt there was nothing to mark in a long political history or the creation, in association with the other colonies, of one of the world's earliest and most successful democracies. There is among some environmentalists a belief that island society will never match the physical environment. One of the founders of the Wilderness Society, a man who wrote lyrically about the southwest, declared: 'I think the political scene is sick and the whole society of Tasmania is diseased and rotten to the core.'[6] John West and his fellow activists might have phrased it more elegantly but could not have expressed it more forcefully. The modern environmental movement has deep roots in Tasmania. It had been latent in the community for a long time. With the decline of class politics in the 1980s and 1990s it burst into life. This is the only way we can understand the sudden efflorescence of the Wilderness Society and the electoral success of the Greens. An enduring patriotism of place found new expression in a politics of place. Tasmanian novelist Richard Flanagan described in 1996 the moment when he sensed the change:

The action seemed to make all the connection I had not found in Tasmanian art, connection between the personal and the political, between the natural world and the human world, between what was and what could be, between my place and myself. This action seemed to suggest that a love of place could be a powerful and commanding moral and creative force. Most of all, it spoke of the possibility of hope in my world. Looking back now, I can see that it was part of the beginning of a politics of place in Tasmania the full potential of which is still to be realised.[7]

A. I. Clark was a forceful exponent of the patriotism of place, but he believed it would give birth to a nationalism that would find expression in republicanism and independence. It did not work out that way. Tasmanians' lack of confidence about their own society made them willing recipients of the imperial propaganda that issued forth from Britain with increasing force in the early 20th century as Britain felt the strain of competition with other powers. Their loyalty to Britain was legendary although not necessarily universal. They retained their local variant of the British blue ensign as the state flag although it contained nothing that related to Tasmania. The heraldic red lion on the fly was a beast unknown in the antipodes. They retained the office of governor with its lilliputian court and attendant protocol and, in more recent times, when it was decided the community needed a Tasmanian day the choice was the day in November when Tasman the Dutch navigator sailed by in 1642. It was as though thousands of years of Aboriginal Tasmania were of no consequence and nothing that had been done in 200 years since the first invasion was as worthy of remembrance as the chance passage around the south coast of ships belonging to a Dutch trading company that showed no interest in the island. Recently, a proposal was put to the Australian Electoral Commission to change the name of the electoral district based on metropolitan Hobart from Denison to Inglis-Clark, from the name of a British imperial official and temporary resident to the native-born Tasmanian statesman. The proposal was publically opposed by the state's most senior Liberal politician and rejected by the commission without explanation.

Tasmanians are surrounded by memorabilia of their colonial past. There is a growing realisation that it is one of the most distinctive features of their society. In the last decades of the 20th century the great store of old buildings found energetic defenders and heritage legislation has hobbled the ambition of would-be developers. The tourist industry has slowly come to realise the attraction of the island's unique history. Even so, there is little local history taught in schools and it is clear that many people feel it is not worth serious consideration. And yet the past lives on in ways and with a strength that are unusual in the rest of Australia.

NOTES

1 FIRST MEETINGS, EXTRAORDINARY ENCOUNTERS

1 N. J. B. Plomley (ed.), *Friendly Mission*, 2nd edn, Queen Victoria Museum, Launceston, 2001, p. 557.

2 ibid., p. 408.

3 N. J. B. Plomley and J. P. Bernier (eds), *The General*, Queen Victoria Museum, Launceston, 1993, p. 289.

4 N. J. B. Plomley (ed.), *The Baudin Expedition and the Tasmanian Aborigines, 1802*, Blubber Head Press, Hobart, 1992, pp. 89–90.

5 Plomley (ed.), *Friendly Mission*, op. cit., p. 408.

6 Plomley, *The Baudin Expedition*, op. cit., p. 890.

7 Plomley (ed.), *The General*, op. cit., p. 280.

8 Plomley (ed.), *The Baudin Expedition*, op. cit., p. 89.

9 E. Duyker (ed.), *The Discovery of Tasmania*, St David's Park Publishing, Hobart, 1992, p. 25.

10 E. Beaglehole (ed.), *The Journals of Captain James Cook*, Cambridge University Press, Cambridge, 1955, vol. 1, p. 53.

11 Plomley (ed.), *The General*, op. cit., p. 208.

12 Plomley (ed.), *The Baudin Expedition*, op. cit., p. 19.

13 ibid., p. 32.

14 Plomley (ed.), *The General*, op. cit., p. 283.

15 Plomley (ed.), *The Baudin Expedition*, op. cit., p. 63.

16 ibid., p. 84.

17 ibid., p. 125.

18 ibid., p. 33.

19 ibid., p. 22.

20 Plomley (ed.), *The General*, op. cit., p. 293.

21 Beaglehole (ed.), *Journals*, op. cit., 1, p.55.

22 Plomley (ed.), *The General*, op. cit., p. 310.

23 Plomley (ed.), *The Baudin Expedition*, op. cit., p. 33.

24 E. Duyker (ed.), *Voyages to Australia and the Pacific 1791–1793*, trans. M. Duyker, Melbourne University Press, Melbourne, 2001, p. 145.
25 A. Delano, *A Narrative of a Voyage to New Holland and Van Diemen's Land*, Cat & Fiddle Press, Hobart, 1973.
26 ibid.
27 Plomley (ed.), *Friendly Mission*, op. cit., p. 408.
28 P. Tardiff, *John Bowen's Hobart*, THRA, Hobart, 2003, p. 142.
29 ibid., p. 112.
30 M. Nicholls (ed.), *The Diaries of the Rev. Robert Knopwood, 1803–1838*, THRA, Hobart, 1977, p. 46.
31 ibid.
32 A. W. H. Humphrey, *A Voyage to Port Phillip and Van Diemen's Land*, The Banks Society, Melbourne, 1994, p. 59.
33 Patterson to King, 26 November 1804, *HRA*, 3, vol. 1, p. 607.
34 ibid.
35 ibid., p. 650.
36 ibid., p. 668.
37 ibid., p. 671.
38 M. Nicholls (ed.), op. cit., pp. 123–5.
39 ibid., p. 104.
40 *HRA*, 3, vol. 1, p. 576.
41 ibid., p. 769.
42 *The Letters of G. P. Harris*, 1803–12, Arden Press, Sorrento, 1994, p. 100.
43 W. Backhouse, *Early Tasmania*, Tasmanian Government Printer, Hobart, 1914, pp. 49–51.
44 P. Tardiff, 'Risdon Cove', in R. Manne (ed.), *Whitewash*, Black Inc. Books, Melbourne, 2003, p. 223.
45 J. Boyce, *Van Diemen's Land*, Black Inc. Books, Melbourne, 2003, p. 38.
46 Plomley (ed.), *Friendly Mission*, op. cit., p. 100.
47 J. West, *History of Tasmania (1852)*, 2nd edn, Angus & Robertson, Sydney, 1971, p. 263.
48 Backhouse, op. cit., pp. 49–50.

2 VAN DIEMEN'S LAND

1 *HRA*, 1, vol. 2, p. 500.
2 *HRA*, 1, vol. iv, p. 12; *HRNSW*, vol. 1, p. 458.
3 D. Collins, *An Account of the English Colony in New South Wales*, 2 vols, London, 1802, vol. 1, pp. 122, 238; vol. 2, p. 26.
4 General Orders, 7 January 1805, *HRA*, 3, vol. 1, p. 529.
5 Collins to King, 11 September 1804, *HRA*, 3, vol. i, p. 281.
6 ibid.

7 Bathurst to Darling, 14 July 1825, *HRA*, 1, vol. xii, p. 21.

8 E. Duyker (ed.), *B. d'Entrecasteaux Voyage to Australia and the Pacific, 1791–3*, trans. M. Duyker, Melbourne University Press, Melbourne, 2001, pp. 140–3, 147.

9 E. de Vattel, *The Law of Nations*, publisher unknown, London, 1758, p. 91.

10 K. M. Bowden, *George Bass, 1771–1803*, Oxford University Press, Melbourne, 1952, p. 76.

11 Plomley (ed.), *The Baudin Expedition*, op. cit., p. 18.

12 *The Letters of G. P. Harris*, op. cit., pp. 58, 98, 100.

13 *HRA*, 3, vol. i, p. 618.

14 *HRA*, 3, vol. i, p. 585.

15 C. Jeffreys, *Van Diemen's Land*, Richardson, London, 1820, p. 16.

16 ibid., p. 94.

17 *Hobart Town Almanac*, 1830, p. 107.

18 H. Widowson, *The Present State of Van Diemen's Land*, Robinson & Joy, London, 1829, p. 108.

19 *Launceston Advertiser*, 15 November 1830.

20 *HRA*, 3, vol. i, p. 665.

21 T. Betts, *An Account of the Colony of Van Diemen's Land, etc.*, Baptist Mission Press, Calcutta, 1830, p. 87.

22 Widowson, op. cit., p. 115.

23 Jeffreys, op. cit., p. iii.

24 Widowson, op. cit, p. v.

25 *Hobart Town Almanac*, 1830, pp. 91, 95.

26 ibid., p. 89.

27 West, op. cit., p. 332.

28 *Hobart Town Courier*, 13 June 1829.

29 W. Mann, *Six Years Residence in the Australian Provinces*, Smith Elder, London, 1839, p. 11.

30 G. W. Evans, *A Geographical, Historical and Topographic Description of Van Diemen's Land*, Souter, London, 1822, p. 26.

31 J. Dixon, *The Condition and Capabilities of Van Diemen's Land*, Smith Elder, London 1839, pp. 28–9.

32 HRA, 3, vol. i, p. 665.

33 Widowson, op. cit., p. xi.

34 *Colonial Times*, 3 September 1825.

35 *Hobart Town Courier*, 30 May 1829.

36 *Colonial Times*, 18 September 1829.

37 *Colonial Times*, 13 February 1829.

38 *Hobart Town Courier*, 10 November 1827.

39 Dixon, op. cit., p. 51

40 10 November 1827.

41 Widowson, op. cit., p. 98.

42 *Colonial Times*, 10 November 1827.
43 E. Curr, *An Account of the Colony of Van Diemen's Land*, Cowie, London, 1824, p. 19.
44 J. Boyce, op cit.
45 *Hobart Town Courier*, 17 April 1830.
46 J. P. Fawkner, *Reminiscences of Early Hobart Town 1804–1812*, Banks Society, Melbourne, 2007, p. 40.
47 *Hobart Town Courier*, 17 April 1830.
48 H. Melville, *History of Van Diemen's Land etc.*, Smith Elder, London, 1835, pp. 320–1.
49 *Colonial Times*, 3 July 1829.
50 *Colonial Times*, 3 July 1829.
51 P. Chapman (ed.), *The Diaries and Letters of G. T. W. B. Boyes, 1820–1832*, Oxford University Press, Melbourne, 1985, pp. 496–7.

3 THE BLACK WAR

1 West, *History*, op. cit., pp. 309–10.
2 J. Dixon, *Narrative of a Voyage to New South Wales and Van Diemen's Land*, Anderson, Edinburgh, 1822, p. 46.
3 *Hobart Town Gazette*, 6 August 1826.
4 J. Jones, in CSO 1/323, AOT.
5 Petition of 2 April 1828, CSO/318, AOT, p. 383.
6 *Colonial Times*, 1 December 1826.
7 West, *History*, op. cit., pp. 272, 333.
8 CSO 1/323, p. 290, AOT.
9 N. J. B. Plomley, *The Aboriginal-Settler Clash in Van Diemen's Land, 1803–1831*, Queen Victoria Museum, Launceston, 1992.
10 J. E. Calder, 'Natives', p. 35, Papers, Mitchell Library, mss A597.
11 H. L. Roth, *The Aborigines of Tasmania*, King, Halifax, 1899, p. 171.
12 Plomley, *The Aboriginal Settler Clash*, op. cit., p. 6.
13 Plomley (ed.), *Friendly Mission*, op. cit., p. 552.
14 Jorgenson to Burnett, 24 February 1831, CSO1/320, AOT.
15 Plomley (ed.), *Friendly Mission*, op. cit., p. 552.
16 Jorgenson to Burnett, op. cit., p. 375.
17 Plomley (ed.), *Friendly Mission*, op. cit., pp. 164–5.
18 Robinson, *Evidence to Aborigines Committee*, 20 January 1831, CBE/1, AOT.
19 Robinson to Colonial Secretary, 11 May 1838, Robinson papers, 49, Mitchell Library, mss A7070.
20 Arthur to Barnes, 19 October 1830, CSO 1/320, AOT.
21 *Hobart Town Courier*, 11 September 1830.
22 J. E. Calder, *Some Account of the Wars, Extirpation, Habits etc, of the Native Tribes of Tasmania*, Henn & Co., 1875, p. 8.

23 Clark to Burnett, CSO1/320/7578, p. 403, AOT.
24 Clark to Burnett, 2 March 1830, CSO 1/ 323, AOT.
25 J. Bonwick, _The Last of the Tasmanians_, Sampson, Low, Son & Marston, London, 1870, p. 226.
26 A. G. L. Shaw (ed.), _Military Operations Against the Aboriginal Inhabitants of Van Dieman's Land, 1831_, THRA, Hobart, 1971, p. 19.
27 _Colonial Times_, 1 December 1826.
28 West History, op. cit., p. 282.
29 _Military Operations_, op. cit., pp. 20–1.
30 West, _History_, op. cit., p. 284.
31 Executive Council minutes, 8 April 1828, AO/EP/230, p. 294, AOT.
32 _Military Operations_, op. cit., pp. 5–7.
33 ibid.
34 GO, 33/7, p. 901, AOT.
35 _Military Operations_, op. cit., p. 11.
36 _Military Operations_, op. cit., p. 290.
37 Executive Council minutes, 27 August 1830, pp. 568–70, AOT.
38 J. Fenton, _History of Tasmania_, Hobart, 1884, p. 106.
39 P. Chapman (ed.), _The Diaries of G. T. W. B. Boyes_, op. cit., pp. 378–80.
40 West, _History_, op. cit., p. 300.
41 ibid, p. 38.
42 _Hobart Town Gazette_, 23 July 1824.
43 _Tasmanian_, 14 December 1827.
44 CSO 1/323, AOT.
45 _Launceston Advertiser_, 26 September 1831.
46 J. Bonwick, op. cit., p. 226.
47 'Legends of a Native Tribune', from _The Mercury_, n.d., Calder Papers, La Trobe Library, ms. 10913.

4 AN INDELIBLE STAIN?

1 Arthur to Glenelg, 6 April 1833, CO 280/41.
2 Arthur to Glenelg, 22 July 1837, CO 280/84.
3 Arthur to Glenelg, 24 September 1832, CO 280/35.
4 Select Committee on the Aboriginal Inhabitants, British Parliamentary Paper, 1837, vol. 7, no. 425, p. 126.
5 Arthur to Glenelg, 22 July 1837, CO 280/84.
6 _Military Operations etc._, op. cit., pp. 6–7.
7 Anstey to Burnett, 4 December 1827, CSO 1/320, AOT.
8 Arthur to Darling, 24 May 1828, GO 33/4, AOT.
9 Parramore to Surveyor-General, 4 December 1827, CSO 38/I, AOT; _Military Operations etc._, op. cit., pp. 4–5.
10 _Colonial Times_, 3 April 1830.

11 Minutes of the Aborigines Committee, 24 October 1831, p. 135, CBE/I, AOT.
12 Robinson Papers, 40, Mitchell Library, mss A7061.
13 Plomley (ed.), *Friendly Mission*, op. cit., pp. 67, 103.
14 ibid., p. 111.
15 K. R. von Stieglitz, *Six Pioneer Women of Tasmania*, Telegraph & Printery, Launceston, n.d., p. 30.
16 Robinson Papers, 40 Mitchell Library, mss A7061, p. 1012.
17 Plomley (ed.), *Friendly Mission*, op. cit., p. 519.
18 Robinson to Burnett, 19 December 1829, CSO 1/328, p. 127.
19 G. A. Robinson, Speech to Aborigines Protection Society, 1838; Bath 1865, pp. 9–10.
20 Arthur to Goderich, 14 March 1833, CO 280/41; West, *History*, op. cit., p. 307; Calder to Reibey, 6 July 1877, Calder Papers, Mitchell Library, mss A597.
21 V. Rae-Ellis, *Black Robinson*, Melbourne University Press, Melbourne, 1988, p. 27.
22 von Stieglitz, op. cit., pp. 27–9.
23 Plomley (ed.), *Friendly Mission*, op. cit., p. 427.
24 ibid., p. 109; Robinson to Colonial Secretary, 17 October 1835, Robinson Papers, Mitchell Library, mss A 7043.
25 Robinson to Montague, 31 July 1835, CSO1/807/1727; Robinson, *Report on Flinders Island*, 1838, CSO 5/39/833.
26 Calder Papers, Mitchell Library, mss A597.
27 N. J. B. Plomley (ed.), *Weep in Silence*, Blubber Head Press, Hobart 1977, p. 747.
28 ibid., pp. 148–9.
29 *Regina v Sioui*, 70 DLR (4th) 427 at 428.
30 R. Hughes, *The Fatal Shore*, Collins, London, 1987, p. 423.
31 Plomley (ed.), *Weep in Silence*, op. cit., p. 329.
32 Plomley (ed.), *Weep in Silence*, op. cit., p. 42; *Fisher Report*, 1842, CSO, 8/11/266, p. 475, AOT.
33 Reports by Nickolls, 7 November 1834, CSO 1/772/16, 503, p. 195, AOT; Fisher, February 1842, CSO, 8/11/266, February–April 1842, CSO 8/11/266, p. 475, AOT.
34 CSO 5/180/4240, AOT.
35 Fisher to Colonial Secretary, 18 January 1842, CSO 8/11/266, AOT.
36 Report, 30 April 1838, Robinson Papers, Mitchell Library, mss A7044.
37 Dove to Colonial Secretary, 26 February 1839, CSO5/182/4352, AOT.
38 Plomley (ed.), *Weep in Silence*, op. cit., pp. 353–5.
39 *Bent's News*, 2 April 1836.
40 Cited by Plomley (ed.), *Weep in Silence*, op. cit., pp. 533–4.

41 West, *History*, op. cit., p. 310.
42 ibid., pp. 331–2.
43 For details of the petition and Walter George Arthur, see H. Reynolds, *Fate of a Free People*, Penguin Books, Melbourne, 2004.

5 THE TRIUMPH OF COLONISATION

 1 *Hobart Town Courier*, 28 October 1836.
 2 ibid.
 3 Minute to Legislative Council, 27/4/36, enclosed in Arthur to Glenelg, 30 April 1836, CO 280/65; Arthur to Glenelg, 4 May 1836, CO 280/66.
 4 *Cornwall Chronicle*, 24 September 1836.
 5 ibid.
 6 P. L. Brown (ed.), *Clyde Company Papers*, vol. 2, 1836–40, Oxford University Press, London, 1952, pp. 31–8.
 7 ibid., p. 31.
 8 ibid., pp. 32–3.
 9 L. Frost (ed.), *A Face in the Glass: The Journal and Life of Annie Baxter Dawbin*, Heinemann, Melbourne, 1992, p. 11.
10 *True Colonist*, 22 January 1836.
11 *Colonial Times*, 29 December 1835.
12 *Launceston Advertiser*, 7 January 1836.
13 Arthur to Glenelg, 4 May 1836, CO 280/66.
14 J. McPhee, *The Art of John Glover*, Macmillan, Melbourne, 1980, pp. 63, 71.
15 P. L. Brown (ed.), *Clyde Company Papers*, op. cit., p. 9.
16 T. E. Burns and J. R. Skemp, *Van Diemen's Land Correspondence*, Queen Victoria Museum, Launceston, 1961, p. 59.
17 *Bent's News*, 7 May 1836.
18 *Bent's News*, 2 April 1836; *The Tasmanian*, 18 March, 27 May 1836.
19 *Cornwall Chronicle*, 5 March 1836.
20 ibid., 16 April 1936.
21 C. Darwin, *Narrative of the Surveying Voyages of the . . . Adventure and Beagle, etc.*, 3 vols, Murray, London, 1839, vol. 3, p. 532–3.
22 *Van Diemen's Land Annual*, 1834, p. 10.
23 ibid., pp. 4–5.
24 *Launceston Advertiser*, 12 May 1836.
25 *Van Diemen's Land Annual*, 1834, p. 10.
26 ibid., p. 56.
27 *Bent's News*, 11 June 1836.
28 ibid., pp. 56–7.
29 *Bent's News*, 13 February 1836.
30 ibid., 26 March 1836.
31 ibid., 13 February 1836.

32 *The Tasmanian*, 23 December 1836.

33 ibid.

34 F. Burkhardt (ed.), *Charles Darwin: The Beagle Letters*; Cambridge University Press, Cambridge, 2008, p. 381.

35 ibid., p. 381.

36 C. Darwin, *Narrative, etc.*, op. cit., vol. 3, p. 535.

37 Arthur to Joseph Hume, 30 December 1835, *Governor's Letterbook, 1833–6*, GO, 52/6, AOT.

38 A. Alexander, *Obliged to Submit: Wives and Mistresses of Colonial Governors*, Montpelier Press, Hobart, 1999, pp. 111–32.

39 W. D. Forsyth, *Governor Arthur's Convict System*, Sydney University Press, Sydney, 1970 (1935), p. 10.

40 Cited by Levy, op. cit., p. 93.

41 ibid., pp. 118–19.

42 *Colonial Times*, 1 March 1836.

43 *True Colonist*, 11 March 1836.

44 *The Tasmanian*, 9 September 1836.

45 *Bent's News*, 26 March 1836.

46 M. Nicholls (ed.), *The Diary of Reverend Robert Knopwood, 1803–1838*, THRA, Hobart, 1977, pp. 646–7.

47 *Colonial Times*, 9 August 1836.

48 See the articles in *Bent's News*, 16 January 1836, and *The True Colonist*, 29 January 1836.

49 *Bent's News*, 9 January 1836.

50 *The True Colonist*, 26 February 1836.

51 *Colonial Times*, 5 January 1836.

52 *Colonial Times*, 18 October 1836; M. C. Levy, *Governor George Arthur*, Georgian House, Melbourne, 1953, p. 138.

53 J. Backhouse, *A Narrative of a Visit to the Australian Colonies*, Hamilton Adams, London, 1843, p. 476.

54 See R. J. Solomon, *Urbanisation; The Evolution of an Australian Capital*, Angus & Robertson, Sydney, 1976, pp. 59–67, 107.

55 P. L. Brown (ed.), *Clyde Company Papers*, vol. 1, op. cit., p. 9.

56 ibid.

57 P. L. Brown (ed.), *Clyde Company Papers*, vol. 2, op. cit., p. 30.

58 Arthur to Glenelg, 4 May 1836, CO 280/66.

59 *Lieutenant Governor's Letterbook, 1833–1836*, GO 52/6, AOT.

60 ibid.

61 Arthur to Glenelg, 4 May 1836, CO 280/66.

62 *Hobart Town Courier*, 5 February 1836.

63 ibid., 26 February 1836.

64 Cited in Levy, *Governor George Arthur*, op. cit., p. 214.

65 J. Dixon, *The Condition and Capabilities of Van Diemen's Land, etc.*, Smith Elder, London, 1839, p. 51.

6 THE POLITICS OF VAN DIEMEN'S LAND

1 Boyes, *Diary*, op. cit., 24 May 1836.
2 Cited by Levy, *Governor George Arthur*, op. cit., p. 349.
3 *Colonial Times*, 31 May 1836.
4 *Bent's News*, 25 June 1836.
5 *Hobart Town Courier*, 27 May 1836.
6 West, *History*, op. cit., p. 135.
7 ibid.
8 ibid., p. 125.
9 The phrase was used by Arthur at the opening of the Wesleyan Sunday School, *Hobart Town Courier*, 22 August 1836.
10 W. Blackstone, *Commentaries on the Laws of England*, 4 vols, W. Strahan, London, 1776, vol. 1, p. 81.
11 Cited by W. D. Forsyth, *Governor Arthur's Convict System*, op. cit., pp. 196–7.
12 Arthur to Glenelg, 12 February 1836, CSO 280/65.
13 Cited by M. C. Levy, op. cit., pp. 127–8.
14 Arthur to Glenelg, 30 April 1836, CO 280/65.
15 Cited by W. D. Forsyth, op. cit., pp. 188–92.
16 ibid., p. 179.
17 *Colonial Times*, 16 March 1836.
18 ibid.
19 West, op. cit., p. 125.
20 *Colonial Times*, 25 May 1831.
21 H. Melville, op. cit., p. 131.
22 *Colonial Times*, 7 November 1845.
23 *Launceston Examiner*, 6 December 1845.
24 *Hobart Town Courier*, 14 September 1850.
25 West, op. cit., p. 221.
26 ibid., p. 209.
27 *Hobart Town Courier*, 8 May 1847.
28 *Launceston Examiner*, 12 May 1847.
29 ibid.
30 ibid., 5 May 1847.
31 J. Lackland (pseud.), *Common Sense, etc.*, Dowling, Launceston, 1847, pp. 2, 21–2.
32 West, op. cit., p. 228.
33 Cited by West, op. cit., pp. 228–9.
34 *Launceston Examiner*, 15 January 1851.
35 Cited by A. G. L. Shaw, *Convicts and Colonies*, Faber, London, 1966, p. 350.
36 *Hobart Town Courier*, 18 October 1851.
37 ibid., 25 October 1851.
38 *Hobart Town Courier*, 29 October 1851.

39 *Launceston Examiner*, 18 October 1851.
40 *Hobart Town Courier*, 5 November 1851.
41 ibid., 18 October 1851.
42 ibid.
43 ibid.
44 *Hobart Town Courier*, 22 October 1851.
45 ibid.
46 *Guardian*, 16 October 1850.
47 ibid., 26 October 1850.
48 ibid., 16 November 1850.
49 ibid., 24 November 1852.
50 ibid., 8 January 1853.
51 *Colonial Times*, 11, 13, 15, 17 August 1853; *Hobart Town Courier*, 11, 13 August 1853; *Launceston Examiner*, 10 August 1853.
52 *Launceston Examiner*, 10 August 1853.
53 ibid.
54 ibid., 13 August 1853.
55 ibid., 17 August 1853.

7 THE CONVICT SYSTEM

1 A. Alexander, *Tasmania's Convicts: How Convicts Built a Free Society*, Allen & Unwin, Sydney, 2010, p. 265.
2 See R. M. Hartwell, *The Economic Development of Van Diemen's Land, 1820–1850*, Melbourne University Press, Melbourne, 1954, p. 68; R. J. Solomon, *Urbanization: The Evolution of an Australian Capital*, Angus & Robertson, Sydney, 1976, p. 107; W. Vamplew (ed.), *Australians: Historical Statistics*, Fairfax, Syme & Weldon, Sydney, 1987, p. 26.
3 G. Rude, *Protest and Punishment*, Clarendon Press, Oxford, 1978.
4 ibid., p. 10.
5 See R. M. Hartwell, op. cit., pp. 201, 238; see also K. Dallas, *Transportation and Colonial Income, Historical Studies of Australia and New Zealand*, vol. 3, 1949, pp. 297–312.
6 *The Guardian*, 26 June 1847.
7 W. R. Allison, 'Remarks on the Transportation Question', published in *The Guardian*, 12 June 1847.
8 Cited by B. Richmond, *John West and the Anti-Transportation*, THRA, 2, vol. 1, November 1952, p. 8.
9 J. Mitchell, *Jail Journal*, Gill & Son, Dublin, n.d., p. 263.
10 Arthur to Glenelg, 4 May 1836, CO 280/66.
11 *Colonial Times*, 1 November 1836.
12 *The Tasmanian*, 25 March 1836.
13 W. D. Forsyth, *Governor Arthur's Convict System*, Sydney University Press, Sydney, 1970 (1935), p. 81.

14 Letter from 'Philo', 7 January 1825.
15 *The Diaries of George Hobler*, 27 February 1828, C & H Reproductions, 1992, Mitchell Library, Sydney, p. 47.
16 ibid., p. 187.
17 See, in general, N. J. B. Plomley (ed.), *Friendly Mission*, THRA, Hobart, 1966.
18 J. Richardson, *A Hobart Mistress and her Convict Servants*, Tasmanian Historical Studies, October 2005, pp. 85–95.
19 Hobler, *Diary*, op. cit., p. 15.
20 Boyes, *Diary*, op. cit., 15 March 1836.
21 Alexander, *Tasmania's Convicts*, op. cit., p. 37.
22 ibid., pp. 41–2.
23 Forsyth, *Governor Arthur's Convict System*, op. cit., pp. 134–5.
24 Darling to Arthur, 7 March 1826, *Letters from Darling, 1825–36*, Arthur Papers, Mitchell Library, A2167.
25 See R. P. Davis, *The Tasmanian Gallows*, Cat & Fiddle Press, Hobart, 1974.
26 P. L. Brown (ed.), *The Narrative of George Russell*, Oxford University Press, London, 1935, p. 53.
27 A. G. L. Shaw, *Convicts and Colonies*, Faber, London, 1966, p. 202.
28 J. Backhouse, *Extracts from the Letters*, 2 vols, London, 1837, vol. 1, p. 4.
29 Shaw, *Convicts and Colonies*, op. cit., p. 201.
30 Forsyth, *Governor Arthur's Convict System*, op. cit., p. 75.
31 Arthur to Buxton, 31 January 1835, *Governor's Letterbook, 1833–1836*, AOT, GO 52/6.
32 Cited by Forsyth, op. cit., p. 142.
33 ibid., p. 75.
34 Backhouse, *Letters*, op. cit., vol. 1, p. 11.
35 Cited by Forsyth, op. cit., p. 95.
36 *Hobart Town Courier*, 8 December 1827.
37 G. Robertson, *Journal, 1–30 January* 1829, pp. 122, 132–4, AOT, CSO 1/331.
38 ibid., pp. 115–17.
39 *Colonial Times*, 25 August 1825.
40 Arthur to Bathurst, 14 September 1825, HRA, vol. 3, no. 4, p. 365.
41 Darling to Arthur, 7 March 1826, *Arthur Papers*, Mitchell Library, mss A2167.
42 Arthur to Bathurst, 11 April 1826, HRA, vol. 3, no. 5, p. 139.
43 R. Tuffin, 'The Post Mortem Treatment of Convicts in Van Diemen's Land, 1814–1874', *Journal of Australian Colonial History (JACH)*, vol. 9, 2007, pp. 99–126.
44 J. Knott, *A Chartist's View of Australia, 1838, The Push From The Bush*, 13, November 1982, p. 7.

45 Denison, *Varieties of Vice-Regal Life*, op. cit., p. 92.
46 *House of Assembly Journals (HAJ)*, V, 1860, p. 76.

8 POST-PENAL DEPRESSION, 1856–70

1 *Launceston Examiner*, 4 December 1856.
2 ibid.
3 W. A. Townsley, *The Struggle for Self Government in Tasmania, 1842–1856*, Tasmanian Government Printer, Hobart, 1951, p. 144.
4 West, op. cit., p. 227.
5 Boyes, *Diary*, op. cit., 8 July 1850.
6 *Hobart Town Courier*, 17 January 1856.
7 *Launceston Examiner*, 21 May 1861.
8 ibid., 18 November 1862.
9 HTA, 12 December 1855.
10 *The Mercury*, 14 April 1857.
11 C. W. Dilke, *Greater Britain*, Macmillan, London, 1869, p. 361.
12 P. D. Edwards and R. B. Joyce, *Trollope's Australia*, University of Queensland Press, St Lucia, 1967, pp. 487–554.
13 J. Martineau, *Letters from Australia*, Longman Green, London, 1869, p. 62.
14 W. May to F. C. May, *Report on the Historical Manuscripts of Tasmania*, vol. 5, University of Tasmania, Hobart, 1964, p. 55.
15 W. Denison, THRA, Hobart, 2004 (1869), p. 106.
16 J. D. Balfe, *Letters of Dion, Hobart Town Advertiser*, Hobart, 1851, p. vi.
17 *Launceston Examiner*, 10 October 1857.
18 *Report of the Chief Inspector of Police*, HAJ, xv, 1868, no. 26.; J. Mitchell, *Jail Journal*, op. cit., p. 244; H. M. Hull, *Experiences of Forty years in Tasmania*, Walch & Sons, Hobart, 1859, pp. 24, 55.
19 *HAJ*, no. 27, 1869, p. xx.
20 ibid., p. 4.
21 *HAJ*, vol. v, no. 98, 1861, p. 6.
22 ibid., p. 5.
23 J. Roberts, *A Mirror of Religion and Society in Tasmania etc.*, Walch & Sons, Hobart, 1858, p. 5.
24 J. B. Walker, *Diary*, 8 September 1865, University of Tasmania, Hobart.
25 'New Chum' (pseud.), *A Ramble in Launceston*, Cornwall Chronicle, Launceston, 1879, p. 49.
26 *Statistics of Tasmania*, 1866, pp. 92–102; 1867, pp. 99–111.
27 R. M. Johnston, *Tasmanian Official Record*, Tasmanian Government Printer, Hobart, 1891, p. 391.
28 See H. Reynolds, 'That Hated Stain: The Aftermath of Transportation in Tasmania', *Historical Studies*, vol. 14, no. 53, October 1969, pp. 29–30.
29 Edwards and Joyce, *Trollope's Australia*, op. cit., p. 505.

30 Select Committee on the Discharge of Prisoners, *HAJ*, 1860, no. 98, pp. 5, 12.

31 Edwards and Joyce, *Trollope's Australia*, op. cit., p. 505.

32 Committee on the Discharge of Prisoners, op. cit., p. 5.

33 'A Home in the Colonies', no. xxvii, *The Statesman of India (Calcutta)*, October 1878.

34 *Hobart Town Courier*, 25 November 1857.

35 For the petitions, see *HAJ*, vol. 2, nos 48, 57, 62, 66, 68, 71, 1857.

36 Comment of Premier W. R. Giblin, *The Mercury*, 24 August 1882.

37 Letters from 'Mechanic' in *Tasmanian News*, 28 February 1884, and J. Richards, in *The Mercury*, 8 August 1887.

38 *Southern Star*, 11 October 1882.

39 S. H. Roberts, *History of Australian Land Settlement*, Macmillan, Melbourne, 1968, p. 37.

40 *The Mercury*, 6 June 1861.

41 G. C. Mundy, *Our Antipodes*, 3rd edn, Richard Bentley, London, 1955, p. 531.

42 W. Henty, *On Improvements in Cottage Husbandry*, Dowling, Launceston, 1849, p. 24.

43 *The Mercury*, 24 August 1885.

44 *The Mercury*, 9 May 1885; Select Committee on Immigration, *HAJ*, vol. 45, no. 105, 1882.

45 Report of the Chief Inspector of Schools, *HAJ*, vol. viii, no. 101, 1861.

46 J. Dunbabin, 'Ploughing Matches and Hop Feasts', *THRA*, vol. 47, no. 2, June 2000, p. 97.

47 K. R. von Stieglitz, *Pioneers of the East Coast*, cited in *The Telegraph*, Launceston, 1955, p. 24.

48 *The Mercury*, 2 May 1885.

49 G. Robertson and E. N. Craig, *Early Houses of Northern Tasmania*, Georgian House, Melbourne, 1966, p. 193.

50 John Leake Papers, *Report on the Historical Manuscripts of Tasmania*, op. cit., vol. 3, p. 29.

51 *HAJ*, vol. xxiii, no. 23, 1872.

52 *HAJ*, vol. xxii, 1872.

53 West, op. cit., p. 105.

54 *The Leader*, 27 March 1875.

55 G. C. Mundy, op. cit., p. 532.

56 *The Leader*, 27 March 1875.

57 Speech by T. D. Chapman on amendment to Master and Servants Act, *The Mercury*, 24 August 1882.

58 *Tasmanian Official Record*, Tasmanian Government Printer, Hobart, 1891, p. 392.

59 ibid.

60 *Tasmanian Mail*, 8 January 1898.

9 REFORM AND RECOVERY

1 See J. L. Stokes, *Discoveries in Australia*, 2 vols, Boone, London, 1846, vol. 2, p. 451.
2 See H. Reynolds, 'Regionalism in Nineteenth Century Tasmania', *THRA*, vol. 17, no. 1, July 1969, p. 17.
3 Cited by J. Martin, 'John Donellan Balfe and the Collective Experience of the Huon, 1850–58', *BA Hons thesis*, University of Tasmania, Hobart, 1968, p. 18.
4 Select Committee on Public Works, *HAJ*, 1864, no. 77.
5 Statistics of Tasmania, Hobart, 1872, p. 194.
6 E. N. C. Braddon, *A Home in the Colonies, etc.*, THRA, Hobart, 1990, p. 30.
7 L. Meredith, *My Home in Tasmania*, 2 vols, John Murray, London, 1852, vol. 2, p. 150.
8 J. Martineau, op. cit., p. 74.
9 *Launceston Examiner*, 11 February 1871; see also W. A. Townsley, 'The Launceston and Western Railway Company', *THRA*, iii, vol. 1, March 1954.
10 *The Mercury*, 13 October 1883.
11 ibid., 12 June 1859.
12 N. Haygarth, '"Grey Gold": James Philosopher Smith and the Creation of Tasmanian Mining Culture', *THS*, no. 2, 2003.
13 *The Mercury*, 1 January 1879, 1 January 1880.
14 ibid., 2 January 1882.
15 *Mining Report*, *HAJ*, vol. xii, no. 57, 1887.
16 *The Clipper*, 2 April 1898.
17 *The Clipper*, 3 September 1898.
18 *Tasmanian News*, 4 December 1889.
19 *Walch's Red Book*, 1890.
20 *Tasmanian News*, 30 July 1884.
21 Letter of 'Watchman', *The Mercury*, 10 January 1890.
22 *Church News*, 1 May 1894.
23 *The Monitor*, 8 September 1894.
24 *Tasmanian Democrat*, 26 October 1891.
25 *The Mercury*, 7 March 1895.
26 J. B. Walker, *Diary*, 3 August 1884.
27 *Tasmanian News*, 31 July 1884.
28 ibid., 11 January 1884.
29 ibid., 4 January 1884.
30 ibid., 31 July 1884.
31 ibid., 26 June 1884.
32 C. W. Dilke, *Problems of Greater Britain*, Macmillan, London, 1890, p. 239.
33 *Tasmanian News*, 23 July 1884.

34 S. Petrow, 'Clark as Attorney-General', in R. Ely et al. (eds), *A Living Force: Andrew Inglis Clark and the Ideal of Commonwealth*, CTHS, Hobart, 2001, p. 38.

35 *The Mercury*, 23 September 1896.

36 *Quadrilateral*, p. 109.

10 FEDERATION AND WAR

1 *The Mercury*, 1 January 1901.

2 'The Struggle in Tasmania', in B. R. Wise, *The Making of the Australian Constitution*, Longman Green, London, 1913, p. 356.

3 A. J. Taylor, 'Shall We Federate?', Hobart, 1898.

4 *Tasmanian News*, 2 June 1898.

5 *Church News*, 1 June 1898.

6 ibid.

7 J. B. Walker, *Diary*, op. cit., 2 June 1898.

8 *Zeehan and Dundas Herald*, 7 June 1898.

9 *Zeehan and Dundas Herald*, 6 June 1898.

10 *The Mercury*, 7 June 1898.

11 Walker, *Diary*, op. cit., 2 June 1898.

12 *The Mercury*, 28 July 1899.

13 *The Clipper*, 29 July 1899.

14 *Launceston Examiner*, 2 June 1898.

15 *The Mercury*, 1 January 1901.

16 *Tasmanian News*, 25 April 1888.

17 A. J. Taylor, *Imperial Federation versus Australian Independence*, *The Mercury*, 1889, p. 8.

18 *The Mercury*, 27 October 1899.

19 W. H. Dawson, *War Songs*, Walch & Sons, Hobart, 1901.

20 *The Mercury*, 3 March, 21 May 1900.

21 Cited by J. Bufton, *Tasmanians in the Transvaal War*, Loone, Hobart, 1905, p. 487.

22 *The Clipper*, 21 January, 18 February 1900.

23 See R. Ely (ed.), *Andrew Inglis Clark and the Idea of Common-wealth*, Centre for Tasmanian Historical Studies (CTHS), University of Tasmania, Hobart, 2001, pp. 237–51.

24 Cited by M. Roe, *The State of Tasmania*, THRA, Hobart, 2001, p. 38.

25 'The Struggle in Tasmania', in B. R. Wise, op. cit., p. 358.

26 Mr. Rooke, reported in *The Mercury*, 24 September 1896.

27 Minutes of the meting of the 4th annual convention of the WCTU of Tasmania, Hobart, 1896.

28 Mr. Stewart, reported in *The Mercury*, 16 September 1903.

29 Roe, *The State of Tasmania*, op. cit., p. 187.

30 *The Clipper*, 10 August 1900.

31 *Zeehan and Dundas Herald*, 3 April 1903.

32 Cited by M. Lake, *A Divided Society*, Melbourne University Press, Melbourne, p. 8.

33 ibid.

34 A. Alexander, 'Patriotism and Enlistment in Brighton, 1914–1918', *THRA*, vol. 55, no. 3, 2008, p. 217.

35 Cited by P. McFie, 'First World War Soldiers of the Richmond Municipality', *THRA*, vol. 55, no. 3, 2008, p. 229.

11 BETWEEN THE WARS

1 See Q. Beresford, '"That Dreaded Plague": Tasmania and the 1919 Influenza epidemic, *THRA*, vol. 29, no. 3, September 1982, pp. 108–15.

2 Cited by Q. Beresford, 'The World War One Soldier Settlement Scheme in Tasmania', *THRA*, vol. 30, no. 3, 1983, p. 97.

3 M. D. McRae, 'The Tasmanian Labour Party and Trade Unions, 1903–1923', *THRA*, vol. 5, no. 1, April 1956, pp. 10–11.

4 E. Lyons, *So We Take Comfort*, Heinemann, London, 1965, p. 145.

5 R. J. May, 'The Politics of Federalism: Financial relations between Tasmanian and the Commonwealth 1901–1933', *Australian Journal of Politics and History* (AJPH), vol. 42, 1996, p. 379.

6 ibid., pp. 380, 387.

7 Cited by W. A. Townsley, in *Tasmania from Colony to Statehood*, St David's Park Publishing, Hobart, 1991, p. 358.

8 N. Batt, 'Unemployment in Tasmania', *THRA*, vol. 25, no. 3, September 1978, p. 66.

9 ibid., p. 52.

10 R. Davis, *Eighty Years Labor: The ALP in Tasmania, 1903–1983*, Sassafras Books, Hobart, 1983, p. 32; see also M. Roe, 'A. G. Ogilvie and the Blend of Van Diemen's Land and Tasmania', *Tasmanian Historical Studies (THS)*, vol. 1, no. 2, 1986, pp. 39–59, and *Albert Ogilvie and Stymie Gaha; World-Wise Tasmanians*, Parliament of Tasmania, Hobart, 2008.

11 I. Terry, 'The Development of the Tarraleah Power Station', *THRA*, 53, vol. 4, December 2006, pp. 197–209.

12 A. Alexander, *The Zinc Works, Pasminco Metals, Risdon* 1992, pp. 7–8; see also J. Reynolds, 'The Establishment of the Electrolytic Zinc Industry in Tasmania', *THRA*, 6, vol. 2, September 1957.

13 D. Young, *Making Crime Pay*, THRA, Hobart, 1996.

14 Cited by M. Walker, 'The Switzerland of the South, etc.', *THS*, vol. 13, 2008, p. 71.

12 POSTWAR TASMANIA

1 R. Solomon, *Urbanization: The Evolution of an Australian Capital*, Angus & Robertson, Sydney, 1976, p. 187.

2 W. A. Townsley, *Tasmania: Microcosm of Federation or Vassal State, 1945–1983*, St David's Park Publishing, Hobart, 1994, p. 216.

3 J. Koshin, *Electric Eric: The Life and Times of Eric Reece: An Australian State Premier*, Bookprint, Launceston, 2009, p. 277.

4 ibid., p. 282.

5 D. Jones, 'The Pedder Tragedy', in R. Green (ed.), *Battle for the Franklin*, Fontana, Melbourne, 1981, p. 67.

6 Cited by M. Mulligan and S. Hill, *Ecological Pioneers*, Cambridge University Press, Cambridge, 2001, p. 248.

7 *Launceston Examiner*, 30 May 1883.

8 L. Malcolm, 'Short notes on the Inhabitants of Cape Barren Island', *Man*, vol. 10, no. 71, 1920, p. 148.

9 *Australian Board of Missions Review*, vol. 17, 15 January 1931, pp. 171–2.

10 Report of A. W. Burbury, 25 September 1929, CSD 22/336/104/37, AOT.

11 L. Ryan, *The Aboriginal Tasmanians*, 2nd edn, Allen & Unwin, Sydney, 1996, p. 253.

12 *The Mercury*, 3 April 1978.

13 *Launceston Examiner*, 16 August 1971.

14 ibid., 11 April 1977.

15 J. Everett, 'Aboriginality', in A. Alexander, *The Companion to Tasmanian History*, CTHS, Hobart 2005, p. 399.

13 TOWARDS THE BICENTENARY

1 J. Koshin, *Electric Eric*, op. cit., p. 332.

2 Cited by P. Hay et al. (eds), 'Environmental Politics in Australia and New Zealand', Occasional Paper 23, Centre for Environmental Studies, University of Tasmania, 1989, p. 198.

3 B. Brown, 'Ecology, Economy, Equality, Eternity', in C. Pybus and R. Flanagan, op. cit., Sun, Sydney, 1990, pp. 249–51.

4 J. West, op. cit., p. 522.

5 M. Angus (ed.), *The World of Olegas Truchanas*, Olegas Truchanas Publication Committee (OTPC), Hobart, 1975, p. 18.

6 K. Kiernan, 'Discovering the Franklin', in R. Green, The Battle for the Franklin, op. cit., pp. 85–6.

7 P. Dombrovskis et al. (eds), *On the Mountain*, West Wind Press, Hobart, 1996, pp. 24–5.

SOURCES

BOOKS, JOURNALS, DIARIES

Alexander, A. 1992, *The Zinc Works*, Pasminco Metals, Risdon.

—— 1999, *Obliged to Submit: Wives and Mistresses of Colonial Governors*, Montpelier Press, Hobart.

—— 2005, *The Companion to Tasmanian History*, CTHS, Hobart.

—— 2008, 'Patriotism and Enlistment in Brighton, 1914–18', *THRA*, vol. 55, no. 3, December.

—— 2010, *Tasmania's Convicts: How Convicts Built a Free Society*, Allen & Unwin, Sydney.

Angus, M. (ed.) 1975, *The World of Olegas Truchanas*, OTPC, Hobart.

Backhouse, J. 1837, *Extracts from the Letters*, 2 vols (vol. 1), Darton & Harvey, London.

—— 1843, *A Narrative of a Visit to the Australian Colonies*, Hamilton Adams, London.

Balfe, J. D. 1851, 'Letters of Dion', *Hobart Town Advertiser*.

Batt, N. 1978, 'Unemployment in Tasmania', *THRA*, vol. 25, no. 3, September.

Beaglehole, E. (ed.) 1955–74, *The Journals of Captain James Cook*, 3 vols, Cambridge University Press, Cambridge.

Beresford, Q. 1982, '"That Dreaded Plague": Tasmania and the 1919 influenza epidemic', *THRA*, vol. 29, no. 3, September.

—— 1983, 'The World War One Soldier Settlement Scheme in Tasmania', *THRA*, 30, vol. 3.

Betts, T. 1830, *An Account of the Colony of Van Diemen's Land, etc.*, Baptist Mission Press, Calcutta.

Blackstone, W. 1776, *Commentaries on the Laws of England*, 4 vols (vol. 1), W. Strahan, London.

Bonwick, J. 1870, *The Last of the Tasmanians*, Sampson, Low, London.

Bowden, K. M. 1952, *George Bass, 1771–1803*, Oxford University Press, Melbourne.

Boyce, J. 2007, *Van Diemen's Land*, Black Inc. Books, Melbourne.

Braddon, E. N. C. 1980, *A Home in the Colonies: Edward Braddon's Letters to India, 1878*, THRA, Hobart.

Brown, B. 1990, 'Ecology, Economy, Equality, Eternity', in C. Pybus and R. Flanagan, *The Whole World is Watching*, Sun, Sydney.

Brown, P. L. (ed.) 1935, *The Narrative of George Russell*, Oxford University Press, London.

—— (ed.) 1952, *Clyde Company Papers, vol. 2, 1836–1840*, Oxford University Press, London.

Bufton, J. 1905, *Tasmanians in the Transvaal War*, Loone, Hobart.

Burkhardt, F. (ed.) 2008, *Charles Darwin: The Beagle Letters*, Cambridge University Press, Cambridge.

Burns, T. E. & Skemp, J. R. 1961, *Van Diemen's Land Correspondence*, Queen Victoria Museum, Launceston.

Calder, J. E. 1875, *Some Account of the Wars, Extirpation, Habits, etc, of the Native Tribes of Tasmania*, Henn & Co., p. 8.

——'Natives', p. 35, papers, Mitchell Library, mss A597.

Chapman, P. (ed.) 1985, *The Diaries and Letters of G. T. W. B. Boyes, 1820–32*, Oxford University Press, Melbourne, 1985.

Chapman, T. D. 1882, Speech by T. D. Chapman on amendment to Master and Servants Act, *The Mercury*, 24 August.

Collins, D. 1971 (1802), *An Account of the English Colony in New South Wales*, 2 vols, Library Board of South Australia, Adelaide.

Curr, E. 1824, *An Account of the Colony of Van Diemen's Land*, Cowie, London.

Dallas, K. 1949, 'Transportation and Colonial Income', *Historical Studies of Australia and New Zealand*, no. 3.

Darwin, C. 1839, *Narrative of the Surveying Voyages of the ... Adventure and Beagle, etc.*, 3 vols (vol. 3), Murray, London.

Davis, R. 1974, *The Tasmanian Gallows*, Cat & Fiddle Press, Hobart.

—— 1983, *Eighty Years Labor: The ALP in Tasmania, 1903–83*, Sassafras Books, Hobart.

Dawson, W. H. 1901, *War Songs*, Walch & Sons, Hobart.

de Vattel, E. 1758, *The Law of Nations*, publisher unknown, London.

Delano, A. 1973, *A Narrative of a Voyage to New Holland and Van Diemen's Land*, Cat & Fiddle Press, Hobart.

Denison, W. 2004 (1869), 'Varieties of Vice-Regal Life', THRA, Hobart.

Dilke, C. W. 1869, *Greater Britain*, Macmillan, London.

—— 1890, *Problems of Greater Britain*, Macmillan, London.

Dixon, J. 1822, *Narrative of a Voyage to New South Wales and Van Diemen's Land*, Smith Elder, Edinburgh.

——1839, *The Conditions and Capabilities of Van Diemen's Land*, London.

Dombrovskis, P. et al. (eds) 1996, *On The Mountain*, West Wind Press, Hobart.

Dunbabin, J. 2000, 'Ploughing Matches and Hop Feasts', *THRA*, vol. 47, no. 2, June.

Duyker, E. (ed.) 1992, *The Discovery of Tasmania*, St David's Park Publishing, Hobart.

—— (ed.) 2001, *B. d'Entrecasteaux Voyage to Australia and the Pacific, 1791–3*, trans. M. Duyker, Melbourne University Press, Melbourne.

Duyker, E. & Duyker, M. (eds) 2001, *Voyages to Australia and the Pacific, 1791–93*, Melbourne University Press, Melbourne.

Edwards, P. D. & Joyce, R. B. 1967, *Trollope's Australia*, University of Queensland Press, St Lucia.

Ely, R. (ed.) 2001, *Andrew Inglis Clark and the Idea of Commonwealth*, Centre for Tasmanian Historical Studies (CTHS), Hobart.

Evans, G. W. 1822, *A Geographical, Historical and Topographic Description of Van Diemen's Land*, Souter, London.

Fawkner, J. P. 2007, *Reminiscences of Early Hobart Town 1804–1812*, The Banks Society, Melbourne.

Fenton, J. 1884, *History of Tasmania*, Walch & Sons, Hobart.

Forsyth, W. D. 1970 (1935), *Governor Arthur's Convict System*, Sydney University Press, Sydney.

Frost, L. (ed.) 1992, *A Face in the Glass: The Journal and Life of Annie Baxter Dawbin*, Heinemann, Melbourne.

Green, R. (ed.) 1981, *Battle for the Franklin*, Fontana, Melbourne.

Hartwell, R. M. 1954, *The Economic Development of Van Diemen's Land, 1820–1850*, Melbourne University Press, Melbourne.

Harris, G. P. 1994, *Letters of G. P. Harris, 1803–1812*, Arden Press, Sorrento.

Hay, P. et al. (eds) 1989, *Environmental Politics in Australia and New Zealand*, University of Tasmania, Hobart.

Haygarth, N. 2003, 'Grey Gold': James Philosopher Smith and the Creation of Tasmanian Mining Culture, THS, no. 2.

Henty, W. 1849, *On Improvements in Cottage Husbandry*, Dowling, Launceston.

Hobler, G. 1992, *The Diaries of George Hobler*, C & H Reproductions, Mitchell Library, Sydney.

Hughes, R. 1987, *The Fatal Shore*, Collins, London.

Hull, H. M. 1859, *Experiences of Forty Years in Tasmania*, Walch & Sons, Hobart.

Humphrey, A. W. H. 1994, *A Voyage to Port Phillip and Van Diemen's Land*, The Banks Society, Melbourne.

Jeffreys, C. 1820, *Van Diemen's Land*, Richardson, London.

Johnston, R. M. 1891, *Tasmanian Official Record*, Tasmanian Government Printer, Hobart.

Jones, D. 1981, 'The Pedder Tragedy', in R. Green (ed.), *Battle for the Franklin*, Fontana, Melbourne.

Knott, J. 1982, 'A Chartist's View of Australia, 1838', *The Push from the Bush*, no. 13, November.

Koshin, J. 2009, *Electric Eric: The Life and Times of Eric Reece, an Australian State Premier*, Bookprint, Launceston.

Lackland, J. (pseud.) 1847, *Common Sense, etc.*, Dowling, Launceston.

Lake, M. 1975, *A Divided Society*, Melbourne University Press, Melbourne.

Leake, J. 1964, *John Leake Papers*, Report on the Historical Manuscripts of Tasmania, 5, University of Tasmania, Hobart.

Levy, M. C. 1953, *Governor George Arthur*, Georgian House, Melbourne.

Lyons, E. 1965, *So We Take Comfort*, Heinemann, London.

Malcolm, L. 1920, 'Short Notes on the Inhabitants of Cape Barren Island', *Man*, vol. 10, no. 71.

Mann W. 1939 (1839), *Six Years Residence in the Australian Provinces*, Smith Elder, London.

Martin, J. 1968, 'John Donellan Balfe and the Collective Experience of the Huon, 1850–58', BA Hons thesis, University of Tasmania, Hobart.

Martineau, J. 1868, *Letters from Australia*, Longman Green, London.

May, R. J. 1996, 'The Politics of Federalism: Financial relations between Tasmanian and the Commonwealth 1901–33', *Australian Journal of Politics and History*, 42.

May W. to F. C. May 1964, *Report on the Historical Manuscripts of Tasmania*, 5, University of Tasmania, Hobart.

McFie, P. 2008, 'First World War Soldiers of the Richmond Municipality', *THRA*, vol. 55, no. 3, December.

McPhee, J. 1980, *The Art of John Glover*, Macmillan, Melbourne.

McRae, M. D. 1956, 'The Tasmanian Labour Party and Trade Unions, 1903–1923', *THRA*, vol. 5, no. 1, April.

Melville, H. 1835, *History of Van Diemen's Land etc.*, Smith Elder, London.

Meredith, L. 1852, *My Home in Tasmania*, 2 vols, Murray, London.

Minutes of the 1896 meeting of the 4th annual convention of the WCTU of Tasmania, Hobart.

Mitchell, J., *Jail Journal*, Gillisons, Dublin, n.d.

Mulligan, M. & Hill, S. 2001, *Ecological Pioneers*, Cambridge University Press, Cambridge.

Mundy, G. C. 1955, *Our Antipodes*, 3rd edn, Richard Bentley, London.

'New Chum' (pseud.) 1879, 'A Ramble in Launceston', *Cornwall Chronicle*, Launceston.

Nicholls, M. (ed.) 1977, *The Diaries of the Rev. Robert Knopwood, 1803–1838*, THRA, Hobart.

Petrow, S. 2001, 'Clark as Attorney-General', in R. Ely et al. (eds), *A Living Force: Andrew Inglis Clark and the Ideal of Commonwealth*, CTHS, Hobart.

Plomley, N. J. B. 1992, *The Aboriginal–Settler Clash in Van Diemen's Land,1803–31*, Queen Victoria Museum, Launceston.

—— (ed.) 1977, *Weep in Silence*, Blubber Head Press, Hobart.

—— (ed.) 1992, *The Baudin Expedition and the Tasmanian Aborigines, 1802*, Blubber Head Press, Hobart.

—— (ed.) 2001, *Friendly Mission*, 2nd edn, Queen Victoria Museum, Launceston.

Plomley, N. J. B. & Bernier, J. P. (eds) 1993, *The General*, Queen Victoria Museum, Launceston.

Rae-Ellis, V. 1988, *Black Robinson*, Melbourne University Press, Melbourne.

Regina v Sioui, 70 DLR (4th) 427 at 428.

Reynolds, H. 1969a, 'Regionalism in Nineteenth Century Tasmania', *THRA*, vol. 17, no. 1, July.

—— 1969b, '"That Hated Stain": The Aftermath of Transportation in Tasmania', *Historical Studies*, vol. 14, no. 53, October.

—— 2004, *Fate of a Free People*, Penguin Books, Melbourne.

Reynolds, J. 1957, 'The Establishment of the Electrolytic Zinc Industry in Tasmania', *THRA*, vol. 6, no. 2, September.

Richardson, J. 2005, 'A Hobart Mistress and her Convict Servants', *Tasmanian Historical Studies*, vol. 10.

Richmond, B. 1952, 'John West and the Anti-Transportation Movement', *THRA*, vol. 2, no. 1, November.

Roberts, J. 1858, *A Mirror of Religion and Society in Tasmania etc.*, Walch & Sons, Hobart.

Roberts, S. H. 1968, *History of Australian Land Settlement*, Macmillan, Melbourne.

Robertson, G. 1829, *Journal*, 1–30 January, pp. 122, 132–4, AOT, CSO 1/331.

Robertson, G. & Craig, E. N. 1966, *Early Houses of Northern Tasmania*, Georgian House, Melbourne.

Robinson, G. A. 1865, Speech to Aborigines Protection Society, 1838, Bath.

Roe, M. 1986, 'A. G. Ogilvie and the Blend of Van Diemen's Land and Tasmania', *Tasmanian Historical Society*, vol. 1, no. 2.

—— 2001, *The State of Tasmania*, THRA, Hobart.

—— 2008, *Albert Ogilvie and Stymie Gaha: World-Wise Tasmanians*, Parliament of Tasmania, Hobart.

Roth, H. L. 1899, *The Aborigines of Tasmania*, King, Halifax.

Rude, G. 1978, *Protest and Punishment*, Clarendon Press, Oxford.

Ryan, L. 1996, *The Aboriginal Tasmanians*, 2nd edn, Allen & Unwin, Sydney.

Select Committee on the Aboriginal Inhabitants, *British Parliamentary Papers 1837*, vol. 7, no. 425.

Select Committee on the Discharge of Prisoners 1860, *HAJ*, no. 98, pp. 5, 12.

Shaw, A. G. L. 1966, *Convicts and Colonies*, Faber, London.

—— (ed.) 1971, *Military Operations Against the Aboriginal Inhabitants of Van Dieman's Land, 1831*, THRA, Hobart.

Solomon, R. J. 1976, *Urbanization; The Evolution of an Australian Capital*, Angus & Robertson, Sydney.

Statistics of Tasmania 1866 and 1867.

Stokes, J. L. 1846, *Discoveries in Australia*, 2 vols, Boone, London.

Tardiff, P. 2003, *John Bowen's Hobart*, THRA, Hobart.

Tardiff, P. 2003, 'Risdon Cove', in R. Manne (ed.), *Whitewash*, Black Inc. Books, Melbourne.

Tasmanian Official Record 1891, Tasmanian Government Printer, Hobart.

Taylor, A. J. 1889, 'Imperial Federation versus Australian Independence', *The Mercury*, Hobart.

Terry, I. 1889, 'The Development of the Tarraleah Power Station', *THRA*, vol. 53, no. 4, December.

Townsley, W. A. 1951, *The Struggle for Self Government in Tasmania, 1842–1856*, Tasmanian Government Printer, Hobart.

—— 1991, *Tasmania from Colony to Statehood*, St David's Park Publishing, Hobart.

—— 1994, *Tasmania: Microcosm of Federation or Vassal State? 1945–83*, St David's Park Publishing, Hobart.

Vamplew, W. (ed.) 1987, *Australians: Historical Statistics*, Fairfax, Syme & Weldon, Sydney.

von Stieglitz, K. R. 1948, 'Six Pioneer Women of Tasmania', *The Telegraph*, Launceston.

—— 1955, 'Pioneers of the East Coast from 1642', *The Telegraph*, Launceston.

Walch's Red Book, 1890.

Walker, J. B. 1865, *Diary*, entry for 8 September, University of Tasmania, Hobart.

—— 1914, *Early Tasmania*, Government Printer, Hobart.

Walker, M. 2008, 'The Switzerland of the South, etc.', *Tasmanian Historical Studies*, 13.

West, J. 1971 (1852), *History of Tasmania*, 2nd edn, Angus & Robertson, Sydney.

Widowson, H. 1829, *The Present State of Van Diemen's Land*, Robinson & Joy, London.

Wise, B. R. 1913, *Making of the Australian Commonwealth*, Longman, London.
Young, D. 1996, 'Making Crime Pay', THRA, Hobart.

NEWSPAPERS, LEAFLETS

Bent's News
Church News
The Clipper
Colonial Times
Cornwall Chronicle
The Courier
The Examiner
The Guardian
Hobart Town Almanac
Hobart Town Courier
Launceston Advertiser
Launceston Examiner
The Leader
The Monitor
The Tasmanian
Tasmanian Democrat
Tasmanian Mail
Tasmanian News
True Colonialist
True Colonist
Van Diemen's Land Annual

PERIODICALS

The Mercury
The Quadrilateral
The Southern Star
The Tasmanian Democrat
The Zeehan and Dundas Herald
Van Dieman's Land Annual

HRA RESOURCES

Arthur to Bathurst, 11 April 1826, *HRA*, 3, no. 5, p. 139.
Arthur to Bathurst, 14 September 1825, *HRA*, 3, no. 4, p. xx.
Bathurst to Darling, 14 July 1825, *HRA*, 1, no. xii, p. 21.
Collins to King, 11 September 1804, *HRA*, 3, no. 1, p. 281.
General Orders, 7 January 1805, *HRA*, 3, no. 1, p. 529.
HRA, 1, no. 2, p. 500.
HRA, 1, no. 4, p. 12; *HRNSW*, 1, p. 458.
HRA, 3, no. 1, p. 576.
HRA, 3, no. 1, p. 585.

HRA, 3, no. 1, p. 618.

HRA, 3, no. 1, p. 665.

Patterson to King, 26 November 1804, *HRA*, 3, no. 1.

AOT RESOURCES

Anstey to Burnett, 4 December 1827, CSO 1/320, AOT.

Arthur to Barnes, 19 October 1830, CSO 1/320, AOT.

Arthur to Buxton, 31 January 1835, *Governor's Letterbook, 1833–36*, AOT, GO 52/6.

Arthur to Darling, 24 May 1828, GO 33/4, AOT.

Arthur to Joseph Hume, 30/12/35, *Governor's Letterbook, 1833–6*, GO 52/6, AOT.

Clark to Burnett, 2 March 1830, CSO 1/323, AOT.

Clark to Burnett, CSO1/320/7578, p. 403, AOT.

CSO 1/323, AOT.

CSO 1/323, p. 290, AOT.

CSO 5/180/4240, AOT.

Dove to Colonial Secretary, 26 February 1839, CSO5/182/4352, AOT.

Executive Council Minutes, 8 April 1828, AO/EP/230, p. 294, AOT.

Executive Council Minutes, 27 August 1830, pp. 568–70, AOT.

February–April 1842, CSO 8/11/266, p. 475, AOT.

Fisher Report, 1842, CSO, 8/11/266, p. 475, AOT.

Fisher to Colonial Secretary, 18 January 1842, CSO 8/11/266, AOT.

GOP 33/7, p. 901, AOT.

J. Jones, in CSO 1/323, AOT.

Jorgenson to Burnett, 24 February 1831, CSO1/320, AOT.

Lieutenant-Governor's Letterbook, 1833–36, GO 52/6, AOT.

Minutes of the Aborigines Committee, 24 October 1831, p. 135, CBE/I, AOT.

Parramore to Surveyor-General, 4 December 1827, CSO 38/I, AOT; *Military Operations etc.*, op. cit., pp. 4–5.

Petition of 2 April 1828, CSO/318, p. 383, AOT.

Report of A. W. Burbury, 25 September 1929, CSD 22/336/104/37, AOT.

Reports by Nickolls, 7 November 1834, CSO 1/ 772/16, 503, p. 195, AOT.

Robinson, Evidence to Aborigines Committee, 20 January 1831, CBE/1, AOT.

HAJ

HAJ, no. 27, p. xxvii, 1869.

HAJ, vol. v, 1860, p. 76.

HAJ, vol. xxiii, no. 23, 1872.

The Mercury, 9 May 1885; Select Committee on Immigration, *HAJ*, 1882.

'Mining Report', *HAJ*, vol. xii, no. 57, 1887.

'Report of the Chief Inspector of Police', *HAJ*, vol. xv, no. 26, 1868.

'Report of the Chief Inspector of Schools', *HAJ*, vol. viii, no. 101, 1861.

Select Committee on Public Works, vol. xx, no. 77, *HAJ*, 1864.

For the petitions, see *HAJ*, vol. ii, nos. 48, 57, 62, 66, 68, 71, 1857.

ARTHUR

Arthur to Glenelg, 12 February 1836, CSO 280/65.

Arthur to Glenelg, 6 April 1833, CO 280/41.

Arthur to Glenelg, 4 May 1836, CO 280/66.

Arthur to Goderich, 14 March 1833, CO 280/41.

Darling to Arthur, 7 March 1826, Arthur Papers, Mitchell Library, mss A2167.

Darling to Arthur, 7 March 1826, *Letters from Darling, 1825–36*, Arthur Papers, Mitchell Library, A2167.

Minute to Legislative Council, 27 March 1836, enclosed in Arthur to Glenelg, 30 March 1836, CO 280/65.

ROBINSON

'Legends of a Native Tribune', from *The Mercury*, n.d., Calder Papers, ms. 10913, La Trobe Library.

Report, 30 April 1838, Robinson Papers, mss A7044, Mitchell Library.

Robinson to Burnett 19 December 1829, CSO 1/328, p. 127.

Robinson to Colonial Secretary, 11 May 1838, Robinson Papers, vol. 49, mss A7070, Mitchell Library.

Robinson to Colonial Secretary, 17 October 1835, Robinson Papers, mss A7043, Mitchell Library.

Robinson to Montague, 31 July 1835, CSO1/807/1727; *Robinson Report on Flinders Island, 1838*, CSO 5/39/833.

Robinson Papers, vol. 40, mss A7061, Mitchell Library.

CALDER

Calder to Reibey, 6 July 1877, Calder Papers, mss A597, Mitchell Library.

Calder Papers, mss A597, Mitchell Library.

INDEX